Disability and Social Change

Disability and Social Change

A Progressive Canadian Approach

edited by

Jeanette Robertson & Grant Larson

FERNWOOD PUBLISHING
HALIFAX & WINNIPEG

Editing: Mark Ambrose Harris
Cover photograph: Jeanette Robertson
Cover design: John van der Woude
Printed and bound in Canada

Published by Fernwood Publishing
32 Oceanvista Lane, Black Point, Nova Scotia, B0J 1B0
and 748 Broadway Avenue, Winnipeg, Manitoba, R3G 0X3

www.fernwoodpublishing.ca

Fernwood Publishing Company Limited gratefully acknowledges the financial support of
the Government of Canada through the Canada Book Fund, the Manitoba Department
of Culture, Heritage and Tourism under the Manitoba Publishers Marketing Assistance
Program and the Province of Manitoba, through the Book Publishing Tax Credit, for
our publishing program. We are pleased to work in partnership with the Province of
Nova Scotia to develop and promote our creative industries for the benefit of all Nova
Scotians. We acknowledge the support of the Canada Council for the Arts, which last
year invested $153 million to bring the arts to Canadians throughout the country.

Library and Archives Canada Cataloguing in Publication

Disability and social change : a progressive Canadian
approach / edited by Jeanette Robertson and Grant Larson.
Includes bibliographical references and index.

ISBN 978-1-55266-813-9 (paperback)

1. People with disabilities—Canada. 2. Social change—Canada.
I. Larson, Grant, author, editor II. Robertson, Jeanette Suzanne, 1962-, author, editor

HV1559.C3D57685 2016   362.40971   C2015-908354-0

Contents

Acknowledgements

We would like to thank all those who have had a part in making this Canadian progressive book on social change and disability a reality. Specifically, we thank the people who have agreed to have their voices and experiences recorded in the book — Kevin Lusignan, Jaclyn Porter, Lorea Regan, Melanie Thomas and Mike Touchie. We also thank the many other people with disabilities who have informed our thinking about this topic and been our teachers over the years. We thank each and every contributing author for their time, expertise and commitment to furthering a more humane, egalitarian and progressive understanding of the experience of those who have been disabled by society's structures, attitudes and behaviours.

And finally, we would like to thank our families and friends who have supported us, listened to our joys and struggles, encouraged us, and also been committed to understanding disability in a new way — June, Bev, Ian, Carla, Kari, Rob, Jeffrey, Sarah, Andrea, Dan, and Jennifer.

Grant Larson and Jeanette Robertson

List of Contributors

Irene Carter is an associate professor, School of Social Work, University of Windsor, whose scholarship focuses on intellectual disabilities, self-help groups, support groups and curriculum development. Her current research projects include children with disabilities and adoptive parents, adult siblings of children with autism, parents of adult children with dual diagnosis and the inclusion of courses and programs about disability in social work in Canada, the U.S., the U.K., Australia, and India.

Peter Dunn is an associate professor at the Faculty of Social Work, Wilfrid Laurier University. He has been involved in five national research projects about disability policies which emphasize empowerment and human rights, funded through SSHRC and Statistics Canada. His extensive writing includes the areas of disability policies, social exclusion, poverty, social housing and holism. He is an enthusiastic dancer, holistic supporter, social justice advocate and pet lover.

Douglas Durst is a professor of social work at the University of Regina and teaches social research and social policy at the undergraduate and graduate levels. Underlying his research is an anti-oppressive approach of giving voice to marginalized peoples, including peoples with disabilities, the elderly, and immigrants and refugees. During his years in the Northwest Territories, he developed a love for the North and its peoples.

Roy Hanes has over thirty years of experience working with and for people with disabilities. He created the first course pertaining to critical disability studies in schools of social work in Canada. He has been and continues to be involved in the promotion of disability studies and disability rights in Canada and abroad. For example, he is a founding member of the Persons with Disability Caucus of the Canadian Association for Social Work Education. He is also a founding member of the Canadian Disability Studies Association and the Committee on Disability and

Abuse (Ottawa, Canada). One of his primary areas of interest is disability history, and he is presently co-editing two books on this topic.

Terri-Lynn Langdon is a disabled social worker and social justice activist working in Toronto. She sits on the Disability Issues Committee at the City of Toronto and works at Eight Branches Healing Arts Centre and Toronto Rehabilitation Institute. She takes a human rights approach to disabled bodies and disability studies. She received her BA and MSW degrees from Wilfrid Laurier University.

Grant Larson is a recently retired associate professor of social work and human service at Thompson Rivers University. His research and teaching interests include mental health, disabilities, international social work, disaster rehabilitation and social work education. Grant utilizes a modern critical theory perspective in teaching and research. He is an individual with a disability who experienced profound hearing loss as an adult.

Kevin Lusignan served as the president of the Family Support Institute of BC, an organization with a parent-to-parent model that supports families who have loved ones with a disability. He is executive director of the Community Ventures Society, a nonprofit agency that serves people of all abilities. He has also been involved as an activist and an advocate in the community living movement in British Columbia for over twenty years.

Judy MacDonald is an associate professor, School of Social Work, Dalhousie University. She identifies as a woman with a (dis)Ability having lived with chronic pain for over twenty-five years. Her scholarship is on access and inclusion for (dis)Abled students, faculty and staff within schools of social work and social work practice and policy with the (dis)Abled.

Jennifer Murphy is a lecturer at Thompson Rivers University. Her teaching interests include social work and law, social policy, and interviewing skills. Her social work background includes working as a family mediator and assisting separated couples to develop a parenting plan for their children. Her research interests are focused on reintegration into community for federal offenders, criminal justice issues and narratives, using a desistance framework for analysis.

Jaclyn Porter graduated from Thompson Rivers University with a bachelor of social work degree. She works in the Calgary Alternative Day Options program at Calgary Alternative Support Services.

Michael Prince is the Lansdowne Professor of Social Policy at the University of Victoria. He is the author of *Absent Citizens: Disability Politics and Policy in Canada,* and he serves on the social policy committee of the Council of Canadians with Disabilities, as well as on the Advisory Committee on Children and Youth with Special Needs, to the Representative of Children and Youth for British Columbia.

Lorea Regan completed a Long Term Care Aide Certificate at Camosun College in Victoria, and she worked in the field for ten years. She was born with one arm missing just below the elbow and has never let this prevent her from achieving whatever goals she has set, defying many of the expectations and limitations placed on her by the medical system and society.

Jeanette Robertson is an associate professor at Thompson Rivers University in the School of Social Work and Human Service, where she has taught disability studies for seventeen years. Before entering academia, she worked as a social worker in the disability field for a number of years. Her experience in the disability field extends to roles of community educator, social work practitioner, program coordinator, Community Living BC council member, and rehabilitation worker in both the voluntary and governmental sector in Alberta and British Columbia (residential settings, day programs, children's respite services and community living services).

Melanie Thomas has a bachelor of arts degree from the University of Toronto, and a master of education degree in Deaf education from the University of British Columbia. She experienced profound hearing loss in her early twenties and received a cochlear implant in her early forties. She continues to be a strong advocate and support to her students as a Teacher of the Deaf and Hard of Hearing in the school district of Kamloops, British Columbia, where she has taught for the past fifteen years.

Mike Touchie is a member of the Ucluelet First Nation in Port Alberni, B.C. He has been a tireless advocate within the nation and the province of British Columbia for people with disabilities since becoming disabled in 1979. He endured a spinal cord injury after a construction accident, which resulted in paraplegia. He is a founding board member of the British Columbia Aboriginal Network on Disability (BCANDS), where he was a member for sixteen years, and served as president for the last six years of his membership. BCANDS is an award-winning, provincial, not-for-profit, charitable society serving the unique and diverse disability and health resource/support service needs of the Aboriginal population of British Columbia. Mike has also had extensive involvement in ensuring accessibility at the municipal level of his home community, Merritt, B.C., where he has resided for the past twenty years.

Introduction

Jeanette Robertson and Grant Larson

It has been said that civilization advances when what had been perceived as misfortune is recognized as injustice. (International Disability Network 2004: xix)

Working with and for people with disabilities has become one of the most important fields of practice in social work and human service practice. Although one may not intentionally set out to work with persons with disabilities, it is inevitable that anyone working in a human service position will provide support to families, children or adults with disabilities in all fields of practice. People with disabilities are the world's largest minority. A global perspective is certainly critical with respect to being informed about the needs and experiences of people with disabilities, as approximately 15 percent of the world's population, or more than one billion people, are reported to live with a disability (World Health Organization 2011). Therefore, it is critical that those preparing for social work and human service professions are challenged to explore their values and attitudes toward people with disabilities to develop knowledge, skills and strategies that will assist people to live meaningful and fulfilling lives with all the protected rights and privileges of citizens in a democratic society. The aim of this book is to provide a basis upon which students can explore essential topics that will assist in the development of an anti-oppressive and anti-ableist framework for working with people with disabilities.

Critical Disability Theory

The orientation of this book promotes a move away from a traditional medical model or tragedy approach to working with people with disabilities. Instead critical disability theory forms the conceptual and theoretical framework for understanding disability, and for determining the kinds of support and responses required to reduce the barriers and limitations imposed by society on people with disabilities. Critical disability theorists argue that disability is socially constructed, and that disabling barriers are located in the environment, social structures and attitudes of society. They reject the objectification of people with disabilities, their portrayal as victims, and the idea that disability emanates from individual deficiency or pathology (Linton 1998; Oliver 2004; Thomas 2014; Titchkosky and Michalko 2009; Wendell 1996). A critical disability approach is commonly referred to as a social model, an anti-oppressive practice perspective, or a structural approach to understanding the experience of persons with disabilities. This approach acknowledges both the immediate practical needs of those with disabilities and the larger environmental and structural factors that create conditions of disadvantage for people with disabilities.

Critical disability theory maintains that discrimination against people with disabilities is so ordinary that it is invisible. Stigma, social exclusion and negative attitudes toward those with disabilities have become so engrained in modern society that most citizens, laws and policies, organizational structures, and indeed, even social programs, actively discriminate against those with disabilities without even knowing they are doing so. Thus, invisibility means one's experiences are not even considered an inconvenience; they are simply not considered at all by society, service providers and important community institutions. A progressive approach to practice then looks not at the individual with the disability, but at societal and institutional structures that create barriers or stand in the way of paid, integrated employment and full participation in the mainstream of life. While people with disabilities in Canada have made modest gains since Section 15 was enshrined in the *Canadian Charter of Rights and Freedoms* (1982), many continue to experience marginalization in society. In Canada and "across the world, people with disabilities have poorer health outcomes, lower education achievements, less economic participation and higher rates of poverty than people without disabilities" (World Health Organization 2011: 5).

It is important to clarify the language used in this book to refer to people with disabilities. The connection between language, ideology and social attitudes cannot be overstated as language and terminology have the power to influence and determine the meaning or value placed on people by the terms used to describe them. Rich discussions have taken place between the editors and contributors during the development process of the book with respect to the most progressive language to employ. Language is embedded in ideological approaches and thus represents how one understands a construct such as "disability" based on the values, assumptions and premises of that particular belief system. It is important, therefore, to consider the underlying values and meanings that are attached to the language we use.

People-first language (people with disabilities) has been the preference and seen as the most acceptable by the majority of disability advocacy groups in Canada, as this language places the person before the disability (Government of Canada 2006; Roeher Institute 1996; Snow 2001–16). This is stated to emphasize that individuals with disabilities are people first and have the same attributes and characteristics as any other citizen rather than individuals who are wholly defined by one characteristic (their disability). Furthermore, language that labels individuals as categories and reduces them to singular identities (such as a paraplegic or a schizophrenic), and terms that exclude persons with disabilities are stigmatizing, disempowering and inappropriate for use in any context.

As well, in keeping with the position that the concept of disability is socially constructed, various contributors to this text argue that terms such as *(dis)Ability* or *disAbility* are more appropriate as they place focus on the ability and strength of individuals rather than on limitations. However, some authors and disability advocates interpret such terms as tokenistic or reflecting niceties that move away from reclaiming the term "disability" in an unapologetic strengths-based manner. Readers will also be introduced to the social model and implications for language that arise from this approach within the book. For example, people with disabilities are reframed as people with impairments, and "disability" is recast as a process that is imposed on people with impairments through disabling barriers and social arrangements (Thomas 2014). Therefore, within this approach, it is acceptable to employ terms such as "disabled persons" as this infers a social process imposed on people by an ableist society and does not reside within the individual (Titchkosky and Michalko 2009). One can see that there are a range of opinions by academics, service providers and people with disabilities about the most appropriate or preferred language that may be employed. Some people with disabilities, for example, are offended by the term "impairment" and prefer the term "disability." Many also object to being referred to as a "disabled person" for the reasons noted above. After considerable thought and reflection, the editors of this book have chosen to employ the terms "person with a disability" and "disabled person" throughout the text. We acknowledge, however, that acceptable language varies between different groups and contexts, and evolves throughout history. Subsequently, what may be acceptable at the time of writing this book may come into question in the future.

Ableism and Assumptions about Disability

In addition to informing the reader about historical and current policy and practice issues in the disability field, the goal of this book is to enable the reader to become conscious of their own perceptions, values and beliefs, and to assist them in critically examining alternative ways of understanding disability and their interactions with people with disabilities. Regardless of where, when or how a person grew up, all have had experiences with people with disabilities, either in school, in family situations or in community activities, or they may personally experience a visible or invisible disability firsthand. The combination of different experiences and the process of societal socialization about disabilities culminate in an individual's beliefs, perceptions and values regarding disability. These beliefs may range from compassion and empathy, to sympathy and pity, to seeing disability as a misfortune, an annoyance or a burden, to accepting and including people with disabilities in social, occupational and community activities. An individual's attitudes may also have been influenced by the inspiration of people such as Terry Fox, Michael J. Fox, Temple Grandin, Rick Hansen, Stephen Hawking, Helen Keller or Christopher Reeve and their successes in overcoming barriers society has created. It is hoped that students using this text will become aware of, and reflect upon, their experiences and attitudes toward people with disabilities to determine what is helpful and what is unhelpful as they work toward developing an anti-ableist perspective. Understanding and awareness of the ableist context of society is essential for effective social work and human service practice.

"Ableism, or disability oppression, is the pervasive system that oppresses people with disabilities while privileging people who do not currently have disabilities. Like other systems of oppression, ableism operates on many levels, including institutional policy and practice, cultural norms and representations, and individual beliefs and behaviors" (Ostiguy, Peters and Shlasko 2016: 299). Anti-ableist and anti-oppressive practice consist of an awareness of and commitment to challenging the pervasive system of discrimination and exclusion that oppresses people with disabilities, as well as a commitment to challenging the "deeply rooted beliefs about health, productivity, beauty, and the value of human life, perpetuated by the public and private media, [which] combine to create an environment that is often hostile" to people with disabilities (Rauscher and McClintock 1997: 98).

In this book, we address both theoretical and practice issues, and provide a unified framework for helping students understand and critically analyze ableism and other forms of oppression to enhance their practice with people with disabilities. The practice contexts may include child welfare, community living, clinical counselling, mental health services, correctional services, residential and day programs, hospitals, employment services, and many others. Social workers and other human service professionals may support or hinder the full inclusion of persons with disabilities through adherence to particular social policies and practice approaches.

> Any of us who identify as "nondisabled" must know that our self-designation is inevitably temporary, and that a car crash, a virus, a degenerative genetic disease, or a precedent-setting legal decision could change our

status in ways over which we have no control whatsoever. (Bérubé, cited in Linton 1998: viii)

The awareness that we are all temporarily able-bodied acknowledges that many people will at some point become disabled (Marks 1999), therefore alerting us to the process of "othering" people with disabilities. This process serves to divide, isolate and create hierarchies consisting of "we — the nondisabled" and "they — the disabled." Unlike other aspects of social location such as race and gender, it is highly likely that most people will become the disabled "other" experiencing this social location of disability at some point in their life.

The following assumptions and premises support the particular philosophical approach to understanding disability presented in this book. Becoming disabled involves major life changes including loss as well as gain, but it is not the end of a meaningful and productive existence. Disability is not inherently negative. People with disabilities experience discrimination, segregation and isolation as a result of other people's prejudice and institutional ableism, not because of the disability itself. Social beliefs, cultural norms and media images about beauty, intelligence, physical ability, communication and behaviour often negatively influence the way people with disabilities are treated. Societal expectations about economic productivity and self-sufficiency devalue persons who are not able to work, regardless of other contributions they may make to family and community life. Without positive messages about who they are, persons with disabilities are vulnerable to internalizing society's negative messages about disability. Independence and dependence are relative concepts, subject to personal definition, something every person experiences, and neither is inherently positive or negative. Disabled persons have yet to be treated like full and equal citizens although law now protects their right to inclusion in the mainstream of our society (Chouinard 2009; Rauscher and McClintock, cited in Adams, Bell and Griffin 1997).

Approach of the Book

The primary audience for this text is social work, human service, child and youth care, and disability studies students. The book is a contributed text that draws on a variety of expertise across a range of contemporary policy and practice areas from a progressive perspective. Contributors to the text include people with disabilities themselves, as well as others with social work and other human service backgrounds, selected on the basis of their background and expertise in the disability field. The book reflects collaboration among people with disabilities, parents, service providers, and Canadian academics that have taught, published or engaged in research on disability related topics.

The twelve chapters included in the book cover a range of topics: first-person accounts from persons with disabilities; historical perspectives and emerging trends; the exploration of disability demographics as "facts"; theoretical approaches to disability; human rights issues; disability legislation and policy in Canada; life experiences and perspectives of families; intersectionality and disability; Indigenous people and disability; mental health disability; and advocacy and strategies for change. Discussion questions are provided at the conclusion of each chapter to provide opportunities for reflection and reinforcement of concepts and approaches. Case examples are also included in selected chapters for further application of content to practice situations. It is important to acknowledge that there are important topics that are not specifically covered in detail in this text, such as the experiences of families and individuals with child welfare and social assistance systems, and the self-determination of people not deemed legally competent. Such topics require further exploration on the part of students and professionals working in the field.

Chapter 1 introduces the voices of persons with disabilities as the foundation for learning about the "lived experience" with disability and provides the insights of people with disabilities about best practices and policy. As such, it highlights the voices, experiences and suggestions of those most affected and celebrates the resilience and strength of people with disabilities who have overcome the barriers society has placed before them. Chapter 2 is focused upon historical perspectives regarding the treatment of people with disabilities from pre-industrialization to institutional care, to the transition to community care and deinstitutionalization, and then to the recent context of care.

Chapter 3 explores the demographics of disability from a critical perspective to demonstrate how privileging a biomedical approach of disability over a socio-political approach has produced negative outcomes for people with disabilities. Some of the recently reported demographics of people with disabilities in Canada are outlined. The aim of this chapter is to explore the costs and controversies in adopting a purely biomedical approach to disability. Chapter 4 explores theoretical approaches to disability such as critical disability theory, anti-oppressive theory, a social model, feminist theory, and a biomedical approach. The author defines and clarifies a "post-social structural model" of disability. Chapter 5 examines human rights issues, disability and the law in Canada. This includes a historical examination of eugenics laws to the current United Nations Convention on the Rights of Persons with Disabilities with a consideration of charity models and citizenship rights.

Chapter 6 assesses disability policy and Canada's record in regards to the treatment and support of people with disabilities. Chapter 7 presents the life experiences and perspectives of families. It focuses on early childhood experiences with disability and the support needed for families. Chapter 8 discusses the everyday lives of people with disabilities and the impact of intersecting aspects of identity such as gender, race, culture, sexual diversity and disability.

Chapter 9 is devoted to a review of the experiences of Indigenous people with disabilities in Canada and presents a case example for analysis as well as recommendations for addressing the complex issues facing Indigenous people with disabilities. Chapter 10 focuses on the "forgotten terrain" in disability studies — mental health disability. The author espouses an anti-oppressive approach to mental health disability and outlines current issues and trends in the field. A case example is presented for reflection and analysis.

Chapter 11 outlines empowering strategies for change and advocacy by and for people with disabilities. The background to Canadian disability advocacy for persons with disabilities, advocacy by nonprofit agencies, families and self-advocates, and the implications for professional social work practice are explored. Chapter 12 summarizes the themes from previous chapters and discusses the challenges for social work and human service practice.

We are pleased to offer this book as a progressive approach to disability through advancing a critical lens for future policy and practice. We hope it will challenge and inspire students and practitioners alike to think "outside the box," and to examine their own attitudes and values toward disability, so they do not inadvertently impose ableist and oppressive practices on one of Canada's most potentially vulnerable populations — a population whose vulnerability is due to the barriers and limitations imposed on them by society. We present the voices of people with disabilities, with the hope that, above all, readers will understand the importance of honouring and hearing the thoughts and experiences of those most affected by disabling barriers and ableist social arrangements in Canadian society.

References

Adams, Maurianne, Lee Anne Bell and Pat Griffin (eds.). 1997. *Teaching for Diversity and Social Justice: A Sourcebook.* New York: Routledge.

Canadian Charter of Rights and Freedoms, Part I of the *Constitution Act,* 1982, Being Schedule B to the *Canada Act 1982* (U.K.) 1982, c. 11 [Charter].

Chouinard, Vera. 2009. "Legal Peripheries: Struggles over DisAbled Canadians' Places in Law, Society, and Space," pp. 217–225. In Tanya Titchkosky and Rod Michalko (eds.), *Rethinking Normalcy: A Disability Studies Reader.* Toronto: Canadian Scholars Press.

Government of Canada. Human Resources and Skills Development Canada. 2006. *A Way with Words and Images: Suggestions for the Portrayal of People with Disabilities.*

International Disability Network. 2004. "International Disability Rights Monitor 2004: Regional Report of the Americas." ohchr.tind.io/record/6605/.

Linton, Simi. 1998. *Claiming Disability: Knowledge and Identity.* New York: New York University Press.

Marks, Deborah. 1999. *Disability: Controversial Debates and Psychosocial Perspectives.*

London: Routledge.

Oliver, Michael. 2004. "If I Had a Hammer: The Social Model in Action." In John Swain, Sally French, Colin Barnes and Carol Thomas (eds.), *Disabling Barriers – Enabling Environments* 2nd edition. London: Sage.

Ostiguy, Benjamin, Madeline Peters, and Davey Shlasko. 2016. "Ableism." In Maurianne Adams, Lee Anne Bell, Diane Goodman, and Khyati Joshi (eds.), *Teaching for Diversity and Social Justice* 3rd edition. New York: Routledge.

Rauscher, Laura, and Mary McClintock. 1997. "Ableism Curriculum Design." In Maurianne Adams, Lee Anne Bell and Pat Griffin (eds.), *Teaching for Diversity and Social Justice: A Sourcebook*. New York: Routledge.

Roeher Institute. 1996. *Disability, Community and Society: Exploring the Links*. North York, ON: Roeher Institute.

Snow, Kathie. 2001–16. "To Ensure Inclusion, Freedom, and Respect for All, It's Time to Embrace People First Language." <http://nebula.wsimg.com/1c1af57f9319dbf909 ec52462367fa88?AccessKeyId=9D6F6082FE5EE52C3DC6&disposition=0&allow origin=1>.

Thomas, Carol. 2014. "Disability and Impairment." In John Swain, Sally French, Colin Barnes and Carol Thomas (eds.), *Disabling Barriers – Enabling Environments* 3rd edition. London: Sage.

Titchkosky, Tanya, and Rod Michalko. 2009. "Introduction." In Tanya Titchkosky and Rod Michalko (eds.), *Rethinking Normalcy: A Disability Studies Reader*. Toronto, ON: Canadian Scholars Press Inc.

Wendell, Susan. 1996. *The Rejected Body: Feminist Philosophical Reflections on Disability*. New York: Routledge.

World Health Organization. 2011. "Summary World Report on Disability." <whqlibdoc. who.int/publications/2011/9789240685215_eng.pdf?ua=1>.

Chapter 1

Privileging the Voices of People with Disabilities

Mike Touchie, Melanie Thomas,

Jaclyn Porter & Lorea Regan

It is only fitting that a book titled *Disability and Social Change: A Progressive Canadian Approach* would begin by hearing the voices of people with disabilities, as they are recognized as the experts in the field of disability and social change. Inclusion of the unique stories, voices and perspectives, as conveyed by Mike Touchie, Melanie Thomas, Jaclyn Porter and Lorea Regan illustrates the diversity of experiences with respect to disability. Such stories convey the presence or absence of enabling environments and disabling barriers, as reflected within individual and societal support and acceptance. Congruent with a progressive approach to disability — their experiences also reflect a consideration of how aspects such as race, class and gender impact their everyday lives in differing ways.

There are also important distinctions to be made between the aspects of acquiring a disability versus being born with a disability. Aspects of identity and self-perception evolve in very different ways for someone who acquires a disability versus someone who has always lived with and accepted their disability. While these authors reflect diversity in this regard, and with respect to different aspects of disability (i.e., mobility and hearing, etc.), it is important to note there are many perspectives not reflected within these stories. There is a danger in assuming that any one person's unique experience will reflect that of another person, although there may be similar structural or attitudinal barriers acknowledged. There are so many diverse factors that influence individuals' daily lives and responses to disability that we must be cautious not to assume homogeneity of experience, while staying alert to the social arrangements which support or curtail people's experiences as valued members of society.

These four individuals were invited to contribute to the book on the basis of their ability and openness to share their stories. There were no limits or alterations placed on their contributions. These stories reflect the writers' candid experiences. While acknowledging Mike, Melanie, Jaclyn, and Lorea's strength and tenacity in general, we must avoid falling into the ableist trap of interpreting these stories through a tragedy lens, as this frames disability as an anomaly to be pitied or risen above or avoided at all cost. This approach lends itself to creating inspirational hero archetypes who have risen above their disabilities and challenged the odds in order to fit into "normal" society. Moreover, one should acknowledge these are individuals who are carrying on with their lives and embracing themselves as full citizens of society despite the pervasive disabling barriers and social arrangements that may thwart their endeavours.

My Disability Is the Least of My Problems
Mike Touchie

This is my story about my life after acquiring my disability. These are things that have happened to me, and this is how I have adapted to a new life. It all started one day in 1980 when I decided to tear apart a small building to rebuild a larger building on our property. I was two months into my nineteenth year of age at the time. I was a student, so this day was not the best day of my life, to say the least.

I had started by tearing off the door and a part of the side wall of this building and then decided to take my crowbar and go to the inside rear of the building to knock off a small board on the rear wall. Much to my dismay, it so happened to be that this wall was supporting the whole building, and the building collapsed on top of me, breaking my back and severing my spinal cord — that being the last day to walk. I was taken by ambulance to our local hospital and diagnosed with a spinal injury and then flown to Vancouver and admitted to the spinal cord unit in Shaughnessy Hospital, where I was treated and very well cared for by the nurses and doctors.

After a week on the spinal cord unit, I was sent for surgery and had two Harrington rods put on my spine, and that was the beginning of my recovery process. I was in the spinal cord unit for three months, then transferred to GF Strong Rehabilitation Centre for rehab for the next seven months. This whole process was very much so a culture shock as I had never been in a large city (Vancouver) in all my life; I had grown up on a First Nations reserve in Port Alberni, British Columbia.

One thing that I learned early in with dealing with my disability was not to blame anyone for an *accident* that had happened. Then to do my best with getting on with life, to do all I could and take advantage of the rehabilitation at GF Strong Rehabilitation Centre.

When you come from a small rural community like so many Aboriginal people, going into the large urban cities is very shocking. You grow up in a small town of maybe one thousand to eighteen thousand people, it is very stressful, to say the least, never mind just having to deal with a huge new problem in your life after being told that you will never be able to walk again at such a young age. I was angry and frustrated at the whole process. I was in constant pain 24/7 as a result of the amount of damage done to the spinal cord. I was prescribed many different pain killers which I really didn't like but had to take — sometimes they helped, and most of the time they didn't help at all. Thirty-three years later I still live with the chronic pain.

I was only two months into my nineteenth year by the time that I had reached rehab. I had already seen so many people from the ages of thirteen to eighty years of age that had spinal injuries from anything from car accidents to tobogganing. Some had similar injuries as I did, and others had more severe low spinal injuries or broken necks. Few walked away from their injuries, and those who did, I was told that they had bruised their cord.

And others had just fractured their vertebrae. Speaking of age groups, the two largest influences on my life were two people who had accidents who were admitted to the spinal unit. One of these people was 13-year-old Jamie. He had been tobogganing and hit a fence post and had broken his neck and was now paralysed from the neck down. I was only on the unit for a week when he was admitted. And then there was Jamima: she was 80 years of age, and she was in a car accident and had also broken her neck and was also paralysed for the neck down. They both had very positive attitudes about what had happened to them. I really looked up to these two people. Both had very serious accidents. At one end of the scale, Jamie, at thirteen, had just started his life, and Jamima was nearing the end of her life, and I was nineteen — really just starting adulthood. I followed their lives for a few years. Jamie ended up living independently, and Jamima went into extended care, and I still think of them today.

In the next seven months of rehabilitation, while in rehab I made a lot of new friends who all ended up being some of the best support a person could ask for as they all had different types of disabilities. I learned a lot about the varying types of disabilities there are in our world. What I never expected was how society would treat people with disabilities in the 1980s. When we were out shopping or pushing our chairs down the sidewalk, people would stare at us or walk around us like we were contagious. After spending the next seven months at GF Strong Rehabilitation Centre I was discharged home where I really started to learn what complications come with the disability, like bed sores, bladder infections and kidney stones. Sores were a result of poor blood circulation, and bladder and kidney infections were from not drinking enough fluids or the wrong kinds of fluids.

This was a huge adjustment in learning what kind of independence that you have. Everyone at home wanted to help me with everything from getting my meals to simple tasks like getting a glass of water. It was hard not to offend people when all they wanted to do was help you out. Trying to explain to everyone that you are quite capable of doing things for yourself was hard for them to accept.

I learned that dairy products contributed to calcium buildup in the bladder and kidneys, resulting in having to go to the hospital to have the buildup crushed and removed, resulting in infections and lots of antibiotics.

After a few months at home I returned to GF Strong for further rehabilitation and to learn how to drive a vehicle with hand controls. I had to take a full defensive driving course. I think it was a six-week in-class course, which today I am very happy to have had the opportunity to participate in, as I continue to drive and it affords me enormous independence.

One year after my accident the Harrington rods in my back became dislodged, and I had to have them removed. As I was waiting for surgery, on the same unit, I met a lady who became my wife, and we had two beautiful daughters. Meeting my wife made me a stronger person; she was so supportive with helping me deal with my disability as it was, only a year after my injury. Which reminds me about when we were trying to have a baby. I didn't know at the time if I could, since there was not all that much research done for people with spinal injuries. As I started to research and talk to professionals about whether it was possible or not, suggestions were made to try, so we did and my wife got pregnant after a year or so, and we had our first child (daughter). About 18 months following this, we were getting ready to have our second child (another daughter).

At this time in 1981 I was also looking for some kind of relief from chronic pain that I was having due to damaged nerves around the spinal cord. I made an appointment with a doctor who specialized in spinal injuries, and my wife and our 1-year-old daughter attended this appointment with me. We had entered the doctor's office and started our appointment, and he proceeded to ask us questions, the first one being, "Is that your baby?" — assuming my wife had our child in a previous relationship. When I assured him that the baby was our child, his immediate response was to reach for his textbook on a shelf behind him. This goes to show that professionals don't know everything. I was a little surprised at his reaction of scepticism and disbelief at the time. As for the problem of experiencing ongoing chronic pain, I had lost so much weight, which was affecting my health — as mentioned earlier, bed sores and kidney and bladder stones. My weight at the day of my injury was around 175 pounds, and by the time that I left rehab I had dropped down to 115 pounds and was as skinny as rake. I even dropped down to as low as 112 pounds, and the surgeon suggested what was called a DREZ lesion (Dorsal Root Entry Zone Lesion), which was an experimental procedure at the time, and I told the doctor that I had nothing to lose so "let's go forward with it."

At the time of my injury there were many expenses that needed to be covered for all my medical equipment through Indian Affairs Health Canada. At times this was quite a procedure to get equipment ordered and delivered to me. Most times when I needed new wheelchairs, I had to order up to a year in advance of receiving it, and this is still the case today. It also is getting tougher as Treaties are being settled with Canada and the province of British Columbia. All kinds of things need to be covered, such as medications, catheters leg bags, connectors, bath benches, cushions and dressings, and on occasion, cushion covers and reachers — all these things are required to live a comfortable life. The other thing that is needed to have an independent lifestyle is hand controls for a vehicle.

Acquiring a disability was a whole learning experience for me over the years. Even today I still find that people are still ignorant about peoples with disabilities. For instance, when my wife and I go to a restaurant, servers still ask my wife, "What would he like to order?" Excuse me, but I have a voice and I can order for myself. Therefore, don't assume just because we have a disability that we cannot speak for ourselves. What I have learned was how to become an advocate on behalf of people with disabilities and to be patient with society, including our government, as they like to change the definition of disability.

Around this time of my life I had found some employment with an organization that counselled to people with disabilities. Finding employment was not an easy task, to say the least, as I found out that society was not ready for people with disabilities to be in the mainstream or to be supporting themselves in the work force. My job was to counsel to Aboriginal peoples with spinal injuries. During my employment with this organization, one of the most shocking things to happen to me as an Aboriginal person was that the organization had a dress code within the office that required employees to wear neckties, slacks and a dress shirt to look professional. Over our history as Aboriginal peoples, of being taken advantage of by many different sectors of white society, Aboriginal peoples have basically learned not to trust anyone who dressed in this manner. Therefore, one of my clients at the time who was from a small community suggested that I was not an Indian (Aboriginal) at all. This statement caught me off guard at the time as I was Indian as Indian gets, being fresh off the reserve myself, having only lived in Vancouver for about a year.

Later on in the day I tried to figure out why my client would say such a thing. It took a while but I figured it out, that it was the way that I was dressing. After I was told this, I tried to dress more casual, which made my clients more comfortable. I worked a few different jobs around Vancouver while I lived there. I worked as a security dispatcher; worked for a pharmaceutical company packing pills; and even tried working for a surveying company.

When we were in rehab in the eighties, it was common to use the term *gimp* as a descriptor of our disabilities and we were not offended at all by this slang, as it is today. I have heard *handicapped, disability, challenged, physically challenged, disabled.* Goodness knows how many more descriptors we will acquire over the years, and there is a definition now for every different disabling condition out there, now known as *syndromes.* The changes in language and descriptors can be very frustrating, so when I address groups I have to be politically correct.

Over the years of dealing with my disability, I became an advocate to address the issues of disabilities. Dealing with society can be one of the most frustrating things for me. I have had arguments and verbal confrontations with people about the parking stalls that were put in place for persons with disabilities. I have almost been bitten by dogs in the backs of trucks and almost had physical confrontations with people while trying to tell them that they were in the wrong parking in parking stalls that were meant for persons with disabilities. I really don't know why society chooses to be so ignorant and confrontational about issues that we are entitled to. As if people with disabilities don't have enough struggles in life.

The Invisible Disability: Advantageous or Not?
Melanie Thomas

It could be argued that hearing loss is an "invisible" disability. It may not be obvious, at least initially. If so, is this an advantage or a disadvantage to the person in question, for example, regarding job opportunities and social situations? Having lived with hearing loss for thirty years, I can say there are advantages *and* disadvantages to not having an "obvious" disability. Ultimately, however, it is society's reaction to the disability that renders the invisibility advantageous or not.

Growing up in a comfortable, upper-middle class suburb in Toronto, disability was not something I ever thought about. I had normal hearing all through my childhood and teenage years, and had a privileged upbringing with a large beautiful home, a huge backyard and pool to play in, good schools, winter vacations in Florida, four siblings and two loving and caring parents. Lots of good friends around the neighbourhood at a time when kids of all ages just played together outside a lot. There was no one with any kind of physical disability in my family, and no one with hearing loss.

My siblings and I were all encouraged to attend university. I was thrilled to be accepted into the University of Toronto's Bachelor of Arts degree program at age twenty-one. I had dreams of becoming a teacher, maybe a high school English teacher, as I loved the great works of literature, especially Shakespeare and the

Brontë sisters. It was there in my first undergraduate year that I noticed I was having trouble hearing the professors in my classes. I certainly didn't recall having any trouble hearing teachers in high school. Was it because the classes were much larger? Most professors didn't use microphone systems. I started to compensate by sitting close to the professors. Losing my hearing was the farthest thing from my mind.

One day specifically stands out to me. I was sitting by our pool with my best friend. We were the only ones home. She was looking at me questioningly and said, "Are you going to answer that?" Apparently the phone was ringing inside the house, but I didn't hear a thing. Also, shortly after that, my mother asked me to unplug the kettle because it had reached a boil. I wasn't hearing that high-pitched, whooshing sound. It was my mom who suggested I get my hearing tested. She thought that I may just have an ear infection, which I was prone to since I swam a lot in our pool.

I was shocked to learn that my first audiogram revealed a moderate, sloping bilateral hearing loss. Overall I was getting along pretty well! For those readers that are not aware, there are basically two kinds of hearing loss. *Conductive* is caused by a blockage of some kind, usually in the middle ear or a deformity to the outer ear. For example, a bad cold can cause a conductive hearing loss due to liquid in the middle ear. Conductive is usually temporary. *Sensorineural* is more dire as it is damage to the inner ear, where the cochlear is located, and this usually entails damage to the nerve/hair cells. Sensorineural is always permanent and can be progressive. The audiologist didn't explain too much, just that it was sensorineural and that I may need hearing aids. *What?*

This was before the days of the Internet with a world of information at your fingertips. My parents were under the impression that I could get some kind of procedure done and "fix it." They arranged to have me see other specialists for other opinions. The end result was always the same: sensorineural, likely progressive. Nothing to be done. Purchase hearing aids. *Are you kidding me?* I was going to be a teacher! How could I hear students? I was twenty-one and about to move out on my own into the world of independent adulthood! This could not be happening! I was in shock and denial, not to mention anger. In fact, looking back I recognized the stages of grief in myself as described by Dr. Elisabeth Kübler-Ross (1969):

- *Denial stage*: Trying to avoid the inevitable.
- *Anger stage*: Frustrated outpouring of bottled-up emotion.
- *Bargaining stage*: Seeking in vain for a way out.
- *Depression stage*: Final realization of the inevitable.
- *Acceptance stage*: Finally finding the way forward.

This journey is individualistic and highly personal. I didn't reach the final stage of acceptance for a long time. Denial was my protective blanket. Well-meaning people told me not to feel sorry for myself. However, I needed to feel sorry for myself, and grieve, because it was like part of me had died. Seeing me like this was hard on my family and friends, because I was a happy, motivated person before, and now I was quiet and miserable. I was going through something I knew they could not possibly relate to. Seeking counselling would have been an obvious avenue now, but it wasn't something that was mentioned then. What I did find myself falling back on was spirituality. I was raised Catholic and found myself praying for a solution. The solution was not as forthcoming as I wanted, however. I found myself angry with God, but luckily I didn't stay angry. Prayer was comforting and a way to help me see through the darkness.

How we take good hearing for granted! Catching the asides, the jokes and banter, not to mention important information, was getting so difficult for me. I gave up on hearing professors. In fact I would purposely sit beside someone with large handwriting so that I could read and piece together what was going on. But it made me feel like a fraud. These weren't my thoughts, I had to rely on someone else's interpretation. More importantly, I loved those literary discussions! Now it was too hard to keep up. But I was determined to do well, and I would go home and pour over the books and the various critics' opinions. It was self-teaching. Then I would be ready to contribute something interesting if the professor called on me out of the blue. Halfway through that first year at the University of Toronto, I did purchase my first set of hearing aids, and when sitting very closely to the professor, I did do better than before. Though I hated admitting I needed them, even to myself. I wore my hair long to cover them and avoided making new friends.

Dating was a daunting prospect as well. I mean, when do you mention, "By the way, I'm going deaf!" I was an attractive girl and had a fair amount of interest. I dreaded those initial phone calls when questions were asked and arrangements were made. What if the restaurant is dark — how could I speech read? What if it is too noisy? What if he wants to see a movie and discuss it after? Phone calls were becoming so difficult anyway. This was a time before texting or emails. I did date here and there but as soon as I felt "exposed" I would stop returning phone calls. I was embarrassed by my hearing loss. I had a couple of long-term boyfriends but only committed when I felt they would be accepting of me the way I was.

I was lucky enough to have good friends that were worried about me and made every attempt to accommodate me. When we went out to dinner or a pub, they would bring little note books and write things down. They knew to only ask me to see foreign films with them, because there would be subtitles. They let me know in no uncertain terms that although this was *horrible and completely unfair*, it was *not* going to impact our friendship. For this I am eternally grateful, and I wish that for anyone facing disability.

My best friend, Veronica, was becoming a teacher and actually worked with some students with special needs. She showed me some sign language, which we used when we were in a situation that was hard for me. That was my first exposure to sign language and it planted a seed in my brain. If I couldn't teach in a regular classroom, could I work with children who had hearing loss and needed sign language? Maybe, just maybe, I could be a role model for them. After all, I wasn't old. I had no idea what the postsecondary options were for teaching the deaf, but I was going to find out.

I graduated with my Bachelor of Arts degree from the University of Toronto but wanted to take some time off before thinking about a new program. I had to work twice as hard as anyone else and needed a break. I went to Europe for a couple months with Veronica, and that was one of the best times of my life. We met a lot of interesting people. What worked well for me in Europe was that many people did not speak English as their first language. Therefore, when someone was speaking to me, their rate of speech was often a bit slower. A moderate rate of speech is very helpful for hard of hearing people. People speaking too fast is always a major impediment to understanding.

I got in touch with the Canadian Hearing Society in Toronto to find out what they could do for me. One of their mandates was to advocate for hard of hearing people in the work realm. They would also work with me and the employer to reach decisions about accommodations. The City of Toronto had an affirmative action policy to hire more people with disabilities. This is how I came to work in the accounts payable department at City Hall. It was a *huge* turnaround for me to present myself as a "person with disability," and the first step towards acceptance for me. Although accounting was the farthest thing from my interests with a BA in English literature, it was good money, and I needed time to re-evaluate my future. There was also a certain comfort in knowing an outside agency was advocating for me and my needs. It wasn't all up to me to inform people. Outside agencies that advocate for people with disabilities are invaluable, because no one should feel powerless and alone in their struggle.

The two years that I worked at Toronto City Hall was a steep learning curve. I had never realized how much information is passed on through auditory means. Although the "outside agency" was there to initially advocate for me, it was still up to me to remind people on a daily basis. People shouldn't forget, but they do. My disability is not evident but is very real. I had to constantly remind people that I needed accommodation. It got tiresome, but I started to realize that it could be worse — after all, I was still relatively very healthy and intelligent. Slowly I was realizing that I did have something to offer. I had researched and found that there was an excellent Teacher of the Deaf program at the University of British Columbia (UBC), and my parents had recently moved out to British Columbia as a transition to retirement. I decided to apply to UBC and see if I even stood a chance of being accepted. I still had to go through the regular Teacher Education program at UBC, before going into Deaf Education, which was a graduate degree. It seemed like such a long haul! My parents taught me that I could do anything I put my mind to, however, and for that I am grateful.

Recently after giving a lecture on my journey to a university social work class, a student asked me if I had felt "double discrimination" in life, because I was disabled *and* female. I had never even considered being female a possible point of discrimination. I was lucky enough to be born at a great time for women, in a progressive country, and into a family that valued the girls and boys equally. However, the sad truth is that this double discrimination is a reality for many disabled women in various other parts of the world.

Moving out west to start a new life was thrilling and terrifying. I did have my parents and also two siblings living in Victoria. I started my Teacher Education program at the University of Victoria (UVIC). There, I felt strong enough to approach the Disability Resource Centre and ask for accommodations. They advocated for me to professors and also arranged for a student to photocopy her notes for me. This was a huge move forward. I was starting to realize that I could *expect* accommodations, but I had to reach out to ask for them.

After the first year there, I transferred to UBC because the Deaf Education graduate program was offered there. I still had to complete two years of the regular Teacher Education program, however, then at least another two years for the Deaf Education graduate program. But because UBC is so much bigger than UVIC, it had a far more comprehensive Disability Resource Centre. They gave a student carbon copy notepaper, so that at the end of each class, all she had to do was rip the top cover off and give it to me right there. This was before technology was available. Now, certainly people can type and send a text right away, or there are other technologies available for hard of hearing students, such as CART (Communication Access Real-time Translation) or SMART Boards (computer projected boards). At the time, however, I was thrilled to have notes given to me immediately after class.

The Teacher Education program was difficult, but I did have some support from the professor who was the director of the Special Education program in Deafness. His name is Dr. Perry Leslie and he became my mentor. It was Dr. Leslie who taught me self-advocacy and encouraged me to become a teacher of the deaf after my Teacher Education program was complete. For the first time, someone saw my disability as a strength, because he said I could be a positive role model to students facing hearing loss.

I worked hard in the undergraduate Teacher Education program to sustain a high overall average, and received excellent reports from my practicum leaders. I was thrilled and proud to be accepted as a graduate student in the Deaf Education program in 1993. What I also loved was the relatively small group that formed the inaugural Master's Degree in Deaf Education program. There were only twelve of us, as it is a selective program, and we were together for all classes. Besides myself, there was one other hard of hearing individual. This was a rebirth of sorts for me, because I was with people who had a special interest in deafness and sign language. More importantly my opinion was sought and valued *because* of my disability. After a decade of feeling shame, embarrassment and anger over my disability, I had made it to a place where I truly had something to offer because of it. Further, we were all learning sign language together, taught by respected members of the Deaf community. I was learning that Deaf people have their own culture — hence the capitalization of "Deaf." Further, Deaf people have their own language, American Sign Language, and *do not* consider their deafness a "disability." This was another milestone for me — realizing that perhaps I'm just different, rather than *disabled*. I certainly didn't feel disabled in a restaurant with my signing friends! I was in on the jokes and banter and part of things.

Another amazing eye-opener was my practicum experience at the B.C. Provincial School for the Deaf in Burnaby. This was a place where everyone signed, and many people wore hearing aids. Many Deaf people choose not to wear hearing aids, but some do wear them. Further, it was a "hub" for the Deaf community of Vancouver. Deaf adults were employed there as teachers or teaching assistants, and, of course, the students thought it was really cool that a new practicum student was deaf. I attended many Deaf social events outside of my practicum hours, just because it was so much fun. There were pub nights, baseball games, picnics and camping. I still keep in touch with many of my Deaf friends from those days.

After two years of graduate school, which included difficult course work, comprehensive examinations and a thesis, I graduated with a Master's of Education in Deaf Education. That year I also started my first teaching job and got married. Yes, I met a young man at the University of Victoria who became my boyfriend and later became my husband. Mike encouraged me to explore the Deaf community and culture even though he is hearing. He took sign language courses and learned about Deaf culture and thought it was all so interesting.

As many people know, buying a house can be difficult for a young couple in Vancouver, B.C. After three years and our first child, we decided to try a smaller place where housing was more affordable. We ended up in beautiful Kamloops, B.C., where I started with the Kamloops school district as a teacher of the Deaf and hard of hearing. I enjoyed meeting new Deaf friends and students. There we had our second child as well. When my kids started school, I realized that I was their advocate on so many levels, but my hearing loss made that so difficult. Not surprisingly, a smaller centre such as Kamloops does not have the same amount of Deaf individuals as does Vancouver. I was back in ""hearing culture" so I wanted a better way to access it. I learned about an amazing new device called a cochlear implant, which actually was not new but had recently undergone rapid and amazing transformations. Soon I realized that might be the right path for me.

I received my cochlear implant in January 2005. It has been incredible and has given me back virtually all the frequencies in my right ear. The cochlear implant team at St. Paul's Hospital in Vancouver were skilled, caring and compassionate. Here in B.C., adults are only eligible for one cochlear implant even though you must be severely to profoundly deaf in both ears to qualify. There isn't enough funding to cover two implants for everyone who needs them. Hopefully that will change because I wouldn't hesitate to have this procedure done in my left ear also. I encourage anyone who has bilateral severe-profound hearing loss to explore this avenue.

There has been some controversy in the Deaf community regarding implanting babies. Babies are screened at birth for hearing loss, and as the cochlea does not grow throughout life, it is indeed possible to implant infants. This has raised ethical questions in the Deaf community. Many Deaf people feel that deaf babies should be allowed to make that decision for themselves when they are old enough to do so. I don't feel this way. The optimal time for oral language learning is between birth and five years of age. Adults who have been deaf since birth and opt for a cochlear implant rarely have significant success. This is because they do not have significant auditory memory. Attaching meaning to sound is a cognitive process that is honed over time throughout life. Who can blame hearing parents for wanting to give their baby this opportunity to hear? Most deaf babies are in fact born to hearing parents. Relatively speaking, congenital deafness is rare. Babies implanted around the age of one year have shown speech and language levels on par with their hearing peers when they reach school age. This is most likely if the baby is bilaterally implanted, which is the norm in some provinces and states.

I continue to wear a hearing aid on my left ear and my cochlear implant speech processor on the right ear. My cochlear implant has given me back a world of sound, although I am still a person functioning with a severe unilateral hearing loss. I am so grateful that I can move between two worlds, hearing and deaf, because I can function as both. This has indeed enriched my life.

Is the invisibility of deafness advantageous? Yes, but only if there is personal acceptance of the disability. *Personal* acceptance helps provide the needed bridge to *societal* acceptance.

Snap Out of It
Jaclyn Porter

Post Diagnosis, Age 17

"Snap out of it!" she yelled, red-faced with her hands on her hips. "Why can't you just snap out of it?"

I looked up at my grandmother's face with tears threatening to fall from my eyes. "Be normal. Be normal. Be normal." I repeat in my head over and over like a Gregorian chamber song. As I looked into my grandmother's eyes, I watched the fear and helplessness behind her question. She is not the kind of woman who is okay with not knowing what to do. Looking back now I know she was trying to help me in the only way she knew how. Having a grandchild with bipolar disorder is never easy. Lucky for me I come from a family of people who never give up.

Downward Spiral, Age 21

Fast-forward four years and I am lying on the sofa in my apartment surrounded by dirty dishes, dust bunnies and empty Slurpee cups. I haven't been outside in days. I haven't showered or taken off my faded, red plaid flannel pyjamas in days either. At this point in my life cable television is my best and only friend. I flip through the channels hoping one of the many programs that I have labelled "my shows" will lift me out of my ever-sinking depression. I carefully select *American Idol*, thinking music will make me feel better. Instead I start comparing myself to the visually perfect contestants on the screen. They seem so happy. I couldn't tell you the last time I felt anything other than numb or down. Secondly, everyone on the stage is glamorous and beautiful. I have spent the past month in some form of elastic waist pants because I am gaining weight so fast I can't wear anything else. I look down at the buttons on my red flannel pyjama shirt and notice that there used to be eight buttons and now there are only four. These buttons had served their purpose for as long as possible. I do not blame the buttons for abandoning ship; they could only stretch to hold my shirt together for so long. Bitterly, I look down at the floor, which was once a toffee-brown shag carpet: it is now lined with a chip-bag-shaped rug, designed by the likes of Frito Lay's. I blame the medication for this transformation of my body. I am constantly wondering what is worse: being fat and numb from medication or thin and dead.

University the Early Years, Age 24

I am sitting in a round-shaped room in the brand-new building at the university. It's the first Friday in the school year, and my professor tells us to share why we want to become Human Service Workers. I watch as people take turns sharing their stories, some personal and moving, others academic in nature. I am one of the last people to share and I have been debating what my answer should be since the moment those words came casually out of my professor's mouth.

"Should I say it?" I think to myself, "No people will think that I'm crazy. Do I really care anymore? Yes, I actually care a lot about what other people think."

"Jaclyn, it's your turn." My professor says with an encouraging smile. I start to question how long it has been "my turn" for.

I finally blurt out, "Hi, my name is Jaclyn Porter, and I want to be a Human Service Worker because I have bipolar disorder and I want to help other people like me." I say this all in one breath and immediately scan the room and try to gauge as many reactions as possible at once. In the moment, everyone's reactions seemed appropriate to me. However, the next several weeks changed my opinion on whether to disclose to others about my illness or not. I was bombarded with questions, which at times were innocent in nature and easy to answer. Others may have been innocent in intent but came across as extremely ignorant.

The most surprising comments and questions came from one girl with big bright-blue eyes and an even larger personality. Her confidence in herself at such a young age intimated me. Actually, everything about this girl intimidated me. A few days after I had disclosed in class, she said to me after everyone had left the room, "I just wanted to let you know my mom has bipolar disorder too. So I know what you are going through — well not really because I don't have it." She laughed and threw her head back in an animated fashion. "I don't have it but I have seen what my mom goes through." She paused and looked slightly confused, most likely because my reaction to her disclosure was a big shit-eating grin.

"What does your mom do?" I ask with much more intent placed in that single sentence than hopefully she could detect.

She grinned and her face lit up like a ray of sunshine, "She's a writer!" The pride in her voice was evident, and I could tell in that short sentence how much she admired her mom.

This was an "A-ha!" moment in my life because it gave me hope. Hope that there are more people like me who are diagnosed with a mental illness who are affected for a fraction of their lives. I do not struggle every day. In fact, I have always felt the expression "struggling with a mental illness" never quite fit for me. I struggle when I can't find my car in a parking lot; I don't feel as though my life is a struggle. I live every day just like everyone else. I will always have a diagnosis of bipolar disorder. Is this all that defines me? Absolutely not, and it doesn't define my friend's mom either, or many of the other people I have met over the years that have a mental illness. If that is the one message I could get people to understand is that mentally ill people do not spend their days thinking about being mentally ill. It does not consume our lives. Sometimes it makes our lives challenging. It can create a lot of headaches and heartache for ourselves and the people we love. But first and foremost we are people. I don't have a birthmark or tattoo on my body that warns people who are uncomfortable or uneducated in the area of mental health that a person with bipolar disorder is in the room. At times I think it would help others if they could physically see that I and millions of others in the world are born with these illnesses. We never asked for them.

Pressure, So Much Pressure, Age 28

I watched my pupils in the mirror fluctuate in size, big and then small. I knew it was happening again but I just didn't want to admit it.

"Fake it until you make it, Jaclyn. Come on! Pull yourself together!" I yell at myself in the mirror like a motivational gym coach.

I was almost done my practicum and I had made a deal with myself months before that I wasn't allowed to get manic until after school was done. All the stress of being in my last semester of school was building every day. My brain was burning the contract we had made a little bit as the weeks went on. At this point my job was to put water on the flames and make sure no one smelled smoke. This proved to be especially challenging at a practicum that dealt with individuals with mental illnesses every day. I had to try to pretend to be a person with a mental illness who wasn't experiencing symptoms until my placement was done, for my own sense of pride, not because my practicum would not accommodate what I was going through.

I clench my teeth and look in the mirror again. My pupils stop dilating and I know I can fake not being hypomanic for another day. Hypomania is the bratty calm before the storm. I think I make my best jokes when I'm hypomanic. Most people think I'm a jerk when I'm hypomanic. This is the big difference between a regular day and hypomania. My perception of what is appropriate and what is not is completely off, which is why if I go to practicum and try to be quiet, then no one will suspect I'm hypomanic. "Fake it until you make it" has been my motto for a long time.

Reflection: Present

You'd think by now I would give up the "I don't need help" but I haven't. I just relapsed at the end of my practicum and I still don't like admitting I need help. Finally admitting I need help got me back to the one place as a social worker I hope to prevent people from going. The psychiatric ward of a hospital isn't that bad but it sure is humbling. As a person with a disability, you can work your ass off and still end up at the bottom. Being successful doesn't make your illness go away and that is a lesson I have recently learned. No matter what I do, bipolar will be here inside me. Sometimes that is not a negative thing — having bipolar has given me a different perspective on life that I'm grateful for. But it has also made me into a different person when I'm manic. A person that is selfish, mean and at times a little scary. I have had friendships and relationships end because of my actions while manic. This is the part of having bipolar that I wish I could get rid of. Depression is easier to understand and manage compared to the monster that is mania. Even if I am manic and acting strangely and people are staring at me in public, I can live with all of that. It's when I hurt my family and friends that I can't stand this illness. I can't take anything that I've said back and that's absolutely the hardest part.

Just Watch Me
Lorea Regan

I was born in 1963 with my arm missing just below my elbow. As I was born with my disability, I adapted without knowing any different. I grew up with two brothers and always thought I could do anything that they could do. I played baseball, rode a bike, climbed trees, water skied, swam and also learned to drive a standard car. Some of these accomplishments, such as learning to drive a standard vehicle, were met with great surprise or dismay by many people.

I never let my disability prevent me from trying to succeed at anything! I raised three children who are all adults now. During my school years, classmates were kind for the most part. A few were not so nice and would tease me somewhat. Sometimes I could see whispering and pointing at my arm, but I just became used to it. I did look different. I think that most people are curious about "what happened?" I feel I was not really treated any different than other kids at home or at school, nor did I want to be. Friends often told me that they forgot I only had one arm because I managed to do everything. People would often ask me to tie my shoes and would watch with amazement.

One of the things that I cannot do to this day is put my hair up in a ponytail and that frustrates me. Thank goodness for hair clips! I also cannot do up the clasps on my bracelets or watches. I have been told many times that I am amazing and an inspiration to others. I had a prosthesis for a while growing up thanks to the Shriners Hospital in Portland, Oregon. We would go to Portland two to three times a year so that I could be fitted for my artificial arm. However, I ended up finding that the prosthesis actually got in my way and chose not to wear it. When I was fourteen, I was also fitted for an arm that had a hand. They matched the size of hand and skin tone to my other arm. I wore it a few times but, again, I felt it got in my way.

At age twenty-three, I decided to go to Camosun College in Victoria, British Columbia, to take the Long-term Care Aide course. I phoned first to enquire about the course to see if my limitations would prevent me from being accepted into the program. At first the woman I was speaking with said that she did not think I could manage the course or the work. I was upset. I then said to her, "You can give me any kind of test first to see if there is anything that I cannot do. If I can't pass that then I will not take the course!" I felt the woman was shocked at this response. I later passed the course at the top of my class. This was huge for me. I was so proud of myself. I was hired at the two hospitals that I had done my practicum at during my studies.

I was a long-term care aide for ten years and received the honorary five-year and ten-year pins they give out, which also made me feel great. I then decided to be a "stay-at-home mom" so I could be there for my children while they were young. Once while I was still working, a woman at the hospital, who had been my partner for a couple of weeks, asked me, "Where did your arm go?" I said, "I was born without it!" She was so shocked and told me that she was sure I had it the day before! I laughed and so did the other girls who overheard this conversation. This was not the only time that people have argued with me that I had both arms. I think that I can hide my arm so well that I can fool people easily.

Recently my daughter found herself using her mouth to aid herself with something she was attempting to do at work. She realized it was something she learned from me and is unaware for the most part when she uses her mouth.

I told a friend that I had my nails done and paid half price. She asked how I get them for half price. I just shook my hand in her face and she remembered that I only had one hand. She felt foolish and we laughed!

I've learned over the years that when people meet me for the first time they are curious and want to know what happened but they don't want to just come out and ask. They often ask someone I am with or someone who knows me. I really don't mind being asked, as we are all curious by nature. To be respectful to one with a disability would be to never assume one can or cannot do something. The person should be asked specifically as each and every situation presents itself, unless someone is totally aware of one's personal limitations. I am most offended when someone has thought I cannot do something. I would rather they think I can do it! If I have difficulty with a task, I ask for help.

Our government gives tax breaks to persons with disabilities. On my original paperwork, which was filled out with my physician, it states I have a "Permanent Disability." Years later I received more paperwork to see if my disability had changed. I was livid! I called the Canada Revenue Agency and asked the woman if they thought that my arm and hand had grown back. I recall being told that everyone was required to re-submit this paperwork every few years. I have never received any more paperwork regarding this issue since then.

Communication is clearly the most important factor with anyone regarding abilities and limitations. I feel that it never hurts to ask someone if there is anything that they might need help with. I am pretty sure that they will let you know one way or another. When you come from the heart, how can you be wrong?

Discussion Questions

1. How does Mike's experience differ with respect to the intersection of race and gender as an Indigenous man from that of Melanie's life?
2. How do jurisdictional matters impact Mike's access to supports and service as compared to non-Aboriginal people with disabilities?
3. What are your thoughts on Melanie's question of whether having an invisible disability is a benefit over having a visible disability? Provide a rationale for your response.
4. How might having an invisible disability benefit Melanie or Jaclyn in the same or different ways? Explain your response.
5. How might Kübler-Ross' stages of grief apply differently to Lorea, who was born with a disability, versus Melanie, who acquired a disability during her late adolescence?
6. What are your thoughts on whether it is acceptable to provide babies with cochlear implants? Explain your rationale for either supporting or opposing this practice.
7. How does Lorea's story capture the role of policy in "making" disability?
8. What are your thoughts regarding sexuality and parenting? Have any of the stories provided new thoughts, insights or questions in this regard?
9. How has your thinking been shaped with respect to addressing the limiting assumptions placed on people with disabilities?
10. How would you best support Mike, Melanie, Jaclyn or Lorea as a social worker if they sought services from a social service organization where you were employed? How might this approach differ or be similar for each individual? What skills and knowledge would you draw on?

References

Kübler-Ross, Elisabeth. 1969. *On Death and Dying*. New York: Macmillan Publishing.

Chapter 2

Looking Back, Rethinking Historical Perspectives and Reflecting upon Emerging Trends

Peter Dunn and Terri-Lynn Langdon

The purpose of this chapter is to provide an overview of some of the trends in disability history prior to the European conquest up to the present in Canada. Specifically, the goals of this chapter are to describe the collectivist approach used by First Nations, the oppression of people with disabilities by European colonizers including the marginalization of individuals in institutions, the pressure for social change, the issues related to deinstitutionalization, which is still incomplete in Canada, and the recent trends and challenges. Another key goal is to outline the evolution of disability paradigms, including the recent trend from institutionalizing people in the community to an alternative innovative approach promoted by the disability movement of ensuring citizenship rights for all.

This chapter explains that prior to European conquest, Aboriginal peoples were noted for respecting individuals with disabilities and providing supports in the community in a collectivist fashion (Dickason and Newbigging 2010; Nelson 2012). However, European colonizers brought with them the demeaning attitudes enshrined in the Poor Laws and later placed people with disabilities in large institutions. Mackelprang and Salsgiver (2009) explain that Europeans considered individuals with disabilities as a menace, a burden or threat to society, as sick, ugly, sexless/over-sexed, incompetent and freakish. In the twentieth century, as a result of the lobbying efforts of activists and the need to save money, many individuals with disabilities were "deinstitutionalized" into the community, often with inadequate supports. Often community programs utilized the same medical and rehabilitation models as the institutions. Today, many of these services throughout Canada do not truly support integration and independence (Dunn 2012). Thus, disability activists have demanded a new model, not of "care" but of human rights (Stienstra 2012). This exciting approach emphasizes personal agency, options and independence for people with disabilities. Innovative responses have been developed at the grassroots level and supported by government policies and funding (Dunn 2012; Lord 2010). Nevertheless, changing an entrenched system with vested interests brings immense challenges, especially in a time of dramatic cuts to funding (Lord and Hutchison 2011).

Early History

For thousands of years before Europeans arrived in Canada, many groups of Aboriginal peoples inhabited the land, each with their own distinct culture. Common among them, however, was a collective approach of meeting everyone's needs — mental, spiritual, emotional and physical. Although the First Nations varied considerably and had disagreements, most stressed equality. Most leaders used persuasion rather than force and focused on the common good. This orientation differs dramatically from the individualist and exploitive approach of the British and French colonizers (Paul 2006; Dickason and Newbigging 2010).

Paul (2006) explains that the traditional view among Aboriginal peoples was that individuals with disabilities possessed special gifts from the Creator, such as healing powers. They were considered part of the community and often given special roles as healers, seers and ceremonial leaders. There was usually little social stigma, as Aboriginal peoples believe that each person has an important role to play (Durst, South and Bluechardt 2006).

Under the 1867 British North America Act (BNAA), the federal government was given exclusive rights to legislate related to Aboriginal peoples. The Indian Act of 1876 gave Indian agents control over every facet of people's lives. First Nations were not involved or consulted in developing this Act. Since then, the exploitation of Aboriginal peoples has continued through industrialization, assimilation and detribalization. Land, resources and traditional culture have been stolen or destroyed. Families were disrupted and cultural assimilation promoted through residential schools and Aboriginal children being removed from their homes in the name of "child welfare." Now, the disability rate among the adult Aboriginal population is about 31 percent, which is almost twice that of the Canadian population as a whole (Durst and Bluechardt 2004; Hirji-Khalfan 2009). Quon (2013) explains that centuries of oppression have left communities susceptible to drug and alcohol addiction and sorely lacking in culturally appropriate resources. The

First Nations Confederacy of Cultural Education Centres (2013) explains that the reasons for the higher rates of disability include poor living conditions brought on by overcrowding and dilapidated housing; chronic health problems such as diabetes and tuberculosis; and higher rates of environmental and trauma-related disabilities.

When Europeans arrived in North America they brought the ideology of the Poor Laws with them. These concepts of individuality, coercion and blame were in stark contrast with the Aboriginal ideas of collectivity and support. Rice and Prince (2013) explain that poverty and social issues were seen as a result of personal weaknesses. This view emphasized that families and charities rather than the whole community should provide supports. These attitudes are still evident in our policies today, including dividing people into categories and stigmatizing them. Social services were viewed as residual and best left to the voluntary efforts of the Church and community, and people were categorized into deserving and nondeserving poor. Although individuals with disabilities were considered deserving, they were stigmatized and seen as incapable of work. No one could receive more assistance than the lowest-paid worker, and the local municipalities were responsible for any government efforts. Many ended up in highly degrading poor houses. According to Guest (1997), almshouses/poor houses, which were objects of fear and loathing, were established in Canada to meet the needs of the insane, the sick, abandoned children and people who were old or feeble.

Guest (1997) explains that despite differences between the regions in pre-Confederation Canada, most of the approaches originating from Britain and France were extremely cruel and harsh. In 1763, Nova Scotia, followed by New Brunswick in 1786, passed Poor Law legislation modelled on Elizabethan legislation. However, lacking highly populated communities with resources to build poor houses, these provinces often contracted out the care of the poor to the lowest bidder. During the early nineteenth century, some areas held annual public auctions of paupers, including people with disabilities. Many people died of willful neglect and abuse. By the mid-nineteenth century, public institutions for the destitute were built in large centres such as Saint John, New Brunswick. Versions of the Poor Laws were also instituted in Prince Edward Island and Newfoundland.

Upper Canada (Ontario) did not legislate Poor Laws, leaving the responsibility up to families. Consequently, jails ended up functioning as poor houses for the "insane and offenders." In Lower Canada (Quebec), the responsibility fell to the Catholic Church. Eventually, institutions for persons considered to be "sick, orphaned, aged and insane" were built and run by the Church. As early as 1717, the Church started the first specialized residence for women with "mental disorders" in Quebec City and in 1747, the first hospital for "the sick, aged, incurable insane and orphaned" in Montreal. People, including those with disabilities, were often stripped of their self-respect, dignity and identity.

Neufeld (2005) explains that there really weren't comprehensive policies for individuals with disabilities in Canada until Quebec passed workers' compensation laws in 1909 for people who were injured. The other provinces soon followed suit. According to the British North America Act of 1867, the provinces and municipalities were responsible for individuals who were disabled, with the exception of Aboriginal peoples, who came under the federal authority of the Indian Act.

Clapton and Fitzgerald (2013) describe the history of disability as a history of "othering." For centuries, certain types of human bodies have been defined as the norm by Europeans, while those outside these criteria were considered the "other." As a result, a "paradigm of humanity" was created; some people fit neatly into the norm, while those who don't often experience a life of isolation and abuse. Individuals who have a disability live on the margins with a history of silence and oppression and with labels such as cripple, idiot and feeble-minded.

There is history that we learn, a history that we never come to know and a history that we need to unlearn (Langdon 2014). The history of disability is the history of bodies and minds seen through the lens of able-bodied people (Clapton and Fitzgerald 2013), a lens distorted by stereotypes. For example, Liz Crow (2000) confronts the stereotypes of disability used in telling the story of Helen Keller (1880–1968) in children's books. Keller, who was deaf and blind, is portrayed as dependent. What is less known is that various authorities considered incarcerating and even killing her because her progressive ideas, which promoted equality, were thought to be dangerous. Perhaps what saved Keller from this particular fate were the ideas at the time that insisted that people with disabilities were incapable and powerless. If Keller was to be incarcerated, the police and other powers would then have to admit that a deaf and blind woman was capable of challenging them and asserting the rights of women and other marginalized people. Crow (2000) goes on to document that Keller was a highly educated, well-travelled and an outspoken individual who advocated for women's suffrage, civil rights, labour rights and socialism.

Institutional Care

According to Graham, Delaney and Swift (2011), the first institution for people with intellectual disabilities in Canada opened in the mid-1800s in Ontario. Over the next century, institutional care was the primary approach throughout Canada for dealing with individuals with developmental (institutions for "idiots") and mental health disabilities ("asylums for the insane") and people with physical disabilities. In 1839, the Ontario government passed the Act to Authorize the Erection of an Asylum within this Province for the Reception of Insane and Lunatic Persons (Ministry of Community and Social Services 2016). This legislation gave the Government of Ontario the authority to build the first provincial institution for persons with developmental disabilities (Ministry of Community and Social Services 2013). Ontario opened the first such institution near Orillia in 1876, named the Orillia Asylum for Idiots, and later renamed the institution the Ontario Hospital School. At the time of its closure in 2009, it was known as the Huronia Regional Centre. At its peak in 1968, it had 2,600 residents. By the mid-1970s, the province of Ontario operated sixteen similar institutions. From the opening of the first institution to the closing of the last ones in 2009 (Ministry of Community and Social Services 2013), Ontario housed over fifty thousand people in these facilities (Peter Park 2004). In 2013 (*Toronto Star* 2013), former residents of the Huronia Regional Centre won a $35 million class action lawsuit against the Ontario government for abuse and neglect. About two thousand children and adults who were buried in the unkempt field by this centre are in numbered or unmarked graves without a name. Medical professionals often tried to talk families into placing their very young disabled children into these types of institutions (Pelka 2012). Families who had done so often coached parents who were wary of institutions to do the same with their children. Tragically, the social systems of the day refused to provide financial support and assistance to families who resisted institutional care for their children.

Illustrating what these facilities were like Peter Park (2004), former president of People First of Canada and co-founder of People First of Ontario, tells his story of spending eighteen years in a highly regimented institution in Ontario in which he was treated like an inmate and slept in a room with eighteen people. He spent about nine years of this time in a locked ward by himself, with no clothes, furniture or bed, for refusing to take experimental drugs and/or for looking at members of the opposite sex. When he was finally put in a paternalistic group home in the community, he had to work for dramatically below minimum wage. He advocated for himself and now lives with his wife in a cooperative apartment of his choosing. He has worked for seventeen years coordinating the national grassroots organization People First of Canada.

By the mid-nineteenth century, the permanent institutions for "lunatics" were opened in the eastern provinces. By the turn of the twentieth century, western Canada had similar institutions (Moran 2013). In 1872, British Columbia opened its first "asylum for the insane" in Victoria (British Columbia Mental Health and Substance Use Services 2013). According to Moran (2013), the authorities believed that especially run asylums could increase the cure rates for many forms of mental illness. For example, "moral therapy" was implemented using strict routines and religious observances away from the stresses of the home environment. This approach was considered an advance over the earlier institutional practice of chaining patients to the wall. Later, other treatments considered progressive were introduced, such as cold baths or showers, electroshock therapy, sulfa drugs and psychosurgery.

Institutions for individuals with disabilities increased dramatically with industrialization (Oliver and Barnes 2012; Barken 2013; Albrecht, Seelman and Bury 2001). Many became seriously overcrowded. It was believed that persons with disabilities could not work or contribute to society, and could not live on their own or with their families. One explanation for the proliferation of institutions is that there was an increased reliance on the scientific method of distinguishing between those considered disabled and individuals considered "able-bodied" (Albrecht, Seelman and Bury 2001). Disability was not viewed as a situation arising from systems of power and disadvantage, but rather as a combination of observable medical facts. Institutions categorized, labelled and separated people with disabilities. They were often hid away from public view. An example was Ontario's London Asylum for the Insane, which opened in 1870. This institution was situated geographically away from "the normals" in society, as were many others.

Institutions soon became a dominant method of holding and storing people with disabilities. It was not only people with developmental and mental health disabilities who were institutionalized; persons with physical disabilities and illnesses such as polio and TB were placed in institutions in isolated and sometimes abusive situations. Overcrowding, poor nutrition and a lack of personal nurturing contact for the residents, including hugs and access to sex and sexual health, was the norm in these institutions. Families were discouraged from visiting (Pelka 2012), and residents had little access to practical supports and medical care. Many faced violence and abuse.

Terri-Lynn Langdon (2014) describes a particular case of institutional abuse of a man with a dual diagnosis who was discharged recently to the community. He was approaching sixty years of age and had spent most of his life in one of the last institutions to be closed in Ontario. He had no front teeth or fingernails, and for a man of his age he looked very "weathered." Institutions routinely removed teeth and fingernails, without consent or pain killers, believing that people with developmental disabilities had violent behaviour and lacked sensations of pain and emotions.

Similar attitudes were reflected in the practice of forced sterilization. When people with disabilities could not be locked up, they were often sterilized against their will. Families with babies with disabilities sometimes left their children to die (Living Archives on Eugenics in Western Canada 2013). Additionally, the offspring of people with disabilities were considered dangerous. These government-sanctioned practices and attitudes were based upon the eugenics movement promoted by Francis Galton, beginning in the 1880s, to improve human hereditary by reducing the reproduction of less-desired people and traits. Sterilization was widespread in institutions throughout North America including western Canada (Living Archives on Eugenics in Western Canada 2013). In the case of *Bell v. Buck* (1927), Carrie Bell, who was labelled feeble-minded, was ordered sterilized by the U.S. Supreme Court, which stated that "population hygiene" and the well-being of the American public was a stake. In 1928, Alberta introduced the Sexual Sterilization Act, promoting surgical sterilization for people — mostly women labelled disabled. This policy remained in effect in Alberta until 1972 and in British Columbia until 1973 (Living Archives on Eugenics in Western Canada 2013). In 1959, Leilani Muir was sterilized without her knowledge by the Government of Alberta while in the "care" of the state. In fact, one of the devastating arguments that helped Muir win a settlement in a legal battle that ended in 1996 was not that her rights had been violated when she was sterilized without her knowledge, but that she had been wrongfully sterilized because, as it turned out, she was not disabled at all (*Muir v. the Queen* 1996). There are still cases in the courts related to the Alberta School for Mental Defectives where Muir was placed. The view that people with disabilities should have limited reproductive rights persists today. Terri-Lynn Langdon (2014) relates "a modern-day expression of eugenics — a neurologist told her that getting pregnant or breastfeeding is not the concern of a woman with disabilities." These are clear examples of the new ableism (Sherry 2008). At the same time, the disability movement has challenged bioethicists for the right of newborns with disabilities to live in the world (Albrecth, Seelman and Bury 2001).

It is important to note that in spite of the routine abuses in institutions, there has always been the formation of friendships, acts of love and acts of resistance in many of these institutions by its prisoners (Reaume 2009). Activists have made changes. For example, St-Amand and LeBlanc (2013) chronicle the life of nineteenth-century activist Mary Huestis Pengilly, whose abuse in a psychiatric institution led her to activist efforts that brought about major changes in government policies.

Not only were people with developmental and mental health disabilities warehoused in these institutions, but also persons with physical disabilities. Tracey Odell (2005) documents the abusive treatment of children and youth with physical disabilities in the facility that was first named, in 1899, the Home for Incurable Children. By 1912, the home offered schooling for residents. In 1957, the facility expanded to include the Ontario Crippled Children's Centre. Some of the individuals interviewed about life in the facility detailed stories of physical and sexual abuse (Odell 2005). After undergoing many social transformations of services, names and locations, the facility is now known as Holland Bloorview Kids Rehabilitation Hospital and has a reputation of providing world-class supports to children with disabilities.

While the deinstitutionalization of persons with disabilities is occurring, it is far from complete. For example, in Nova Scotia, over seven hundred individuals with developmental disabilities are housed in adult residential care centres. Nova Scotia currently has seven institutions housing people with physical, developmental and mental health disabilities (Barken 2013). The Manitoba Developmental Centre states on its website that it provides resident-centred services for over 220 individuals with developmental disabilities. The facility in Manitoba has been the focus of deinstitutionalization watch by People First of Canada (2013). In Alberta, the Michener Centre, which was built in 1923 as a training school for "mental defectives," is scheduled to close. Historically, it was part of the Alberta government's eugenics program, in which 2,844 people were sterilized (Wingrove 2013). The 125 residents still living there will be placed in community care (Wingrove 2013). Once the Michener Centre is closed, Manitoba, Quebec and Nova Scotia will be the only provinces still using large-scale institutions for the care and control of persons with disabilities (Wingrove 2013).

It should be pointed out that the conditions of many large institutions improved over the twentieth century, with more humane treatment and professional care. Reforms helped shift the focus away from custody toward treatment. Eventually, the psychodynamic approach emphasized understanding the social causes of mental health problems, and asylums for the insane were replaced by modern psychiatric hospitals (Denton 2000). However, the values of medicalization, categorization and dependency usually persisted (Dunn 2012).

Transition to Deinstitutionalization

Deinstitutionalization began in the 1960s in Canada and accelerated in the 1970s and 1980s. Sizeable numbers of people were discharged from large-scale institutions into the community. This process occurred as a result of the efforts of disability advocates, the changing ideas about institutions and the development of psychopharmacology (Denton 2000). However, many believe that the prime motivation for deinstitutionalization was to save money, since institutions of the day were no longer cost-effective (Barken 2013). Many people with disabilities left institutions without adequate supports and resources. People First of Canada (2013) has highlighted the lack of supports in the community and the increasing number of people who eventually became homeless.

In Canada today, the move to services in the community for many persons with disabilities means relying on multiple, fragmented, paternalistic, and contradictory social welfare programs and disability-specific charities (Langdon 2014; Torjman 2007). Many in the cross-disability community resent this situation as they try to move away from the image of the "good poster child" and the pervasive idea that persons with disabilities are all Tiny Tims (Hickman 2011; Lathrop 2013). In Charles Dickens' book *A Christmas Carol,* Tiny Tim is only pitied and viewed as an object of charity. Langdon (2014) explains that from her personal experiences, navigating social services is exhausting. The way that social systems are administered in Canada means that persons with disabilities must regularly engage with the medical profession to "prove" that they are disabled. The reporting requirements for financial assistance are often difficult, ongoing and humiliating. The social service systems in Canada today tend to be needs-based rather than rights-based services, and the determination of need is often based on letters of support from a designated medical professional. Those who do not have a medically verified diagnosis are often without support. Furthermore, many charities are disability-specific, which means that persons with rare or multiple disabilities often have less access to funding for community supports and assistive devices. Many larger organizations that serve people with disabilities do not have human rights offices or inform individuals of their rights. Many people have become institutionalized within the community, experiencing the same conditions of dependency, categorization, separation, isolation and stigma as individuals in institutions (Dunn 2012).

A move to services in the community is not the end goal of the disability movement. Instead, real social change means recognizing the rights and self-determination of people with disabilities. These rights including full inclusion in the economy — starting with far better access to employment and more comprehensive and enforceable disability rights legislation. Many individuals with disabilities live in inappropriate long-term care facilities, nursing homes and hospitals. The lack of resources for aging families caring for disabled family members has been identified for decades now. Despite the best efforts of persons with disabilities and their allies, the dramatic policy shift needed to address these very important issues has been extremely slow and limited (Lord 2010).

Pressure for Social Change

Nevertheless, many positive changes have occurred as a result of the disability movement. During the 1960s and 1970s, the disability movement gained strength and demanded that people be deinstitutionalized and be able to exercise their human rights. Initially, disability-specific mainstream agencies, parent organizations and disability activist agencies banded together to pressure governments for new policies. These efforts arose partly from the increased awareness of social injustices highlighted by the human rights movement in the 1950s and 1960s (Peters 2004). Stienstra (2012) traces how disability activists eventually strengthened the rights of Canadians with disabilities as the disability movement became increasingly controlled by people with disabilities.

One of the key social movements has been the independent living movement, which has had a major impact on human services in Canada (Dunn 2012). This movement began in the United States in the early 1970s with the creation of three Independent Living Centers (ILCs). Some of the initial self-advocates had physical disabilities; however, the centres increasingly serve individuals with a wide range of disabilities. By the 1990s, there were several hundred centres in the United States. This growing movement lobbied for deinstitutionalization and full participation in all aspects of society (Pfeiffer 2003). In Canada, the independent living movement grew quickly from a few centres in the early 1980s. The Independent Living Centres in Canada follow four principles: consumer control, a cross-disability approach, community-based services, and the promotion of integration and full participation. The centres are run by and for people with disabilities (Hanes 2010; Lord 2010; Walters 2010). They have created innovative programs in which citizens with disabilities are responsible for developing and managing their own services (Hutchison et al. 2000; Lord 2010). In 1986, the Canadian Association of Independent Living Centres (now called Independent Living Canada) was created as a national coordinating body for the movement. This organization provides training, support, lobbying, networking with government and nongovernmental organizations, and information dissemination.

The community living movement, another key movement in Canada, has its roots in the 1960s, a time when parents and caregivers of children with developmental disabilities lobbied for their children's right to education and recreation, adequate residential and vocational programs, and small residences and group homes instead of institutions. Services which were initially segregated, such as specialized education and sheltered employment, were integrated into mainstream organizations in the community. People First of Canada (2013) played a critical role by demanding an end to institutional care and sheltered workshops that institutionalized people in the community. They advocated for more integrated options for independent living, inclusive education, supported employment and recreation. Activists emphasized rights, choices, individual preferences, social networks and empowerment, as well as individualized planning and funding (Dunn 2012).

Denton (2000) describes how reforms in institutions for psychiatric consumer/survivors shifted from custody towards treatment. The community mental health movement followed with a focus upon services in the community, preventing long-term hospitalization, and coordinating local, integrated services. Community programs were initiated to help individuals who found themselves isolated and unsupported after their discharge from institutions (Nelson 2012). Since the 1980s, the psychiatric consumer/survivor movement in Canada was developed in response to people's experiences of alienation and oppression within the mental health system (Lord 2000). Its approach stresses empowerment and community integration through self-help, mutual aid, peer support, advocacy and stakeholder participation. It critiques the expert-driven and segregated strategies of case management and clubhouses as not responsive to the social conditions faced by consumer/survivors. Organizations such as the National Network for Mental Health have played a key role in promoting this self-advocate approach (Everett 2000; Nelson 2012; Nelson, Lord and Ochocka 2001).

There have been many other key disability advocacy efforts in Canada that will be covered in later chapters, such as the British Columbia Aboriginal Network on Disability Society (BCANDS), DisAbled Women's Network (DAWN), Canadian Association of the Deaf (CAD), and Alliance for Equality of Blind Canadians (AEBC). Provincial and national organizations have helped coordinate and promote these initiatives (Dunn 2012). For example, the Council of Canadians with Disabilities (CCD), formerly named the Coalition of Provincial Organizations of the Handicapped (COPOH), is a coalition of provincial and national disability organizations. It was established as a national coordinating body that advocates for citizen rights, self-determination, control and equality. It has had a major impact on disability rights and service delivery systems throughout Canada (Beachell 2013). Peters (2004) points out that the disability rights movement in Canada has had major successes such as ensuring that disability was included in the equality provisions of the *Charter of Rights and Freedoms* and creating the Ontarians with Disabilities Act and later the Accessibility for Ontarians with Disabilities Act. The overall movement in Canada has transformed notions of disability issues, developed an alternative vision of services, and created innovative interventions operated by self-advocates (Lord 2010).

Changing Paradigms and Models

As a result of social change, the paradigms or ideas about disability have evolved in Canada. These shifting ideas have influenced human service organizations and government policies, creating new models of programs in Canada. Three major paradigms have evolved in Canada: the medical and rehabilitation paradigm, the traditional community service paradigm, and the critical disability paradigm based upon the social model of disability. The latter two paradigms are often confused because they both take place in the community; however, the principles underlying them are dramatically different. Many people feel that simply having services in the community such as group homes, sheltered workshops and clubhouses are adequate. However, disability activists argue that these approaches only transfer forms of institutional segregation to the community and are not empowering (Dunn 2012).

The medical and rehabilitation paradigm, initiated with institutionalization, viewed people with disabilities as deviant and/or sick. In considering disability as a sickness, it emphasizes the limitations of individuals, their inabilities in the tasks of daily living, and their lack of compliance with medical directives. The existing economic and political order is not questioned, since problems are seen as primarily those of the individual. Flowing from this paradigm is a model of "care" that stresses medicalization, separation and isolation, and social policies emphasizing institutional care and charity. People with disabilities are labelled and treated as the "other." They are socialized into the role of being sick and dependent, and separated from mainstream society. Even though many larger "custodial" institutions have been closed, this approach continues in hospitals, rehabilitation centres and other facilities. Individuals are considered "patients," with medical and rehabilitation practitioners in charge of their "care" (Lord 2010; Dunn 2012).

The second paradigm and model of intervention is the traditional community service approach. It continues to view and treat individuals with disabilities as dependent and in need of "care." Disability is evaluated in terms of the ability to perform activities of daily living. Problems are viewed as the lack of abilities and/or inadequate specialized care in the community. As people with disabilities are deinstitutionalized into the community, they experience some of the same oppressions as in institutions: categorization, separation, isolation, and stigma. Professional staff are in charge. Furthermore, community programs are often unresponsive, complex and fragmented, with staff advocating for only incremental changes. McKnight and Block (2010) feel that many people have been, in essence, institutionalized within the community. In this model, policies emphasize segregated and specialized services, including group homes, sheltered workshops, special education and specialized transit (Dunn 2012; Council of Canadians with Disabilities 2010).

Disability activists, on the other hand, have developed an alternative analysis based on a social construction of disability (Hiranandani 2005; Pothier and Delvin 2006). This paradigm, the critical disability approach, locates pathology in the environment rather than in the individual: in unprotected rights, overdependency on relatives and professionals, and lack of responsive services (Hanes 2010; Barnes and Mercer 2010). This approach challenges ableism, capitalism, racism, sexism, homophobia and other oppressive conditions. It values citizen rights, social inclusion, social identity, independent living and quality of life. Barnes and Mercer (2010) explain that individuals with disabilities do not wish to receive charity, but rather gain social rights and inclusion. They wish to be in charge of their lives and fully included in all aspects of society. This model emphasizes that people can lead productive lives in the community through self-help, peer support, advocacy and the removal of barriers (Rioux and Prince 2002; Walters 2010). It proposes social policies and programs that emphasize citizen control (Lord, Snow, and Dingwall 2005). Later chapters in this book will discuss more of the theory and the evolution of the critical disability paradigm, including its intersection with postmodernism, feminism, Marxism and other critical theories.

Current Trends, Challenges and Possibilities

Instead of "well-meaning care" in the community, requiring individuals with disabilities to behave as "clients" and recipients of social services, activists are demanding to provide their own programs based upon self-direction, choice and options. Traditional community services are not sufficient, as they often perpetuate the old ways of separation, isolation, compliance and hierarchy. Many people feel controlled and regulated (Dunn 2012). Lord and Hutchison (2011) encourage the shift of power to individuals with disabilities, including building social networks and promoting empowerment.

One positive example of this social change is the development of Independent Living Centres in Canada. They are run by individuals with disabilities and utilize peer support and peer-driven programs. Each centre responds to the needs of its particular community, providing four common programs: information and refer-ral, peer support, independent living/empowerment skills and development, and research and demonstration. The majority of staff and board members are individu-als with disabilities (Hanes 2010; Lord 2010; Walters 2010). Another example of innovations is individualized funding for personal supports. Traditionally, agen-cies have provided "personal care" in the community when and how they deem appropriate. These supports are usually not portable from one area to another, making it hard for self-advocates to travel or move (Yoshida et al. 2006). Now, individuals with disabilities are given money directly so that they can hire, fire and direct their own personal supports. Independent Living Centres provide training for self-advocates in organizing and finding these supports (Dunn 2012; Lord and Hutchison 2007; Torjman 2007). Activists are also advocating that mainstream transport be accessible, including buses, trains, subways, taxis, cars and airplanes, and that there be a range of accessible transportation options and not just special-ized vans (Dunn 2012). Instead of special education for children with disabilities in segregated schools where students are labelled and isolated, advocates are demanding integration in regular schools where students can develop friendships and social connections (Reid and Knight 2006).

Activists are also advocating the end of sheltered workshops and the right to live where they like and with whom they like (Park 2004). They argue that sheltered workshops are segregated, often pay dramatically below minimum wage and make people dependent. Research shows that persons with disabilities in Canada have abysmal incomes (Sherry 2008) because many people with disabilities are forced into cheap labour. Studies show a statistically significant link between rates of dis-ability, poverty and an early death (Sherry 2008). Thus, advocates are calling for more concerted efforts in promoting supported employment in Canada (Lord and Hutchison 2007).

Perhaps it is time to phase out group homes. They are segregated services which foster dependence. At one point of time group homes were seen as progressive, as were the large institutions before them. Yet, increasingly, activists are saying that individuals with disabilities can live somewhere other than a group home, have options in their lives and be integrated into the community (Park, 2004). Individualized funding, supported employment and affordable housing options would allow people to live truly "textured lives in the community" (Pedlar et al. 1999).

There are many challenges in transforming the current services in the community, including making major changes to government policies along with ensuring adequate funding and supports. Sheltered workshops and group homes cannot be closed without alternatives, as many people with disabilities might then become jobless and homeless. This transition must be thoughtful and as seamless as possible.

The role of social workers should also change. More students with disabilities need to be educated in social work and hired for meaningful social work jobs (Dunn et al. 2008). The role of able-bodied social workers may also require change, to one of ally rather than "case manager" or service provider. Finally, it is essential that disability communities continue to develop their own culture (Longmore 1995), building on the writing, art and vision of disabled icons as reflected in events such as Mad Pride, the Disability Pride March and disability film festivals. Ultimately, we require a new vision for the future that ensures that all individuals live truly integrated lives in Canada with adequate, empowering and accessible personal supports, housing, education, income, transportation and community services (McRuer 2003; Sherry 2008).

Chapter Summary

This chapter outlined some of the important changes in disability history, from the collectivist orientation of Aboriginal peoples to the individualistic focus of European colonization and widespread institutional care and then deinstitution-alization. The current move towards fully integrating people with disabilities into the community marks a progressive return to a more collectivist orientation. These changes in attitudes and policies are the result of activist pressure, coalition building and social movements. However, much more needs to be done to advance a model of policies and programs in the community that support independent living. The myth that disability is a tragedy persists, along with the outdated notion that people with disabilities must be cared for and cannot govern their own lives. The vision of a community where everyone has a valued role needs constant reinforcement in an industrialized, capitalist culture that values able bodies. The gap between the rich and the poor continues to grow with individuals with disabilities being increasingly marginalized. It is time to create a truly barrier-free society with concrete rights and social justice for all.

Discussion Questions

1. What do you feel are the major changes in disability history in Canada?
2. What can we learn from First Nations communities?
3. Have conditions for individuals with disabilities gotten better or worse in Canada?
4. How have social workers added to the problems?
5. What role should social workers play?
6. Think of a current policy or program in Canada that does not fully support the rights of persons with disabilities. What do you think can be done to change this situation?
7. Do you feel we should get rid of sheltered workshops and group homes? If so, what are some of the issues and solutions in making these changes?
8. What would a truly inclusive society look like?
9. What impedes us from creating an inclusive society in Canada?
10. What are some of the challenges to coalition building and how might we create an effective system in Canada which promotes individual control, self-direction, choice and flexibility?

References

Albrecth, Gary, Katherine Seelman and Michael Bury. 2001. *Handbook of Disability Studies*. California: Sage Publications.

Armitage, Andrew. 2003. *Social Welfare in Canada Revisited*. Toronto, ON: Oxford University Press.

Barken, Rachel. 2013. "A Place to Call Home: Intellectual Disabilities and Residential Services in Nova Scotia." *Canadian Journal of Disability Studies* 2, 1.

Barnes, Colin, and Geof Mercer. 2010. *Exploring Disability*. Cambridge, UK: Polity Press.

Beachell, Laurie. 2013. ccd *Annual Report*. Winnipeg, MB: Council of Canadians with Disabilities.

British Columbia Mental Health and Substance Use Services. 2013. "History." <bcmhsus. ca/history >.

Clapton, Jayne, and Jennifer Fitzgerald. 2013. *The History of Disability: The History of "Otherness."* <ru.org/human-rights/the-history-of-disability-a-history-of-otherness.html>.

Council of Canadians with Disabilities. 2010. *Canada Ratifies United Nations Convention on the Rights of Persons with Disabilities*. Winnipeg, MB: Council of Canadians with Disabilities.

Crow, Liz. 2000. "Helen Keller: 'Re-thinking the Problematic Icon.'" *Disability and Society* 15, 6.

Denton, L. 2000. "From Human Care to Prevention." *Canadian Journal of Community Mental Health* 19, 2.

Dickason, Olive, and William Newbigging. 2010. *A Concise History of Canada's First Nations.* Toronto: Oxford University.

Dunn, Peter. 2012. "Canadians with Disabilities." In Anne Westhues and Brian Wharf (eds.), Canadian Social Policy: Issues and Perspectives. Waterloo: Wilfrid Laurier University Press.

Dunn, Peter, Roy Hanes, Susan Hardie, Don Leslie and Judy MacDonald. 2008. "Best Practices in Promoting Disability Inclusion within Canadian Schools of Social Work." *Disability Studies Quarterly* 28, 1.

Durst, Doug, and Mary Bluechardt. 2004. "Aboriginal People with Disabilities: A Vacuum in Public Policy." *SIPP Briefing Note* 6. Regina, SK: Saskatchewan Institute in Public Policy.

Durst, Douglas, Shelly M. South and Mary Bluechardt. 2006. "Urban First Nations Peoples with Disabilities Speak Out." *Journal of Aboriginal Health* (September).

Everett, Barbara. 2000. *A Fragile Revolution: Consumers and Psychiatric Survivors Confronting the Power of the Mental Health System.* Waterloo, ON: Wilfrid Laurier University Press.

First Nations Confederacy of Cultural Educational Centres. 2013. <abdc.bc.ca/uaed/backgroundinfo>.

Graham, John, Roger Delaney and Karen Swift. 2011. *Canadian Social Policy: An Introduction.* Toronto: Prentice Hall Allyn and Bacon.

Guest, Dennis. 1997. *The Emergence of Social Security in Canada.* Vancouver: UBC Press.

Hanes, Roy. 2010. "Social Work and Persons with Disabilities." In Stephen Hick (ed.), *Social Work in Canada: An Introduction.* Toronto: Thompson Educational Publishing.

Hickman, Louise. 2011. "Jerry's Orphans." <louisehickman.wordpress.com/2011/11/04/jerrysorphans-piss-on-pity-nablopomo-4/>.

Hiranandani, Vanmala. 2005. "Towards a Critical Disability Theory in Social Work." *Critical Social Work* 6, 1.

Hirji-Khalfan, Raihana. 2009. "Federal Supports for Aboriginal People with Disabilities." York University Library. <pi.library.yorku.ca/ojs/index.php/ccd/article/viewFile/23386/21577>.

Hutchison, Peggy, Alison Pedlar, Peter Dunn and John Lord. 2000. "The Impact of Independent Living Resource Centres." *International Journal of Rehabilitation Research* 23, 2.

Landon, Terri-Lynn. 2014. Personal Communication. Toronto: Author.

Lathrop, Douglas. 2013. "Empowering Tiny Tim: Pathetic Cripple? Ha! Crafty Little Con Artist Is More like It." *Mainstream Magazine.* <mainstream-mag.com/1297tim.html>.

Living Archives of Eugenics in Western Canada. 2013. <eugenicsarchive.ca/>.

Longmore, Paul K. 1995. "The Second Phase: From Disability Rights to Disability Culture." <independentliving.org/docs3/longm95.html>.

Lord, John, 2000. "Is that All There Is? Searching for Citizenship in the Midst of Services." *Canadian Journal of Community Mental Health* 19, 2.

_____. 2010. *Impact: Changing the Way We View Disability: The History, Perspective, and Vision of the Independent Living Movement in Canada.* Ottawa, ON: Independent Living Canada.

Lord, John, and Peggy Hutchison. 2007. *Pathways to Inclusion: Building a New Story with People and Communities.* Toronto, ON: Captus Press.

Lord, John, Judith Snow and Charlotte Dingwall. 2005. *Building a New Story: Transforming Disability Supports and Policies.* Toronto, ON: Individualized Funding Coalition of Ontario.

Mackelprang, Romel, and Richard Salsgiver. 2009. *Disability: A Diversity Model Approach in Human Service Practice.* New York, Lyceum Books.

Manitoba Developmental Centre. 2013. <gov.mb.ca/fs/pwd/mdc.html>.

McKnight, John, and Peter Block. 2010. *The Abundant Community.* San Francisco, CA: Berrett-Koehler Publishers.

McRuer, Robert. 2003. "AIDS, Christopher Reeve and Queer/DisAbility Studies." In J.J. Cohen and Weiss Gail (eds.), *Thinking the Limits of the Body.* New York: State University of New York Press.

Moran, James. 2013. "History of Madness and Mental Illness: A Short History of Care and Treatment in Canada." <historyofmadness.ca/index.php?option=com_content&view =article&id=80&Itemid=19&lang=en>.

Nelson, Geoffrey. 2012. "Mental health Policies in Canada." In Anne Westhues (ed.), *Canadian Social Policy: Issues and Perspectives* 5th edition. Waterloo, ON: Wilfrid Laurier University Press.

Nelson, Geoffrey, John Lord and Joanne Ochocka. 2001. *Shifting the Paradigm in Community Mental Health: Towards Empowerment and Community.* Toronto, ON: University of Toronto Press.

Neufeld, Aldred. 2005. "Disability Policy (Canada)." In J. Herrick and P. Stuart (eds.), *Encyclopedia of Social Welfare History in North America.* Boston: Beacon Press.

Odell, Tracey. 2005. *Not Your Average Childhood: Lived Experience of Children with Physical Disabilities Raised at Bloorview Hospital Home and School 1960–1989.* York University, Toronto, Canada.

Oliver, Michael, and Colin Barnes. 2012. "The New Politics of Disablement." In *The Rise of Disabling Capitalism.* New York: Palgrave.

Ontario Ministry of Community and Social Services. Institutions in Ontario. 2012. <mcss. gov.on.ca/en/dshistory/firstInstitution/huronia.aspx>.

Park, Peter. 2004. "The Difference SRV Made in My Life." *International Journal of Disability, Community and Rehabilitation* 3, 1.

Paul, Daniel. N. 2006. *First Nations History: We Were Not the Savages.* Halifax: Fernwood Publishing.

Pedlar, Alison, Larry Haworth, Peggy Hutchison, Andrew Taylor and Peter Dunn. 1999. *A Textured Life: Empowerment and Adults with Developmental Disabilities.* Waterloo, ON: Wilfrid Laurier University Press.

Pelka, Fred. 2012. *What We Have Done: An Oral History of the DisAblity Rights Movement.* University of Massachusetts Press.

People First of Canada. 2013. "Institutional Watch." <institutionwatch.ca/>.

Peters, Yvonne. 2004. *Twenty Years of Litigating for Disability Equality Rights: Has It Made a Difference?* Winnipeg, MB: Council of Canadians with Disabilities.

Pfeiffer, David. 2003. "The Origins of Independent Living." *Ragged Edge* 1–2 (July).

Pothier, Diane, and Richard Delvin. (eds.). 2006. *Critical Disability Theory: Essays in Philosophy, Politics, Policy and Law.* Vancouver, BC: UBC Press.

Quon, Anna. 2013. "Aboriginal People with Disabilities." *Abilities.* <abilities.ca/

the-path-to-healing/>.

Reaume, Geoffrey. 2009 [2000]. *Remembrance of Patients Past: Patient Life at the Toronto Hospital for the Insane, 1870–1940.* Toronto: Oxford University Press Canada.

Reid, Kim, and Michelle Knight. 2006. "Disability Justifies Exclusion of Minority Students: A Critical History Grounded in Disability Studies." *Educational Researcher* 35.

Rice, James, and Michael Prince. 2013. *Changing Politics of Canadian Social Policy.* Toronto: University of Toronto Press.

Rioux, Marcia, and Michael Prince. 2002. "The Canadian Political Landscape of Disability: Policy Perspectives, Social Statuses, Interest Groups, and Rights Movement." In A. Puttee (ed.), *Federalism, Democracy, and Disability Policy in Canada.* Montreal, QC, and Kingston, ON: McGill-Queen's University Press.

Sherry, Mark. 2008. *Disability and Diversity: A Sociological Perspective.* New York: Nova Science Publishers

St-Amand, Neree, and Eugene LeBlanc. 2013. "Women in 19th Century Asylums: Three Exemplary Women." In Brenda A. LeFrançois, R. Menzies and G. Reaume (eds.), *Mad Matters: A Critical Reader in Canadian Mad Studies.* Toronto: Scholars Press.

Stienstra, Deborah. 2012. *Disability Rights.* Winnipeg: Fernwood Publishing.*Swanson, Jean 2001. *Poor Bashing: The Politics of Exclusion.* Toronto. Between the Lines.

Torjman, Sherri. 2007. *Five-Point Plan for Reforming Disability Supports.* Ottawa, ON: Caledon Institute.

Toronto Star. 2013. "Huronia Institution Cemetery a Painful Reminder of Neglect and Abuse." *The Toronto Star News.* September 17.

Walters, Tracy. 2010. *Independent Living Canada Annual Report.* Ottawa, ON: Independent Living Canada.

Wingrove, Josh. 2013. "Alberta's Michener Centre Can't Shake Sordid History." *Globe and Mail.* (Spring).

Yoshida, Karen, Vic Willi, Ian Parker and David Locker. 2006. "The Emergence of Self-Managed Attendant Services in Ontario." In Marry Anne McColl and L. Jongbloed (eds.), *Disability and Social Policy in Canada.* Toronto, ON: Captus Press.

Chapter 3

Exploring the Conceptualization of Disability and Demographics as "Facts"

Jeanette Robertson

Critical attention to the ways we constitute facts about disability makes possible a reflection on what it means for readers and for writers, disabled or not, to be confronted with disability as a totalized entity; an entity framed and treated as nothing more or less than a problem of a medical nature. (Titchkosky 2007: 47)

This chapter will address the controversy of how disability is conceptualized, how people become classified as people with disabilities, and how these aspects are constructed. As noted by Dunn and Langdon in the previous chapter, responses to disability have evolved since the 1970s from segregated institutional and educational approaches to community and educational inclusion. However, the combination of a neoliberal ideology based on individualism and the perpetuation of disability as nothing more than a problem of a medical nature contributes to an ableist societal context, which discriminates in favour of the able-bodied. Although progress has occurred since deinstitutionalization and the promotion of integration, society continues to discriminate and exclude many people with disabilities from accessing the same benefits as their able-bodied counterparts, as well as neglecting to address the oppressive social arrangements that cause or greatly contribute to the barriers of full inclusion. Consequently, one may conclude that it may be important to understand the prevalence of people with disabilities and their circumstances in order to ascertain the required resources and support, and to confront the disabling barriers that exclude them from full participation in society.

Conversely, in reviewing disability demographics, the reader is wise to acknowledge that the process for arriving at a definition of disability, and the paradigm through which disability is understood, is hotly contested and fraught with controversy. There is no generally accepted definition of disability in Canada or within the international community (WHO 2011; Center for International Rehabilitation 2004). The conceptualization of disability is complex and multidimensional, and is continuously debated. Thus, it is necessary to understand how disability is defined within particular surveys or reports when reviewing demographics, as the way in which disability is defined has a direct bearing on the quantification of a given population and the everyday lives of the people being counted or discounted.

In fact, "the definition of *disability*, like the definition of *illness*, is inevitably a matter of social debate and social construction: as humans have defined *normal* in as many ways as there are human cultures" (Bérubé cited in Linton 1998: p. viii). There is a broad range of what society deems as a disability, encompassing a huge diversity of conditions, some of which may include:

- Perceptual (such as visual and hearing impairments or learning disabilities)
- Illness-related (such as multiple sclerosis, cystic fibrosis or HIV/AIDS)
- Physical (such as cerebral palsy or spina bifida)
- Neurological (such as epilepsy)
- Developmental (such as Down syndrome or disorders on the autism spectrum)
- Psychiatric (such as bipolar depression or schizophrenia)
- Mobility (such as quadriplegia or paraplegia)
- Environmental (such as asthma or sensitivities to allergens/scents and chemicals in the environment)

However, individuals may or may not consider themselves as disabled and they may or may not use this specific term to describe themselves or their experiences, as has been illustrated in the first-person accounts in Chapter 1.

The aim of this chapter is to alert the reader to the ways in which the conceptualization and demographics of disability are a matter of social debate and social construction. One must consider the manner in which disability is constituted, the purpose and methods of data collection of various surveys, and who is in/excluded in the research design and process. An overview of the global and Canadian demographic "estimates" of people with disabilities, as outlined within various sources, is provided with attention to how disability is defined and the discrepant results and variability across these sources. Reported demographic breakdowns with respect to age, gender, region and types of disability within Canada are also provided as reported in the 2012 Canadian Survey on Disability (Statistics Canada 2015), with the caveat that one must exercise caution and critical judgement in accepting these numbers as objective "facts." Moreover, one needs to be alerted to the process of objectifying and homogenizing a population as nothing more than a "problem" of a medical nature. Also, an assumption is often made that the population being classified and counted is without strengths, and may pose a threat to society or themselves due to the level of resources and supports they will require. This approach neglects to acknowledge the strengths and contributions of people with disabilities, as well as the barriers imposed on them by society.

Demographic "Estimates" of Disability

The reader may be surprised to learn that people with disabilities are reported to be the world's largest minority. A global perspective is certainly critical with respect to being informed about the needs and experiences of people with disabilities, as approximately 15 percent of the world's population, or more than one billion people, are reported to live with a disability (WHO 2011). Furthermore, as noted by Larson in Chapter 10, one of the most common forms of disability facing the globe is the incidence of mental illness. The majority of disabilities are acquired (97 percent) through illness, disease or injury as opposed to being present at birth, although the number of individuals with acquired disabilities is increasing through medical advances, population growth and the ageing process (Peters, Wolbers and Dimling 2008). The number of people with disabilities will undoubtedly continue to be influenced by aspects such as the spread of disease, civil wars, terrorism and natural disasters throughout the globe. According to United Nations (2006), 80 percent of persons with disabilities live in developing countries, and there is a correlation between disability rates and poverty, as rates of disability are significantly higher among groups with lower educational attainment. Twenty percent of the world's poorest people have a disability and tend to be regarded in their own communities as the most disadvantaged (United Nations 2006).

In most Organisation for Economic Co-operation and Development (OECD) countries, women report higher incidents of disability than men. "Girls and women of all ages with any form of disability are generally among the more vulnerable and marginalized of society" (United Nations 2000: 20). As will be addressed by MacDonald in Chapter 8, women with disabilities are acknowledged to be multiply disadvantaged, experiencing exclusion because of their gender and their disability, and women and girls with disabilities are particularly vulnerable to abuse. In addition, 30 percent of street youth are reported to have some kind of disability (United Nations 2006).

There have been numerous national disability reports conducted in Canada by Statistics Canada and other governmental departments since the International Year of Disabled Persons in 1981. The reported demographics of three such disability surveys will be reviewed within this chapter. These include the 1991 Health and Activity Limitation Survey (HALS) (Statistics Canada 1991a, 1991b), the 2006 Participation and Activity Limitation Survey (PALS) (Statistics Canada 2002, 2013), and the 2012 Canadian Survey on Disability (CSD) (Statistics Canada 2015). Depending on the report under review, the percentage of Canadians with disabilities has been reported to range from 14.7 percent in 1991 (HALS) to 12.4 percent, or 3.6 million Canadians in 2001 (Statistics Canada 2002), to 14.3 percent, or 4.4 million Canadians in 2006 (Human Resources and Skills Development Canada 2011), to recent estimates of 13.7 percent, or 3.8 million Canadians in 2012 (Statistics Canada 2015). Furthermore, in 2002, as noted by Larson in Chapter 10, approximately 20 percent of Canadians experience a form of mental disability sometime in their lifetime (Health Canada 2002).

One is lead to question the variability between the findings of each of these reports. For example, how is it that there were 0.6 million less people with disabilities between 2006 and 2012? This discrepancy is unusual given that the population with disabilities is considered to increase with age. Thus, it is critical to understand the various influences, such as how disability was conceptualized, and how such influences impact the outcomes of these and other surveys of disability. Moreover, the discrepancies between the demographic findings of various surveys provide further evidence of the social construction of disability. The social construction of disability refers to the meanings, notions or particular connotations that are assigned to people with disabilities that evolve over time, and that appear to be natural and obvious to people who accept these meanings. However, these meanings may or may not represent reality, so they remain largely an invention or pretense of a given society. Likewise, related and additional influences include the methods of surveying, and respondents included in the survey, among many other aspects.

Regardless of how disability is defined, it appears that people with disabilities are reported to comprise a large proportion of the global and Canadian population. The following tables reflect the results of the Canadian Survey on Disability (Statistics Canada 2015), which was conducted by Statistics Canada in the fall of 2012. The tables provide estimates of Canadians reporting a disability by age, gender, region and type of disability. Readers will note the total percentage of Canadians with disabilities in 2012 was reported to be 13.7 percent, and this increased with age, ranging from 4.4 percent for respondents from 15–24 years of age, to 42.5 percent for those 75 years and over (Figure 3.1). Furthermore, females reported a higher

Figure 3.1 Population with a Disability, by Age, 2012 (percent)

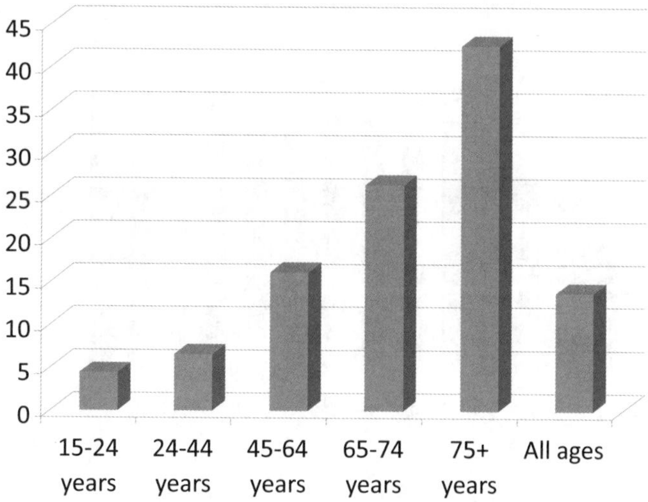

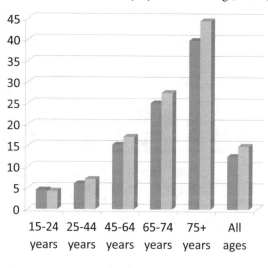

Source: Statistics Canada, 2013, "Canadian Survey on Disability 2012: Tables," Table 1.1 *Prevalence of Disability for Adults by Sex and Age Group*, Canada 2012, Catalogue no. 89-654-X, Ottawa.

Figure 3.2 Population with a Disability, by Gender and Age, 2012 (percent)

Source: Statistics Canada, 2013, "Canadian Survey on Disability 2012: Tables," Table 1.1 *Prevalence of Disability for Adults by Sex and Age Group*, Canada 2012, Catalogue no. 89-654-X, Ottawa.

Figure 3.3 Population with a Disability, by Region, 2012 (percent)

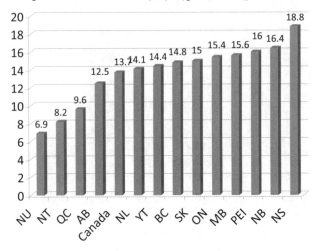

Source: Statistics Canada, 2013, "Canadian Survey on Disability 2012: Tables," Table 1.1 *Prevalence of Disability for Adults by Sex and Age Group*, Canada 2012, Catalogue no. 89-654-X, Ottawa.

Figure 3.4 Persons With a Disability, by Type, 2012 (percent)

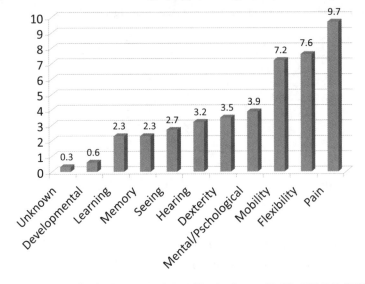

Source: ESDC, calculations based on Statistics Canada, 2013, "Canadian Survey on Disability 2012: Tables," Table 3.1 *Adults with Disabilities by Type, Sex and Age Group*, Canada 2012, and Table 2.1 *Adults With and Without Disabilities by Sex and Age Group*, Canada, 2012, Catalogue no. 89-654-X, Ottawa 2013.

prevalence of disability in almost all age groups (except the 15–24 age group), with 14.9 percent of females and 12.5 percent of males reporting a disability. This disparity grew further among the oldest Canadians (those 75 and older) with 44.5 percent of women and 39.8 percent of men reporting a disability (Figure 3.2). Also worth noting is that respondents from Nunavut reported the lowest rate (6.9 percent) of disability, with respondents in Nova Scotia reporting the highest rates at 18.8 percent (Figure 3.3). As for the types of disabilities reported, pain, flexibility and mobility were the three most widely reported disabilities among adults aged 15 and over. Again, women reported more of these types of conditions than men. The most prevalent types of disabilities (noted in Figure 3.4) varied by age. While those aged 45–64 reported pain (12.7 percent), flexibility (9.8 percent) and mobility (8.6 percent) the most, young people (15–25) mostly reported mental/psychological disabilities (2.2 percent), learning disabilities (2.0 percent), and pain (1.9 percent).

According to the World Health Organization:

> Robust evidence helps to make well informed decisions about disability policies and programmes. Understanding the numbers of people with disabilities and their circumstances can improve efforts to remove disabling barriers and provide services to allow people with disabilities to participate. (2011: 21)

Although the demographics may elicit valuable information or "evidence" with which to develop strategies for providing services and addressing disabling barriers, a number of questions arise. For example, one might query how the data for the survey was collected. Was this an online or face-to-face survey? Was there an interview process? How was disability defined? Who was included or excluded from the study? Were people with disabilities consulted in the process of defining disability? One might also wonder where the lives of Aboriginal Canadians are reflected within these statistics. While 13.7 percent of Canadians reported having a disability, how many of these respondents were Aboriginal? As referenced by Durst in Chapter 9, the last comprehensive survey to focus primarily on Aboriginal people was conducted in 1991, and the findings indicated that 31.4 percent of Aboriginal respondents reported having a disability (Statistics Canada 1994), while the Canadian Survey on Disability indicates 18.6 percent of Aboriginal respondents living off-reserve reported having a disability (Statistics Canada 2015). Durst also confirms that the 2012 Canadian Survey on Disability (Statistics Canada 2013) did not include the population of First Nations living on reserves. However, it is worth noting that in 2009, according to Health Canada, nearly one-quarter (22.9 percent) of First Nations adults living on-reserve reported having at least one disability (Health Canada 2009). Durst speaks further to the demographic dis-parities and the ex/inclusion of on- and off-reserve Aboriginal peoples (Chapter 9). Furthermore, one might also ponder why it is that respondents in Nova Scotia reported a significantly higher incidence of disability (11.9 percent higher) than respondents in Nunavut. In light of this, one is lead to ponder the elements within the survey process and the conceptualization of disability that influence the dif-ferent outcomes.

Conceptualization of Disability: A Matter of Social Debate

The reader is wise to acknowledge and be informed about the process for arriving at a definition of disability, and the paradigm through which disability is understood. Notwithstanding, it is important to acknowledge the diverse range of disabilities and societal and individual responses to disability, as people with disabilities are not a homogenous group and their experiences reflect this diversity. As discussed by MacDonald in Chapter 8, it is also necessary to consider how intersectional factors such as race, class, gender, sexual orientation and age, as well as other aspects of identity such as culture and religion, impact the everyday lives of people with dis-abilities. Likewise, whether a disability is congenital (present at birth) or acquired later in life (following an accident, hereditary or acquired progressive illness or disease) also influences the diversity of experience and response to disability, as illustrated by the first-person accounts in Chapter 1.

Moreover, "any of us who identify as 'nondisabled' must know that our self-designation is inevitably temporary, and that a car crash, a virus, a degenerative genetic disease, or a precedent-setting legal decision could change our status in ways over which we have no control whatsoever" (Bérubé, cited in Linton 1998: viii). The awareness that we are all temporarily able-bodied acknowledges that many people will at some point become disabled (Marks 1999). Nevertheless, the question about "the disabled" subject is embedded within relations of power in modern societies (Tremain 2005). Subsequently, a number of classification sys-tems have been developed and applied to the categorization of disability, each with different underlying assumptions and motivations throughout history. The range of classification systems have included such crude aspects as measuring people's skulls and attributing the circumference of their skull to their level of intelligence, and administering intelligence quotient (IQ) tests to newly arrived immigrants before they disembarked from their vessel. These procedures were inevitably biased with respect to class, race and gender, as the IQ test was primarily based on white, middle class, Judeo-Christian, patriarchal culture, and administered in English, which was not the first language of many respondents (Whiting 1996). Likewise, several conceptual models and classification systems have influenced the definition of disability and the resulting interpretation of demographics throughout history to the present day. The medical model has had a powerful influence on the conceptualization of disability and reflects the assumption that disability is a condition solely residing in the individual. According to Withers (2012), the medical model approach diagnoses people as "problems." Disability is seen as a medical issue emerging from a deviant anatomy. Thus, the attention is directed at the condition itself with the primary goal of decreasing the prevalence of disability in society. People are perceived to be *deficient, sick, afflicted or suffering* from a disability, and treatment and prevention are the primary goals. The person with a disability is considered dependent or passive with little input into their needs and aspirations. Medical personnel are the experts with the medical knowledge, and they are placed in charge of assessment and treatment.

With the aim of decreasing the prevalence of disability or assisting people to approximate the lives of able-bodied people as much as possible, the interventions may include surgery, drug therapy, prenatal screening, and rehabilitation therapies such as physiotherapy, occupational therapy and other clinical services. As will be addressed by Larson in Chapter 10, the *Diagnostic and Statistical Manual of Mental Disorders* (DSM) published by the American Psychiatric Association has also played a prominent role in the diagnosis of mental disability. Medical personnel often act as gatekeepers to needed services and supports with the power to assess whether individuals are deemed to be legitimately disabled or not. Most importantly, the manner in which disability is defined directly impacts the person's everyday lived experience.

Oliver (2009) refers to the medical model as the medicalization of disability and attributes this process to an individual model of disability — underpinned by what he calls a *personal tragedy theory of disability*. He argues that it is crucial that we reject the medicalization of disability both in practice and in theory. "Medicalization (or the application of medical knowledge to an increasing range of social problems) emerged as a key aspect in the social control of disabled people" (Barnes and Mercer 2003: 27). Examples of this include institutionalization, segregated schooling and special education. The medicalization of disability served to promote the development of the professionalization of disability services and the growth of many programs and services for people with disabilities, as well as an expansion of the professions allied to medicine, education and social welfare fields (Barnes and Mercer 2003). In short, approaches based solely on the medical model do not consider oppressive social conditions and often produce power imbalances between persons with disabilities and the service providers.

With this understanding of the medical model in mind, let us turn our attention to examining the conceptualization of disability within the three surveys. In addition to directing our attention to how disability is interpreted as an intrinsic characteristic of individuals with disabilities (medical model), consideration will also be directed to whether the role of the social and physical environment in the disabling process (social model) is reflected within the surveys. The first survey to be reviewed is the Health and Activity Limitation Survey (Statistics Canada 2002). Until 2001, the HALS (conducted as a post-census survey in 1986 and 1991) was considered the most comprehensive data source on people with disabilities and was intended to go beyond simply identifying the presence of disability to provide more detail as to the nature and extent of disability. Respondents 15 years and older were selected through the use of census information on the basis of pre-identification of disability within the census. The types of disabilities included in the survey were hearing, seeing, speaking, mobility, agility and "other." There was no specificity for the "'other'" category within the survey as it applied to mental health conditions, learning disabilities, intellectual impairments or labelling by others (Office for Disability Issues, Government of Canada 2003).

The target population for the 1991 survey was all persons with a physical or psychological disability who were living in Canada at the time of the census, including residents of the Yukon and the Northwest Territories, and permanent residents of most collective dwellings and health care institutions. First Nations reserves, residents in penal institutions, correctional facilities, military camps, campgrounds and parks, soup kitchens, merchant and coast guard ships and children's group homes were not included in the study (Statistics Canada 1991b). HALS employed the International Classification of Impairments, Disabilities and Handicaps (ICIDH 1980) definition of disability, which defines disability as "any restriction or lack (resulting from an impairment) of ability to perform an activity in the manner or within the range considered normal for a human being" (Office for Disability Issues, Government of Canada 2003: 9).

The ICIDH, developed by the World Health Organization (WHO), has been a broadly used conceptual framework for disability. The framework is described in three interrelated dimensions — Impairment, Disability and Handicap:

> *Impairment:* Any loss or abnormality of psychological, physiological or anatomical structure or function.
>
> *Disability:* Any restriction or lack (resulting from an impairment) of ability to perform an activity in the manner or within the range considered normal for a human being.
>
> *Handicap:* A disadvantage for a given individual, resulting from an impairment or a disability, that limits or prevents the fulfilment of a role that is normal (depending on age, sex, and social and cultural factors) for that individual. (WHO 1980)

The ability of the ICIDH, not only to classify an individual's circumstance, but to provide a theoretical framework to interrelate impairment, disability and handicap, made it a powerful tool for a range of applications. However, it was not without its criticisms. The framework created the impression that the concepts of impairment, disability and handicap stood in conceptual isolation from each other, which is not the case (Roeher Institute 1996). Although this conceptualization of disability was seen as progressive by many proponents at the time of its introduction, this framework still fell within the medical model approach.

As the reader will note, impairment as framed above is considered to occur at the individual level, and assessment requires judgement of mental and physical functioning of the body and its component parts according to particular standards. The classification of *impairment*, on the other hand, is hierarchical and noted to allow considerable specificity (such as any loss or abnormality of structure or function). *Disability* is concerned with functional performance or activity, and limitations therein, affecting the whole person. The disability aspect attempts to encompass those activities considered important in daily living. Like impairment, the classification of disability is hierarchical, but allows for an additional parameter to record the severity of disability. *Handicap* reflects the interaction with and adaptation to the person's surroundings and focuses on the person as a social being. The handicap definition attempts to classify those consequences that place an individual at a disadvantage in relation to their peers.

However, due to criticisms that the ICIDH framework focused solely on the individual as the source of change, without consideration of the inhibiting or disabling broader social factors (Roeher Institute 1996), the classification system was reviewed, and later revised in 1993, and was renamed the International Classification of Functioning, Disability and Health (ICF) framework of disability (Office for Disability Issues, Government of Canada 2003). In addition to concerns regarding the use of the ICIDH framework within the HALS, the resulting statistics from the survey have also been noted to contain sampling errors (Statistics Canada n.d.). These aspects bring the results of the survey into question.

The second Statistics Canada post-census survey to be considered, the PALS (2006) included a sample of respondents from private and some collective households who answered "yes" to the 2006 census disability filter questions. This survey employed the ICF conceptualization of disability. The ICF framework is stated to recognize the role of environmental factors and defines "disability as the relationship between body structures and functions, daily activities and social participation, while recognizing the role of environmental factors" (Statistics Canada 2007b: 8). "PALS conceptualizes disability as activity limitations and participation restrictions associated with long-term physical or mental conditions or health-related conditions" (2007b: 7). Thus, the new PALS (which replaced the HALS), by employing the ICF conceptualization of disability, was considered to increase the focus on environmental factors of disability by reflecting the shift to a social model definition of disability. However, as noted by Barnes (2014: 41), "impairment is still the primary focus of analysis and 'a significant variation from the statistical norm.' This of course ignores the fact that the identification and labelling of impairment as socially deviant is subject to ideological, political and cultural forces." Hence, this approach continues to reinforce the medical model in positioning disability as an individual pathology without sufficient consideration of the role of the social and physical environment in the disabling process.

In addition to employing the ICF definition of disability versus the ICIDH definition, there were also other major differences between the 1991 HALS and the PALS. For example, the sample for the 2006 PALS differed slightly from the HALS in that it did not include persons living in institutions, and included all three territories, as well as a number of Aboriginal communities. However, PALS was similar in that it included persons residing in private and some collective households in the ten provinces. Although it is acknowledged by Statistics Canada that the PALS cannot be compared to the HALS (Statistics Canada 2002), there is the assumption that the PALS 2006 results can be compared to the 2001 PALS survey to identify trends between these five years, although it is important to note that there were methodological and content changes between the 2001 and 2006 PALS (Statistics Canada 2007a).

The third and most current survey conducted by Statistics Canada to be examined, the Canadian Survey on Disability, shared in Tables 1–4 (Statistics Canada 2015), is reported to have incorporated significant changes from the way disability was defined within the 2006 PALS survey. The 2012 CSD comprised all Canadians aged 15 or older as of May 10, 2011, who were living in private dwellings. Thus, the demographics should be interpreted accordingly, as people residing in mental health and care facilities were not included. Although both the PALS and CSD employed the ICF framework for the conceptualization of disability, the CSD is reported to have utilized a new set of disability screening questions. These questions are said to reflect a fuller implementation of the social model of disability. Greater consistency in disability identification by type, and improved coverage of a full range of disability types, especially mental/psychological and cognitive (learning and memory) disabilities are noted to be included. Thus, Statistics Canada (2013) states that comparisons between the CSD and PALS cannot be made. Specifically, comparisons of the prevalence of disability over time are not possible or recommended.

Although the ICF framework used for the CSD is stated to consider the relationship between body function and structure, daily activities and social participation, while recognizing the role of environmental factors, impairment is still the primary focus of analysis and interpreted to vary from the statistical norm. This again "ignores the fact that the identification and labelling of impairment as socially deviant is subject to ideological, political and cultural forces ..." (Barnes 2014: 41). Titchkosky and Michalko go further in problematizing the focus on disability as the "problem" to alter the gaze towards rethinking our conceptualization of normalcy to question the "dangerous illusion about the meaning of normalcy" (Finkelstein, cited in Titchkosky and Michalko 2009: 1).

Moreover, as illustrated across the three surveys, "the definition of *disability*, like the definition of *illness*, is inevitably a matter of social debate and social construction: as humans have defined *normal* in as many ways as there are human cultures" (Bérubé cited in Linton 1998: viii). However, the meanings attached to these labels may or may not represent reality, so they remain largely an invention or pretense of a given society.

An Alternative Paradigm

A second school of thought or approach, addressed at length by Hanes in Chapter 4, based on the social construction of disability is the social model of disability. This approach emerged to provide a counter perspective (Frazee, Gilmour and Mykitiuk, cited in Pothier and Devlin 2006) to the medical model. This paradigm, referred to as the social model, locates barriers and the creation of disability in the environment rather than in the individual (Barnes and Mercer 2003; Oliver 2009; Thomas 2014; Wendell 1996). Within this model there is a distinction made between the concepts of "impairment" and "disability." Disability is reformulated to constitute the social disadvantages and exclusions that people with impairments experience that are imposed on top of their impairment. Disability is reframed as an entirely socially caused phenomenon (Thomas 2014).

In fact, the term "disability" has been reclaimed from medical professionals. "In wrenching this term from the powerful grip of doctors and social workers who believed that disability *was* the impairment itself or resided in restrictions of activity *caused by* impairment," disabled activists such as Paul Hunt and Vic Finkelstein reconstructed its meaning to reflect the social exclusion encountered in their lived experience (Thomas 2014: 9). This social understanding of disability had a transformative effect for people with disabilities both personally and politically. Adoption of the social model paved the way for readily observing and addressing the socially created barriers and exclusions within aspects such as education, employment, housing, transportation, civil rights, negotiation of the built environment and so forth. According to Crow, on a personal level, the social model has had a transformative effect:

It has enabled a vision of ourselves free from the constraints of disability (oppression) and provided a direction for our commitment to social change. It has played a central role in promoting disabled people's individual self-worth, collective identity and political organization. I don't think it is an exaggeration to say that the social model has saved lives. (cited in Thomas 2014: 10)

However, the social model is not without its criticism (Morris 1991; Thomas 2014). Authors such as Morris have argued that the shift in perspectives and the adoption of the social model resulted in the experience of impairment (the biological) being taken underground, as will be noted by Hanes in Chapter 4. The emphasis of disability as purely a social phenomenon implied that the impairment itself was not disabling, as disablement had nothing to do with the body. "Indeed, to dwell on impairment in DS (disability studies) or the disabled people's movement was viewed as hazardous because to do so gave credence to the medical preoccupation with bodily matters, deflecting attention away from disablist social barriers" (Thomas 2014: 13). Asch (2001) proposes a human variation approach suggesting that instead of maintaining the dichotomy — disabled or not disabled — we should determine how to modify the environments so that they are not disabling. One begins to develop a clear sense of how the varying conceptualizations of disability have a direct impact on whether one is included or excluded from disability demographics.

The God Trick

Titchkosky asserts that it is critical to consider the active participation in meaning-making, in "making up the meaning of people" (2007: 6). She alerts us to how the "god trick" is employed within government documents through the authoritative statement of facts that constitute disability as a condition readily identifiable in people in the form of rates within a population. Through the use of statistics, government data constructs disability as an individual problem. She provides a compelling critique of how people construct meaning about disability with the exploration of the construction of disability as "problem" within medical discourse. The god trick is used to present "authoritative facts" that go unquestioned, and these facts define the body in a manner that is totalizing and reductive. Titchkosky asserts that the god trick allows authors to disguise truths and provide information uncritically.

According to Titchkosky, disability as conveyed no longer names a type of self or a way of being: it is now a name for reduced ability to do, resulting from a lack of functionality in one's normal bodily comportment. Disability is constructed as happening to the body, not an active participation, nor a choice in claiming disability as an identity. Disability is conveyed as merely something that happens to the body. Titchkosky invites us to consider treating disability as a way of perceiving and orienting to the world rather than conceiving of it as an individual functional limitation, as this will uncover how we might encounter disability in new ways (2007). Measuring people's unfortunate problems and ascertaining their location within the social whole in order to address their personal accommodation needs is the kind of work done by those professions committed to the study of disability (Titchkosky 2007). This sort of work seeks to minimize the negative effects of disability to "help" disabled people "fit" into "normal" society.

However, critical disability theory questions the reduction of disability to finite categories to be counted, and defined using such critical divisions as normal versus pathological or the competent citizen versus the ward of the state (Linton 1998).

Consequences for the Counted or Discounted

As has been illustrated by Dunn and Langdon in the previous chapter, the consequences of being classified as "disabled" in the past often resulted in placement in poor houses, work houses or institutions, sterilization in many cases, and death within Hitler's eugenics program during World War II (Chadwick 2003). As in the example of the three surveys reviewed, there are an array of definitions of disability used across local, provincial and federal programs and services. Often times, social work and other human service professionals are involved directly or indirectly within the process of defining disability through administering various assessments, and through the resulting provision or curtailment of access to resources and services.

Within the current context, there are a variety of both negative and positive consequences that may result from being classified as "disabled." For example, on the negative side, this classification may result in being discriminated against, labelled, stigmatized or stereotyped, as well as being excluded from certain activities like mainstream education, driving a motor vehicle or participating in certain leisure activities — it is this process that "others" people with disabilities. On the other hand, this classification may provide access to needed services and resources such as additional educational, medical or financial support. However, the process often serves to divide, isolate and create hierarchies consisting of "we — the non-disabled" and "they — the disabled." As illustrated in the first-person accounts in Chapter 1 and the family experiences in Chapter 7, as well as the historical accounts in Chapter 2, people deemed to be "disabled" have endured much antagonism and oppression throughout history and to this present day.

Furthermore, according to Wendell (1996), social arrangements and expectations make essential contributions to the absence or presence of disability. Disability cannot be defined purely in biomedical terms. The interaction between social factors and our bodies affect health and functioning, but social arrangements can make a biological condition more or less relevant to almost any situation (Wendell 1996). Tremain sheds light on Foucault's notion of the disabled person as being embedded within the relations of power in modern societies (2005). Wendell calls "the interaction of the biological and the social to create (or prevent) disability 'the social construction of disability.'" (1996: 35). Thus, altering social arrangements and relations of power will have a direct impact on whether one is included or excluded from disability demographics. One begins to develop a clear sense of how the varying conceptualizations of disability within an ableist society have a direct bearing on whether one is counted or discounted within demographic findings.

Chapter Summary

It is critical to acknowledge that disability demographics represent snapshots in time. These snapshots only provide a limited and skewed representation of "facts" based on how disability is defined, the respondents included in the surveys, and the interpretations applied to these responses. Furthermore, there is no generally accepted definition of disability in Canada or within the international community. Through the exploration of three government surveys conducted in 1991, 2006 and 2012, this chapter has addressed the controversy of how disability is conceptualized, how people become classified as people with disabilities, and how these aspects are constructed within government surveys. In reviewing disability demographics, the reader has been introduced to how the influence of a medical or social model lens greatly alters the process for arriving at a definition of disability, and the paradigm through which disability is understood. As discussed, disability as interpreted through a medical model lens constitutes disability as an intrinsic characteristic of individuals, whereas a social model lens directs attention to the role of the social and physical environments in the disabling process.

Consequently, it is necessary to understand how disability is defined within particular surveys or reports when reviewing demographics, as the way in which disability is defined has a direct bearing on the quantification of a given population and the everyday lives of the people being counted or discounted. In fact, "the definition of *disability*, like the definition of *illness*, is inevitably a matter of social debate and social construction" (Bérubé, cited in Linton 1998: viii). Moreover, the discrepancies between the demographic findings of various surveys provide further evidence of the social construction of disability.

Individuals deemed as having a disability may or may not consider themselves as having a disability, and they may or may not use this specific term to describe themselves or their experiences. Thus, one must exercise caution and critical judgement in accepting demographics as objective "facts." Moreover, one needs to be alerted to the process of objectifying and homogenizing a population as nothing more than a "problem" of a medical nature. Also, an assumption is often made that the population being classified and counted is without strengths and may pose a threat to society or themselves due to the level of resources and supports they will require. This approach neglects to acknowledge the strengths and contributions of people with disabilities, as well as the barriers imposed on them by society.

Titchkosky alerts us to how the "god trick" is employed within government documents through the authoritative statement of facts that constitute disability as a condition readily identifiable in people in the form of rates within a population. Through the use of statistics, government data constructs disability as an individual problem. The god trick is used to present "authoritative facts" that go unquestioned, and these facts define the body in a manner that is totalizing and reductive. She asserts that disability as conveyed no longer names a type of self or a way of being: it is now a name for reduced ability to do, resulting from a lack of functionality. We are invited to consider treating disability as a way of perceiving and orienting to the world rather than conceiving of it as an individual functional limitation, as this will uncover how we might encounter disability in new ways.

Often times, social work and other human service professionals are involved directly or indirectly in the process of defining disability through administering various assessments, and through the resulting provision or curtailment of access to resources and services. Thus, it is necessary to be cognizant of the direct impact of the conceptualizations of disability on the lives of the people who are counted and discounted, as this has direct implications for service and program provision and the everyday experience of people with disabilities.

Discussion Questions

1. People with disabilities are reported to be the largest minority in the world. What percentage of the world's population are reported to have a disability? How does this number compare to the most current demographic reports in Canada?

2. What factors influence how people are counted as having disabilities in various surveys?

3. What are the dangers in interpreting demographics as "facts"?

4. How is disability interpreted within the medical model and how does this differ from the social model?

5. What is meant by the social construction of disability? How might disability be socially constructed?

6. How do the ICIDH and the ICF definitions of disability differ? What are the criticisms of these approaches?
7. What does Titchkosky mean by "god trick" and how does this apply to demographics?

References

Asch, Adrienne. 2001. "Critical Race Theory, Feminism, and Disability: Reflections on Social Justice and Personal Identity." *Ohio State Law Journal* 62, 1.

Barnes, Colin. 2014. "Reflections on Doing Emancipatory Disability Research." In John Swain, Sally French, Colin Barnes and Carol Thomas (eds.), *Disabling Barriers – Enabling Environments* 2nd edition. London, UK: Sage.

Barnes, Colin, and Geof Mercer. 2003. *Disability*. Cambridge: UK: Polity.

Center for International Rehabilitation. 2004. "International Disability Rights Monitor 2004: Regional Report of the Americas." <bbi.syr.edu/publications/blanck_docs/2003-2004/IDRM_Americas_2004.pdf>.

Chadwick, Patricia. 2003. "Disability Social History Project." <disabilityhistory.org/timeline_new.html>.

Frazee, Catherine, Joan Gilmour and Roxanne Mykitiuk. 2006. "Now You See Her, Now You Don't: How Law Shapes Disabled Women's Experience of Exposure, Surveillance, and Assessment in the Clinical Encounter." In Dianne Pothier and Richard Devlin (eds.), *Critical Disability Theory: Essays in Philosophy, Politics, Policy and Law*. Vancouver: UBC Press.

Health Canada. 2002. "A Report on Mental Illnesses in Canada." <phac-aspc.gc.ca/publicat/miic-mmac/pdf/men_ill_e.pdf>.

____. 2009. "A Statistical Profile on the Health of First Nations in Canada: Self-Rated Health and Selected Conditions 2002 to 2005." <www.hc-sc.gc.ca/fniahspnia/alt_formats/pdf/pubs/aborig-autoch/2009-stats-profil-vol3/2009-stats-profil-vol3-eng.pdf>.

Human Resources and Skills Development Canada. 2011. "Disability in Canada: A 2006 Profile." <esdc.gc.ca/eng/disability/arc/disability_2006.pdf>.

Linton, Simi. 1998. *Claiming Disability: Knowledge and Identity*. New York: New York University Press.

Marks, Deborah. 1999. *Disability: Controversial Debates and Psychosocial Perspectives*. London: Routledge.

Morris, Jenny. 1991. *Pride Against Prejudice: Transforming Attitudes to Disability*. London: Women's Press.

Office for Disability Issues, Human Resources Development Canada. 2003. "Defining Disability: A Complex Issue." <publications.gc.ca/collections/Collection/RH37-4-3-2003E.pdf>.

Oliver, Michael. 2009. "The Social Model in Context." In Tanya Titchkosky and Rod Michalko (eds.), *Rethinking Normalcy: A Disability Studies Reader*. Toronto, ON: Canadian Scholars Press Inc.

Peters, Susan, Kimberly Wolbers and Lisa Dimling. 2008. "Reframing Global Education From a Disability Rights Movement Perspective." In Susan Gabel and Scot Danforth (eds.), *Disability and the International Politics of Education*. New York: Peter Lang.

Roeher Institute. 1996. *Disability, Community and Society: Exploring the Links*. North York, ON: Roeher Institute.

Statistics Canada. n.d. "Health and Activity Limitation Survey: Data Quality Statements (HALS)." <23.statcan.gc.ca/imdb-bmdi/document/3251_D1_T2_V1-eng.pdf>.

____. 1991a. "Health and Activity Limitation Survey: Household Component (HALS)." <23.statcan.gc.ca/imdb/p2SV.pl?Function=getSurvey&SurvId=1352&InstaId=5661&SDDS=3251>.

____. 1991b. "Health and Activity Limitation Survey: Institutional Component (HALS)." <23.statcan.gc.ca/imdb/p2SV.pl?Function=getSurvey&SDDS=3252>.

____. 1994. "1991 Aboriginal People's Survey: Disability and Housing." Catalogue 89-535. Ottawa: Minister of Industry, Science and Technology.

____. 2002. "A New Approach to Disability Data: Changes Between the 1991 Health and Activity Limitation Survey (HALS) and the 2001 Participation and Activity Limitation Survey (PALS)." <5.statcan.gc.ca/olc-cel/olc.action?ObjId=89-578-X2002001&ObjType=46&lang=en>.

____. 2007a. "Participation and Activity Limitation Survey 2006: Analytical Report." <statcan.gc.ca/pub/89-628-x/89-628-x2007002-eng.htm>.

____. 2007b. "Participation and Activity Limitation Survey 2006: Technical and Methodological Report." <statcan.gc.ca/pub/89-628-x/89-628-x2007002-eng.pdf>.

____. 2013. "The 2012 Canadian Survey on Disability (CSD) and the 2006 Participation and Activity Limitation Survey (PALS)." <23.statcan.gc.ca/imdb-bmdi/document/3251_D6_T9_V1-eng.htm>.

____. 2015. "A Profile of Persons with Disabilities Among Canadians Aged 15 Years or Older, 2012." <statcan.gc.ca/pub/89-654-x/89-654-x2015001-eng.htm>.

Thomas, Carol. 2014. "Disability and Impairment." In John Swain, Sally French, Colin Barnes and Carol Thomas (eds.), *Disabling Barriers — Enabling Environments* 3rd edition. London, UK: Sage.

Titchkosky Tanya. 2007. *Reading & Writing Disability Differently: The Textured Life of Embodiment* Toronto, ON: University of Toronto Press.

Titchkosky, Tanya, and Rod Michalko. 2009. "Introduction." In Tanya Titchkosky and Rod Michalko (eds.), *Rethinking Normalcy: A Disability Studies Reader*. Toronto, ON: Canadian Scholars Press Inc.

Tremain, Shelly. 2005. "Foucault, Governmentality, and Critical Disability Theory: An Introduction." In Shelley Tremain (ed.), *Foucault and the Government of Disability*. Michigan: University of Michigan Press.

United Nations. 2000. "General Assembly, Resolution S23/3." <un.org/womenwatch/daw/followup/ress233e.pdf>.

____. 2006. "Convention on the Rights of Persons with Disabilities: Some Facts about Persons with Disabilities." <un.org/disabilities/convention/facts.shtml>.

Wendell, Susan. 1996. *The Rejected Body: Feminist Philosophical Reflections on Disability*. New York: Routledge.

Whiting, Glynis. 1996. *The Sterilization of Leilani Muir (film)*. National Film Board of Canada.

Withers, A.J. 2012. *Disability Politics & Theory*. Black Point, NS: Fernwood Publishing.

WHO (World Health Organization). 1980. "International Classification of Impairments,

Disabilities and Handicaps: A Manual of Classification Relating to Consequences of Disease." <whqlibdoc.who.int/publications/1980/9241541261_eng.pdf>.

____. 2011. "World Report on Disability." <who.int/disabilities/world_report/2011/report.pdf>.

Chapter 4

Critical Disability Theory: Developing a Post-Social Model of Disability

Roy Hanes

The following draws attention to the politics of disability discourse and offers a social work paradigm for theorizing, researching and practising social work from a radical or anti-oppressive perspective. This chapter should help to generate student debate on the way disability discourse is constructed in most schools of social work, by drawing attention to dominant disability theories such as the social model (Oliver 1990) and suggesting that this "radical" theory does not go far enough when it comes to changing approaches to research, analysis and practice. I borrow from Maurice Moreau's structural approach to social work to show how this model not only offers a progressive analysis, akin to a social model, but also gives social work a critical disability theory for practice. In this study, I combine elements of the social model and the structural approach to create a post-social model of disability, where critical disability theory and radical social work practice are merged. In brief, this chapter examines the theoretical debate as well as issues of practice.

Since the early 1970s a number of issues pertaining to the analysis of disability have emerged in Canada, the United States and other Western industrialized countries. Many critical theorists have linked disability to race, ethnicity and culture, gender, sexual orientation and social policy (Scheer and Groce 1988; Oliver 1990; Wendell 1996; Hanes and Moscovitch 2004; Hansen 2002; Samuels 2003; Smith and Hutchison 2004; Prince 2009). Notwithstanding the vast array of research emerging from the academic disciplines of social work, sociology, women's studies, disability policy, gender studies, political science, history, disability studies and several other fields of enquiry, the primary discourses of disability emerging in Canada over the past twenty-five to thirty years are rooted in two opposing paradigms (Hanes 1995, 2004; Meister 2003; Hick 2008; Leslie, Hanes, Dunn and MacDonald 2008; McAllan and Ditillo 1999; Prince 2004; Puttee 2004; Reynolds Whyte and Ingstad 1995; Titchkosky and Michalko 2007). On the one hand, there is a rehabilitation paradigm, where disability and impairment are depicted as medicalized and individualized problems; and on the other hand, the independent living model, where disability is portrayed as individual difficulties arising from economic, cultural, historical, social and political barriers and oppression. Gerben Dejong drew attention to these paradigms in his seminal article "Defining and Implementing the Independent Living Concept" (1978). Within a short time other authors from the United States and Canada were adding their voices to the independent living philosophy (Crewe and Zola 1983; Coalition of Provincial Organizations of the Handicapped 1984).

In Britain, Michael Oliver — writing from a Marxist perspective — added to disability debates in his analysis of the "Personal Tragedy and Social Models of Disability" (1990). Like the rehabilitation paradigm, the personal tragedy model focuses on medicalized social constructs of disability as a tragic life event where all means must be employed to help, fix or cure the disabled individual. Although more radical and political in analysis than the independent living philosophy, the social model of disability does share a similar theoretical foundation, in that environments, relationships and social interactions between disabled and nondisabled people are viewed as the root cause of the problems experienced by people with disabilities.

Throughout the past decade the social model has emerged as the dominant theory within most disability studies programs in Canada, the United States and abroad. The influence of this model has been far-reaching and its weight in the study of disability is noted in many fields of study. Despite its rise to dominance, in recent years there has been a mounting critique of the social model, with many disability theorists feeling that it does not adequately speak to the lived experiences of disabled individuals, though it provides a well-informed framework for the analysis of disability issues at the socio-political, cultural and economic levels (French 1993; Crow 1996; Thomas 1999; Corker and Shakespeare 2001).

This chapter attempts to bridge the divide between the social and individualized models with a social work theory encompassing the lived experiences of disabled individuals as well as the contextual relevance of disability embedded in society. This theory, encapsulating both the "personal and the political," is referred to as the structural approach to social work (Middleman and Goldberg 1974; Goldberg Wood and Tully 2006; Moreau 1979; Moreau and Leonard 1989; Mullaly 2007, 1997; Lundy 2004). While the structural approach is most noted for its focus on socio-political and economic analysis and change — thus providing principles for critical analysis and broader societal change, both in the field and among disability theorists — it also stresses the importance of exploring and understanding the day-to-day lived experiences of disabled people. And it connects the lived experiences of disabled individuals with the wider socio-economic, cultural and political milieu that, in effect, impedes the life-fulfilling opportunities of all disabled people.

It is this "conjoint element" that is missing from many contemporary disability debates, and my goal in this chapter is to add new dimensions to the discourse by shifting to a "post"-social model, where individual lived experiences can be linked with the wider socio-economic context. The chapter will show that an exploration of lived experiences without the "social" sphere, and vice versa — the examination of the social sphere without individual experiences — severely restricts analysis and action. This chapter presents the case, moreover, that the personal and social contexts are not mutually exclusive but complementary, and will show that the structural approach provides a framework for the examination of the lived experiences of disabled individuals and their families, as well as the systemic barriers and oppressions arising from social spheres. In summary, this chapter examines existing paradigms of disability discourse and offers a new one, incorporating a convergence of the individualized and social models, thus arriving at a post-social/structural approach model of disability.

Disability Rights Movements and Changing Discourses

Disability rights movements in Canada and the United States were influenced by the emergence of social action and political activism of the late 1960s and the early 1970s (Crewe and Zola 1983; Peters 2003; Stienstra and Wight-Felske 2003; Valentine 1994). For the most part, between the early 1900s and the early 1970s, the "problems" of people with disabilities were largely defined as individual and medical issues (Zola 1992). During this time, tens of thousands of disabled children and adults were placed in an assortment of institutions, including hospitals, asylums and chronic-care facilities. In this period, we find the rise of specialized and professionalized services, special and segregated education, segregated recreation programs, support services and so on. And throughout the development of all these programs we find the dominance of the ideologies of individual pathology and the interests of the medical/rehabilitative professions. It is this trend that Zola (1992) referred to as the "medicalization of disability," and that led Henry Enns to warn that the medical dominance and interest in individual pathology were so pervasive in the lives of people with disabilities that, for many, it became what he termed a lifelong "cradle to grave" relationship.

By the late 1960s, inspired by the growing power of social action — as exemplified in the university students', labour, civil rights, peace, gay rights and women's movements — many people with disabilities began to question their socio-political and economic exclusion as well as the roles of institutionalization and of professional and medical dominance. They examined their lot in life in terms of oppression and the lack of political rights, and subsequently began to challenge medical and professional dominance. And rather than accepting labels, such as "defective, flawed, invalid or sick," they argued that they should be seen as members of an oppressed and disenfranchised minority group (Dejong 1978; Hanes 2008). "Many persons with disabilities," observed Frieden, "considered themselves members of a minority group related not by colour or nationality but by functional limitation and similar need" (1983: 55). Over time, these shifts in identity politics led to the deconstruction of disability definitions, methods of treatment, and mechanisms of service delivery, and to challenges to medical dominance and the medicalization of disability (Crewe and Zola 1983).

From the late 1970s, disability rights advocates and theorists have attempted to draw attention to the oppression of disabled people, which has contributed to their high levels of unemployment, undereducation, poverty and exclusion from mainstream society. The disability rights movements that emerged in the United States and Canada during the mid-1970s helped people with disabilities and their advocates change their view of disability from that of a rehabilitative construct to an independent living ideology, which emphasized political rights and empowerment rather than medical treatment and care (Dejong 1978; Crewe and Zola 1983; Coalition of Provincial Organizations of the Handicapped 1984; Driedger 1989). The shift from a rehabilitative to a socio-political paradigm under the umbrella of the movement for independent living contributed to a corresponding shift away from policies and social programs fixed in individualized physical, mental and character flaws to the development of social and political strategies for intervention, support and research.

The movement for independent living, often referred to as the civil rights movement for disabled people, conveys two opposing views of disability (Dejong 1978). On the one hand, there is the professionally dominated rehabilitation model — the belief that disability is primarily a medical problem and that the agent of change should be the disabled individual. And, on the other hand, the rights-based model — that the adversities experienced by disabled people stem primarily from the socio-political and economic contexts and the agent of change should be at the contextual level (Dejong 1978; Crewe and Zola 1983; Oliver 1996). The transition from a rehabilitative to an independent living paradigm became more than just a new way of defining disability, as it also gave way to a new way of presenting and researching disability issues, and in so doing offered new avenues for social action and political change (Dejong 1978).

Social and Personal Tragedy Models of Disability

The social model of disability originated in Britain during the 1990s, and like the independent living paradigm, it offers two dominant streams of analysis. On the one hand, as Oliver (1990) argues, a "personal tragedy model" supports the social construct of disability as a catastrophic life event. Similar to the rehabilitative paradigm (Dejong 1978), the personal tragedy model also builds on medicalized notions of pathology and personal loss and promotes the need for rehabilitation and individual change through the services of medical and/or affiliated professionals (Oliver 1990, 1996; Barnes and Mercer 2003).

According to Michael Oliver, a personal tragedy perspective explains the sufferings incurred by people with disabilities as the direct consequences of individual impairment and personal failures — including the inability to cope and adapt — as decided on an individualized, incremental, medically diagnosed and professionally prescribed basis. Needs and access to supports and services are determined by medical and/or rehabilitation specialists, including, but not limited to, psychiatrists, social workers, psychologists, occupational therapists and physiotherapists. From a personal tragedy perspective, the social position of people with disabilities is one of an "invalid outsider." The dominant message is that it is the people with disabilities who must be changed, fixed or cured and it is they who should adapt to society and its existing socio-economic order. The importance of major societal change is not recognized from this perspective, and thus it is considered that piecemeal adjustments and minor structural and policy reforms are sufficient. In this sense the disability category can be viewed as socially constructed, with the problematic identity located within the individual (Oliver 1990, 1996; Barnes and Mercer 2003; Titchkosky 2007).

Against the personal tragedy model, Oliver (1990) offered a critical theory of disability referred to as the "social model." It recognizes that the disadvantages of disabled people arise from socio-political and economic inequality, which contributes to the powerlessness of people with disabilities as individuals and as a collective. The primary argument is that their needs would be best met through broader changes in society and the economy rather than in themselves as individuals. On the basis of this analysis, it is recognized that people may have impairments, but it is society and its social organizations that oppress and "handicap" people with disabilities. Accordingly, the emphasis is on changing environments and attitudes so that people with disabilities can be included in all aspects of society, rather than on changing disabled people so they can cope and fit in as best as they can (Oliver 1990; Barnes, Mercer and Shakespeare 1999).

A social model of disability views the root cause of problems faced by disabled people as stemming from social oppression, leading in turn to discrimination — not unlike the discrimination incurred by people in other minority groups. Policy development incorporating an analysis based on a social model focuses on the human rights and inclusion of disabled people. For example, strategies seated in a social model address human rights legislation, employment equity issues, disabled people's direct involvement in policy development, independent living programs, public awareness campaigns and policies aimed at greater accessibility and inclusion. In short, the focus of policy development and intervention is on "alleviating oppression rather than compensating victims" (Oliver 1990: 2).

Increasingly, disabled people's self-help organizations are relying on a social model in their attempts to challenge their exclusion from the mainstream. Disability rights advocates conclude that individualized medical models do not adequately address exclusionary practices stemming from attitudinal and physical barriers, as well as the role and influence of professional dominance, the consequences of medicalization, and the negative impact of disability industries, which often keep disabled individuals in subservient roles under their care providers. Those who support the social model believe that an individual "tragedy/loss/pathology" framework will never challenge the social reality of people with disabilities and that socio-political and economic change is required to achieve full inclusion.

Despite the merits of a social model of disability, one must not lose sight of the disabled individual in the proverbial inaccessible forest. A fundamental critique of the social model is that the individual's lived experiences become minimized and/or lost in the promotion of a disability analysis based solely on societal issues, and many authors have noted that people with disabilities often live with pain and with loss and that their primary concern is getting through one day to the next (Crow 1996; Oliver 1996; Thomas 1999, 2007). Recognizing and providing for the day-to-day needs of disabled people in these situations is paramount, but a social model does not adequately focus on disabled people's lived experiences. In recognition of the shortcomings of both the social and personal tragedy models, it seems appropriate to try to incorporate both the personal and the political in a model for disability analysis and action. The binary separation of the social and personal tragedy models tends to dominate much of the disability discourse, and as a consequence, a lot of the debate becomes a reductionist, esoteric discourse where subjective, social constructionist analyses devalue disabled people's lived experiences. This argument does not deny that notions of disability and impairment are socially constructed worldwide, but it is intended to raise the possibility of debates exploring the objective reality of disabled people. The day-to-day realities of people with disabilities and the social contextual elements must be connected; there is a need for a person-centred political approach where the subjective interpretations and objective realities of disability converge. Such an analysis and intersections are found in the structural approach to social work.

The Structural Approach

As with other developments in society of the early 1970s, the rise of the structural approach can be traced to a paradigm shift in Canadian society. Indeed, the argument can be made that the structural approach grew from the same elements of discontent, which also affected people with disabilities, and grew from the same socio-political influences, such as the rise of the women's movement, the poor people's campaigns, and the anti-Vietnam War and consumer movements.

Collectively, these social movements influenced changes in social work theory, education, training and practice. Many social work practitioners, educators and researchers recognized that individualized problem definitions with individualized methods of intervention had minimal impact on the day-to-day lives of their clients. One of the greatest transformations came at the level of analysis, as problem definitions moved from individual blame to a contextual focus, and this radical shift in analysis brought about further advances in the realm of intervention — from individual to community-scale systemic interventions and socio-political change (Moreau 1979; Moreau and Leonard 1989).

The establishment of the structural approach corresponded to a paradigm shift in social work, where psychoanalytical case work, for example, gave way to a focus on ecosystems theory, with social work educators adopting concepts from social ecology and systems theory (Lecomte 1990). They explored the need for environmental and contextual change as well as individual, couple and family change. While a dominant concern of the structural approach is the belief that the structures of society should be changed so that the needs of people can be met, it equally recognizes that because of the damaging characteristics of classism, heterosexism, racism, sexism and ableism, many individuals are psychologically and emotionally hurt and therefore in need of assistance, guidance and support (Moreau and Leonard 1989). Historically, the structural approach led to a swing away from individualized to community and socio-political models of intervention and then to the incorporation of the personal into socio-political models of analysis, intervention and research (Moreau 1979; Lecomte 1990). In this regard, it represented a convergence of the individual, experiential and socio-political contexts, and is just as concerned with the lived experiences of individuals as it is with the socio-political inequalities of society at large.

Linking the Personal and the Political: Tiers of Analysis and Practice

The structural approach advocates for supportive interventions to enable individuals to deal with their personal needs and eventually contribute to changing their environments, life circumstances and, hopefully, social inequalities. It emphasizes two fundamental tiers of analysis and practice, where the first tier focuses on work with individuals with disabilities and significant others, such as family, and the second tier is aimed at attitudinal barriers, accessibility issues, disability policy concerns, and institutional, organizational, as well as socio-political, cultural, ideological and economic change — as Moreau and Leonard (1989) wrote, "change [to] promote greater inclusion and access for people with disabilities." They summarized the two-tiered process of the structural approach as follows: "concretely, the approach was described as involving a two-tiered interrelated process — one tier, more short term aimed at immediate individual tension relief, and a second tier, longer term, aimed at institutional and structural change and tension elimination" (18).

The structural approach recognizes the importance of linking the personal with the political and as such it promotes the importance of striving for agency and institutional change, working as allies with clients, getting involved in socio-political movements, and becoming activists as well as counsellors and resource providers. The structural approach maintains that social workers should, as much as possible, be allies, not hindrances, to their clients and that assistance should be provided through supportive counselling rather than psychotherapeutic interventions based on notions of individual pathology.

A core principle of the approach is that most people adopt the values, behaviours and beliefs of the dominant culture. For example, in free-market, competitive capitalist societies such as Canada's, people are taught that if they work hard they will be successful and if they fail to be successful it is their own fault. From an early age people are taught that Canada is a fair and just society where all people, regardless of race, class, gender, sexual orientation or ability, are provided with equal opportunities to develop their lives but that it is up to the individual to make the best of these opportunities to pursue the "Canadian Dream." Because people are taught to accept these values throughout their lives, there is a tendency to blame themselves and/or others for their hardships. Rarely do people, regardless of their life circumstances, examine the economic and ideological factors that contribute to their difficulties.

In many ways, such social conditioning creates a double-bind situation for disabled people and their families. Despite the social, political, economic, attitudinal and physical barriers that must be dealt with on a daily basis, they are expected to participate in the mainstream and to develop to their "full potential." They are expected, moreover, to be stoic and "not give in" to adversity. But despite these societal messages, they are often told that they must accept their lot in life. Interestingly, when disabled people are assertive and fight for their rights, they are depicted as being angry and aggressive, and if they accept their disability, they are accused of giving in and giving up. Hence, for many disabled people, life symbolizes a series of disempowering and oppressive contradictions, paradoxes and no-win situations, which can lead to depression, anxiety and other emotional difficulties. In addition to these difficulties, the reality for many people with disabilities is that, because of disease, impairment or injury, they have to cope with severe physical pain, constant fatigue and progressive debilitating impairments.

As noted above, the structural approach acknowledges that disabled people's hardships are entrenched in inequality and oppression, but presents the challenge of focusing on individual issues as well as the more encompassing issues of social justice and societal change. The structural approach lays stress on the narratives and lived experiences of people with disabilities and recognizes the relevance of depression and the psychological and physical pain that often accompanies many different forms of impairment. Likewise, it recognizes the personal consequences of the stigma of disability, of being undereducated or underemployed, living in an inaccessible world and being relegated to the social role of an outsider. All of these elements can be deconstructed in terms of the oppression of disabled people, but while it is vital to overturn conditions of inequality and oppression, it is also imperative to deal with the personal consequences of being unemployed, devalued or an outsider. All of these elements can contribute to one's self-image, and if there is an internalization of negative self-worth, there may be a need for assistance to resolve these issues and feelings.

Convergence of Structural Social Work and Disability

The structural approach to social work is concerned with social oppression but equally with the immediate needs of clients, and it offers disability theorists as well as practitioners a way of connecting the missing pieces of the social and personal tragedy models, as well as those of independent living and rehabilitation.

The structural approach recognizes the central position of both individual lived experiences and the social and political spheres of disability. Neither one is more relevant or more important than the other. However, it should be emphasized that the structural approach is not based on a "liberal compromise" between the medical and social models. Though like the social model, it is entrenched in critical theory and hence recognizes the importance of socio-economic and political change; the structural approach accepts the central role of the day-to-day lived experiences of disabled people. And it is more than a theoretical paradigm of analysis — it is action-oriented and calls for individual as well as societal change.

It cannot be denied that social work practice and social policy development have followed the personal tragedy and medical model concepts of disability, and that that is why social work practice, education and research have traditionally focused on direct services, especially individual and family counselling, and paid little attention to the need for greater political change. Similarly, social policies intended to support disabled people and their families are limited by an individual pathology analysis of disability. Consequently, because problems are constructed as individual-centred or, at best, family located, the tendency is to develop policies and programs to meet the diagnosed and/or prescribed needs of individuals. Despite the fact that disabled people are covered under federal and provincial human rights legislation in Canada, most government-sponsored programs are focused on the individual and family and rarely ever challenge systemic oppression and ableism.

Fundamentally, the structural approach maintains that researchers, academics and policy developers, as well as practitioners, must try to keep the experiences of the disabled individual steadfastly in view. Totally shifting to a rights-based focus and subsequently developing programs that deal solely with accessibility issues risks discounting the lived experiences of disabled individuals. Critiques of the social model clearly make this point. For example, Jenny Morris (1991) asserts the following: "While environmental barriers and social attitudes are a crucial part of our experience of disability — and do indeed disable us — to suggest that this is all there is, is to deny the personal experience of physical and intellectual restrictions, of illness[,] or the fear of dying" (10). Similarly, disabled feminists assert that the social model does not incorporate a gendered analysis of disability; likewise, disabled people of colour contend that it does not adequately deal with issues of race and racism. In contrast, the structural approach recognizes the significance of race and gender as well as class and sexual orientation when addressing the needs and concerns of disabled people. In this sense, the structural approach is more comprehensive.

Notwithstanding these critiques, it remains this writer's contention that a social model analysis provides social work and disability studies with an excellent beginning point to explore how disability is framed as a social category. And a social model provides a more in-depth analysis of disability than medical model alternatives. What is required is a "post-social model," based in structural social work, which recognizes the significance of individual and familial experiences and the contextual interrelationship of these experiences with socio-political variables. For example, the provision of care to individuals, couples and families to help deal with day-to-day issues such as coping with loss, adjusting to trauma or living with chronic pain, through information, counselling or other mechanisms of immediate support, is just as important as advocating for more extensive socio-political and economic changes, such as the provision of universal supportive care programs, accessible transportation, decent employment, accessible, affordable housing, or barrier removal.

Maurice Moreau and Lynne Leonard (1989) stressed this interrelationship by focusing on the significance of "immediate relief" and "elimination of oppression." Addressing one sphere without the other, Moreau argued, would not and could not lead to beneficial changes for individuals, families or society. A post-social model of disability oriented in the structural approach, which does away with binary divisions between the socio-political and the individual/familial realms, allows for a more holistic analysis of disability than a social model. It links personal experiences to social and political inequality and in so doing responds to critiques of the social model. And it is grounded in praxis, linking theory and practice with the aim of bringing about change at the individual as well as societal levels.

A Post-Social Model for Practice

The structural approach moves beyond the social and personal tragedy/medical models of disability. Through its focus on a two-tiered system of analysis and action, it provides opportunities for individual as well as systemic analysis and change. For example, the first tier or level of analysis and activity is identified as immediate support, or as what Moreau (1979) referred to as "immediate tension relief." At this level of praxis, the focus is primarily on the individual, couple and/ or family, and the social worker's role is primarily one of resource provider and supportive counsellor to the disabled individual and his or her family. To meet the immediate needs and concerns of a disabled person, the worker could be engaged in individual or significant-other supportive counselling and/or social work activity, which might include advocacy work to gain important required resources. Immediate tension relief focuses on the present, and the involvement with clients is expected to last days, weeks or months. The aim of the intervention is for the social worker to move out of the lives of disabled people as soon as possible and not to engage in "client making."

The second level of involvement espoused by the structural approach involves long-term change through collective action and group activity (Moreau 1979). As indicated earlier, the structural approach combines both individual and societal change, but it stresses the process of collective action over individual intervention to bring about societal change. This is based on the contention that greater societal change is more likely to occur through the action of the collective rather than the individual. The structural approach suggests that group action helps disabled individuals and their families redefine problem areas as those of structural inequality rather than of personal inadequacy. By stressing the relevance of group activity, moreover, the structural approach recognizes the importance of group and collective action in the development of mutual support as well as personal empowerment. The importance of group and collective action has been central to disabled persons' movements since the early 1970s, and a significant benefit of group and collective action has been the great potential for human growth and the increased sense of purpose and self-esteem. In Canada, these elements have been the cornerstone of the social justice activities of disabled people and their advocates for the past twenty to thirty years.

Chapter Summary

Social workers are often criticized by people with disabilities for their limited focus on individual and family counselling and their long-standing adherence to rehabilitation and medical constructs of disability where the disabled person is identified as having or being the problem. Similarly, social workers are criticized because of the limited attention they pay to social and political change. And in many ways social workers are viewed as being part of the problem, not the solution. Increasingly, disability rights activists and academics have had a significant impact on challenging medical model constructs of disability and some have presented challenges to social work education, training, research and practice (Dunn et al. 2006; Leslie et al. 2008). And as a result of these challenges, many social work educators have incorporated a rights-based focus into their research and course content. For example, social worker educators, students, social workers and disability activists from across Canada came together in Ottawa in 1993 to develop the Persons with Disabilities Caucus of the Canadian Association of Schools of Social Work. Since that time, most of the MSW and BSW disability-related courses that have been developed in Canada have incorporated social model and anti-oppressive paradigms. Increasingly, social workers are getting involved in a wide spectrum of activities on behalf of disabled people, including counselling and support, assistance in obtaining resources, community organizing and social action.

As this chapter has shown, disability research over the past few decades has challenged the social model of disability as being too engaged with the social and political spheres of disability analysis and discourse. As noted throughout, the social model is severely limited in its analysis, as it has not recognized the day-to-day needs or the lived experiences of disabled people. Rooted in these critiques and discourse has been the recommendation to include more of the narratives of people with disabilities. The social model, without the analysis of the lived experiences of disabled people, becomes a limited, one-theme entity, only highlighting the shortcomings of social contexts. Interestingly, while many authors give their critiques of the social model, they offer limited alternatives as to what should and can be done to rectify the status quo. The structural approach moves beyond a critique of the social model and offers a framework of convergence to engage both the personal and political, not only for the purposes of critical analysis, but also for action. The two-tiered framework of the structural approach offers disability theorists, as well as social work researchers, academics and practitioners, a mechanism for analysis and action in both the personal and the socio-political spheres.

Discussion Questions

1. What are the core elements of the social model of disability and what are the strengths and weaknesses of this approach?

2. What are the core elements of the personal tragedy model of disability and what are the strengths and weaknesses of this approach?

3. What are some of the core principles of the structural approach and how does it differ from the social and personal tragedy model?

4. Create case studies and compare how a social worker might work with clients with disabilities — borrowing from the personal tragedy/rehabilitation and social model/independent living movement approach.

5. Apply these case examples to demonstrate how a social worker might be involved with clients with disabilities by focusing on short-term immediate relief and longer-term social political involvement.

References

Barnes, Colin, and Geoff Mercer. 2003. *Disability*. Maldon, MA: Blackwell Publishers.

Barnes, Colin, Geoff Mercer and Tom Shakespeare. 1999. *Exploring Disability: A Sociological Introduction*. Oxford: Blackwell Publishing.

Coalition of Provincial Organizations of the Handicapped. 1984. *Independent Living: Made in Canada*. Ottawa: Coalition of Provincial Organizations of the Handicapped.

Corker, Mary, and Tom Shakespeare. 2001. *Disability/Postmodernity: Embodying Disability Theory*. London: Continuum Press.

Crewe, Nancy, and Irving Zola. 1983. *Independent Living for Physically Disabled People*. San Francisco: Jossey Bass.

Crow, Liz. 1996. "Including All of Our Lives: Renewing the Social Model of Disability." In Colin Barnes and Geoff Mercer (eds.), *Exploring the Divide*. Leeds: Disability Press.

Dejong, Gerben. 1978. "Defining and Implementing the Independent Living Concept." *Archives of Physical Medicine and Rehabilitation* 60: 435–46.

Driedger, Diane. 1989. *The Last Civil Rights Movement: Disabled People's International*. New York: St Martin's Press.

Dunn, Peter, Roy Hanes, Susan Hardie and Judy MacDonald. 2006. "Creating Disability Inclusion within Canadian Schools of Social Work." *Journal of Social Work in Disability and Rehabilitation* 5,: 1–19.

French, Sally. 1993. "Disability, Impairment or Something In Between." In John Swain, Colin Barnes, Sally French and Carol Thomas (eds.), *Disabling Barriers — Enabling Environments*. London: Sage.

Frieden, Lex. 1983. "Independent Living in the United States and Other Countries." *Handicaps Monthly*, April: 54–61.

Goldberg Wood, Gale, and Carol Tully. 2006. *The Structural Approach to Direct Practice in Social Work: A Social Constructionist Perspective*. New York: Columbia University Press.

Hanes, Roy. 1995. "Linking Mental Defect to Physical Disability: The Case of Crippled Children in Ontario, 1890–1940." *Journal on Developmental Disability* 4.

_____. 2004. "The Criminalization of Cripples in 19th Century Ontario." *Disability Studies Review* (Summer).

_____. 2008. "Social Work with Persons with Disabilities." In Steven Hicks (ed.), *Social Work in Canada*. Toronto: Thompson Educational Publishing.

Hanes, Roy, and Allan Moscovitch. 2004. "Disability Supports and Services in a Social Union." In Allan Puttee (ed.), *Federalism, Democracy, and Disability Policy in Canada*. Kingston: McGill-Queen's University Press.

Hansen, Nancy. 2002. "Passing through Other People's Spaces: Disabled Women, Geography and Work." PhD thesis, University of Glasgow.

Hick, Steven. 2008. *Social Work in Canada*. Toronto: Thompson Educational Publishing.

Lecomte, Roland. 1990. "Connecting Private Troubles and Public Issues in Social Work Education." In Brian Wharf (ed.), *Social Work and Social Change in Canada*. Toronto: McClelland and Stewart.

Leslie, Donald, Roy Hanes, Peter Dunn and Judy MacDonald. 2008. "Disability Related Best Practices in Promoting Disability Inclusion within Canadian Schools of Social Work." *Disability Studies Quarterly* (Winter).

Lundy, Colleen. 2004. *Social Work and Social Justice: A Structural Approach to Practice*. Toronto: Broadview Press.

McAllan, Leslie, and Deborah Ditillo. 1999. "Addressing the Needs of Lesbian and Gay Clients with Disabilities." In Robert P. Marinelli and Arthur E. Dell Orto (eds.), *The Psychological and Social Impact of Disability*. New York: Springer Publishing.

Meister, Joan. 2003. "An Early Dawning (1985–1994)." In Deborah Stienstra and Aileen Wight-Felske (eds.), *Making Equality: History of Advocacy and Persons with Disabilities in Canada*. Concord, ON: Captus Press.

Middleman, Ruth, and Gale Goldberg. 1974. *Social Service Delivery: A Structural Approach to Social Work Practice*. New York: Columbia University Press.

Moreau, Maurice. 1979. "A Structural Approach to Practice." *Canadian Journal of Social Work Education* 5: 78–94.

Moreau, Maurice, and Lynne Leonard. 1989. *Empowerment through a Structural Approach: A Report from Practice*. Ottawa, ON: School of Social Work, Carleton University.

Morris, Jenny. 1991. *Pride against Prejudice*. London: Women's Press.

Mullaly, Bob. 1997. *Structural Approach: Ideology, Theory and Practice*. Toronto: University of Toronto Press.

_____. 2007. *The New Structural Social Work*. Toronto: University of Toronto Press.

Oliver, Michael. 1990. *The Politics of Disablement*. London: Macmillan Press.

_____. 1996. "The Social Model in Context." In *Understanding Disability: From Theory to Practice*. New York: St Martin's Press.

Peters, Yvonne. 2003. "From Charity to Equality: Canadians with Disabilities Take Their Rightful Place in Canada's Constitution." In Deborah Stienstra and Eileen Wight-Felske (eds.), *Making Equity: History of Advocacy and Persons with Disabilities in Canada*. Concord, ON: Captus Press.

Prince, Michael. 2004. "Canadian Disability Policy: Still a Hit-and-Miss Affair." *Canadian Journal of Sociology* 29.

_____. 2009. *Absent Citizens: Disability Politics and Policy in Canada*. Toronto: University of Toronto Press.

Puttee, Allan. 2004. *Federalism, Democracy, and Disability Policy in Canada*. Kingston, ON: McGill-Queens University Press

Reynolds Whyte, Susan, and Benedicte Ingstad. 1995. *Disability and Culture*. Berkeley: University of California Press.

Samuels, Ellen. 2003. "My Body, My Closet: Invisible Disability and the Limits of Coming-Out Discourse." GLQ: *A Journal of Lesbian and Gay Studies*.

Scheer, Jessica, and Nora Groce. 1988. "Impairment as a Human Constant: Cross-Cultural and Historical Perspectives on Variation." *Journal of Social Issues* 44: 23–37.

Smith, Bonnie G., and Beth Hutchison. 2004. *Gendering Disability*. New Brunswick, NJ: Rutgers University Press.

Stienstra, Deborah, and Eileen Wight-Felske. 2003. *Making Equity: History of Advocacy and Persons with Disabilities in Canada*. Concord, ON: Captus Press.

Thomas, Carol. 1999. *Female Forms: Experiencing and Understanding Disability*. Buckingham: Open University Press.

____. 2007. *Sociologies of Disabilities and Illness: Contested Ideas in Disability Studies and Medical Sociology*. New York: Palgrave Macmillan.

Titchkosky, Tanya. 2007. *Reading and Writing Disability Differently*. Toronto: University of Toronto Press.

Titchkosky, Tanya, and Rod Michalko. 2007. *Rethinking Normalcy: A Disability Studies Reader*. Toronto: Canadian Scholars Press.

Valentine, Fraser. 1994. *The Canadian Independent Living Movement: An Historical Overview*. Ottawa: Canadian Association of   Independent Living Centres.

Wendell, Susan. 1996. "Who Is Disabled?" and "The Social Construction of Disability." Chapters 1 and 2 of *The Rejected Body: Feminist Philosophical Reflections on Disability*. New York: Routledge.

Wharf, Brian. 1990. *Social Work and Social Change in Canada*. Toronto: McClelland and Stewart.

Zola, Irving. 1992. "The Medicalization of Aging and Disability." In Gary Albrecht and Judith Levy (eds.), *Advances in Medical Sociology: A Research Annual* Vol. 2. School of Public Health, University of Illinois.

Chapter 5

Human Rights, Disability and the Law in Canada

Jennifer Murphy

The long struggle for people with disabilities to reframe their discourse from one of charity and pity towards a context of entitlement within a human rights framework is a continuing process even within wealthy developed countries. Global initiatives in the form of United Nations Declarations have made great strides in changing the overarching narrative of disability as individual "deficiency" to one of a discussion of the social construction of disability within an ableist society. An important factor is the placement of disability within a human rights context that recognizes the need for equal access to a myriad of rights, including civil, cultural, political, social and economic rights (WHO 2011). This is also, of course, an important principle in developing national laws and policy. The major issue remains, however, the need to move towards a model of citizenship in which people with disabilities would be treated as fully equal and participating members of society whose human rights could not be constrained by a consideration of their disabilities as "deficiencies" to be managed and/or "cured."

This chapter focuses on the development of a human rights approach to laws affecting people with disabilities in Canada. In order to provide a context for current laws and case law, the historical treatment of people with disabilities is reviewed, including eugenics policies in Canada and globally. The post-World War II UN Declarations that have affected national legislation on equality issues and discrimination are also discussed, along with the impact of the *Charter of Rights and Freedoms* (1982) and subsequent case law in Canada. Finally, pressing current issues and ethical considerations around disability are raised within the context of the need for substantive equality for people with disabilities, not merely equality of opportunity or nondiscriminatory practice.

From Eugenics to the UN Convention

One of the most contentious issues to consider in the historical context of disability and human rights is the rise of the eugenics movement in the nineteenth century and its influence on legislation and policy that continued into the twentieth century. Influenced by Darwin's theory of evolution superimposed on human development theories and the emerging field of genetics, eugenicists in nineteenth-century England focused on the concept of selective breeding as a means to improve the human race. This pseudo-scientific approach posited that the human race was at risk of degeneration and decay if groups of people deemed to be "feeble-minded" were allowed to have children (Roeher Institute 1996). The Darwinian concept of "survival of the fittest" was applied to human society in an effort to ensure that a wide range of conditions that were considered to be hereditary — for example, deafness, blindness, epilepsy and "mental retardation" — could be eradicated by sterilizing members of these populations.

Definitions of those who should not be allowed to reproduce, however, were not confined to determining "hereditary traits" but were placed within moral and social ideas about the "deserving" and "undeserving" in a similar fashion to the English Poor Laws of the sixteenth and seventeenth centuries. The lives of post-Industrial Revolution working-class families in England in the second half of the nineteenth century were mired in poverty and disease, and the response of scientists of the day, and in particular the founder of the eugenics movement in England, Francis Galton, was to pathologize the poor rather than acknowledge the systemic social causes of poverty (Pichot 2009). The political solution that was advanced with significant support from scientists, politicians, religious communities, and the middle and upper classes was to prevent further proliferation of the "degenerate" poor.

The eugenics movement had two differing approaches: positive and negative eugenics (Carlson 2001). Positive eugenics, supported by Galton, focused on convincing the "best" people — that is, the brightest, most talented and healthiest — that they had a moral duty to reproduce in order for British society to flourish and advance. This approach was popular in a country with a stratified class system, encompassing a hereditary aristocracy at the summit and limited social mobility. Negative eugenics, on the other hand, focused on the prevention of perceived hereditary defects through sterilization and segregation of the "feeble-minded" from the rest of society (for a further discussion of this issue, see the Leilani Muir case discussed in Chapter 2 and Chapter 8). This approach was more popular in the

United States where a less rigid class system promoted the belief that anyone who worked hard could be successful and that, concomitantly, the poor were deficient in some manner, exemplified by a lack of mental or physical capacity or through a moral failing of some kind, such as lack of motivation, for example.

While the eugenics movement started in England, it was widespread throughout Europe, the United States and Canada by the early twentieth century. The first laws that dealt with eugenics were promulgated in the United States and focused on two areas: sterilization of the "unfit," for example, by virtue of mental illness, mental incapacity or criminality; and the prohibition of marriage between the "unfit," which included the same categories as for compulsory sterilization in addition to a ban on miscegenation, or interracial marriage, to ensure "racial purity," Fears around the degeneration of the human race were so widespread that in a thirty-year period (1907 to 1937), two-thirds of U.S. states passed compulsory sterilization laws in addition to laws that prohibited marriages on the basis of eugenics (Largent 2008). Although many state laws were challenged on constitutional grounds and occasionally overturned, they were usually rewritten to circumvent court decisions, sometimes through several rewritings and further court challenges over a decade or more. In total, Largent (2008) estimates that at least 63,000 Americans were sterilized under the state laws that were in effect in the majority of American states.

In Canada, similar attitudes towards eugenics were popular, and Alberta was the first province to introduce compulsory sterilization legislation in 1928: the Sexual Sterilization Act. Similar legislation was enacted in British Columbia in 1933: An Act Respecting Sexual Sterilization. The legislation in both provinces allowed the compulsory sterilization of inmates in "insane" asylums and houses of detention, to be determined by a board chosen by the Lieutenant Governor. Both these laws were in effect until repealed in the 1970s and led to the forced sterilization of, for the most part, women and girls who were deemed to be intellectually disabled. In British Columbia, it is estimated that the Eugenics Board ordered the compulsory sterilization of several hundred people (Harris-Zsovan 2010). Alberta, however, under the political leadership of Social Credit's William Aberhart and later Ernest Manning, dispensed with the need to obtain consent from guardians or patients and sterilized almost three thousand people. Not only was consent not obtained, but many patients were not informed that the surgery they were to undergo was, in fact, sterilization. Although Alberta and British Columbia were the only two provinces in Canada to enact legislation to formalize a policy of sterilization, other provinces also sterilized people determined to be mentally disabled without their consent (Roeher Institute 1996).

These laws also restricted other basic rights of citizenship, such as the right to vote, marry and own property (Roeher Institute 1996). From a human rights perspective, the restriction of these fundamental rights to certain classes of citizens only exemplified the discrimination faced by people with disabilities in every aspect of their lives. Furthermore, the withholding of basic rights on the basis of a perceived disability determined by doctors, medical boards and/or family members increased their vulnerability to being provided with inhumane care in institutions and asylums. The loss of these human rights and the justification for this abrogation of civil and political rights added to the barriers that people with disabilities and their supporters had to overcome in order to be seen as deserving of inclusion into society as full citizens.

Although the eugenics movement was widely supported from the nineteenth century until well into the twentieth century in Europe, the United States and Canada, the scale and scope of eugenics policies in Nazi Germany was unprecedented, and the subsequent murder of millions of people based on their supposed inferiority in terms of race and mental/physical disability illustrated the dehumanizing and criminality inherent in this ideology. However, the laws that supported the sterilization of those deemed "mentally defective" remained in effect in Canada until the 1970s, and in both provinces where sterilization was enshrined in legislation, there was considerable political opposition to compensating surviving victims of sterilization (Harris-Zsovan 2010). In 1998, Ralph Klein, Alberta's premier at the time, even attempted to use the notwithstanding clause of the *Charter of Rights and Freedoms* to limit compensation to victims, until voter outrage forced him to withdraw the legislation.

International Conventions and Agreements

The post-World War II development of international conventions to define and support human rights, exemplified by the 1948 Universal Declaration of Human Rights, must be placed in the context of the abrogation of human rights in Nazi Germany for those deemed less than human based on race/nationality (Jews, Roma) and ability (those perceived to be physically and mentally disabled persons), along with opponents of the regime on political or religious grounds. The principles and values inscribed in the Declarations shape and influence national laws and policies that address the same issues. For this reason, a discussion of the principal U.N. documents on disability rights is important, even though both the UN Declaration of Human Rights and the 1971 UN Declaration on the Rights of Mentally Retarded Persons could be seen as resulting from a charitable ethos rather than a rights ethos. For example, both Declarations limit those persons labelled "disabled" in exercising their rights and limit the ability of the state to provide accommodations (Rioux and Valentine 2006; Rioux and Heath 2014). Essentially then, the Declarations acknowledged the need to recognize the rights of persons with disabilities without providing a framework that would ensure the fundamental enjoyment of those rights.

The UN Declaration of Human Rights set the framework for the recognition of all people as having inherent rights to freedom from discrimination, as outlined in the following section:

> Everyone is entitled to all the rights and freedoms set forth in this Declaration, without distinction of any kind, such as race, colour, sex, language, religion, political or other opinion, national or social origin, property, birth or other status. (U.N. 1948: Article 2)

While this article did not explicitly proscribe discrimination on the basis of physical and mental disability, the placement of disability within a human rights framework evolved from the original Declaration. Rioux and Heath (2014) argue that there was widespread support within disability movements to advocate for disability rights within this human rights framework because of its fundamental principles and values of the inherent worth of all human beings, even for those labelled as "deficient" or "different."

The first international attempt to formalize the rights of disabled persons was the UN Declaration on the Rights of Mentally Retarded Persons (1971). This document stated that disabled people had the same rights as all other human beings wherever feasible, including the right to education, medical care, employment, and economic security (U.N. 1971). Although this Declaration reaffirmed the worth and dignity of all human beings, the concluding section is more problematic in its depiction of the possible restriction of rights of some disabled people:

> Whenever mentally retarded persons are unable, because of the severity of their handicap, to exercise all their rights in a meaningful way or it should become necessary to restrict or deny some or all of these rights, the procedure used for that restriction or denial of rights must contain proper legal safeguards against every form of abuse. This procedure must be based on an evaluation of the social capability of the mentally retarded person by qualified experts and must be subject to periodic review and to the right of appeal to higher authorities. (U.N. 1971: Section 7)

Any evaluation of the efficacy of this Declaration must take into account the ways in which the document could be undermined and ignored by signatory nations who could determine whose rights could be denied or restricted on the basis of their disability. Furthermore, it could be argued that this provision about the denial of rights to persons with disabilities on the basis of the severity of their disability sets up a multi-tiered system of differentiation between levels of disability that is analogous to the stratification of a class system, dependent upon a definition of the "severity" of their disability and the ability to exercise their rights "in a meaningful way."

The UN Declaration on the Rights of Disabled Persons (1975), however, provided a shift in approach to link the rights of disabled people to the fundamental principles in the UN Declaration on Human Rights of the inherent self-worth and dignity of all human beings and the principle of nondiscriminatory treatment for all, along with social and political rights. Rioux and Valentine (2006) argue that the increased international focus on disability rights contributed to a clearer contextual understanding of disability as a rights-based issue, as distinguished from charitable or medical issues. A number of subsequent U.N. initiatives, including the UN Declaration of the Decade of Disabled Persons (1983–1992) and the UN Standard Rules for the Equalization of Opportunities for People with Disabilities (U.N. 1993) mark a transition to promoting the rights of persons with disabilities as opposed to the charity model of protection and paternalism. The underlying principle then of continuing to develop international policies on disability rights focuses on the need for real equality for persons with disabilities, as opposed to nondiscriminatory national and international laws.

The change in approach from a charity-based model to a human rights model coalesced in the UN Commission on Human Rights Resolution 2000/51 that placed disability issues within a framework of equality, citizenship and full participation (Rioux 2009). The move away from nondiscriminatory laws in both the international and national context towards the promotion of substantive legal equality for persons with disabilities represents a significant challenge to nations to provide the resources that would allow for equal participation within all sectors of society. Rather than focus only on access to employment or education, for example, the discussion was broadened to a more encompassing terminology of citizenship: those rights that come from full equality and participation in all aspects of a community.

The 2006 UN Convention on the Rights of Persons with Disabilities (CRPD) acknowledges the further shift in theoretical approaches from a biomedical explanation of disability to a structural model which posits that disability resides within social structures that create disability: the first explanation pathologizes individual "difference," while the second views persons with disabilities as being "disabled by society rather than their bodies" (WHO 2011: 4). The CRPD, therefore, views disability as a complex interaction between "persons with impairments" (WHO 2011: 4) and a society replete with barriers to full participation and equality as a result of social policies and environments that do not support equality. This shift in the definition of disability is more than a semantic change; it is designed to remove the term "disability" from being a personal attribute to an interaction between individuals and the society they inhabit. In other words, if "disability" resides within the person, the onus is on medical science to "cure or fix" people with disabilities, whereas if "disability" resides within the structures of society, social, political and legal reforms can be drafted to provide real equality to all members of society.

Further, the International Disability Rights Monitor (IDRM) tracks and reports on the progress — or lack thereof — of disability rights in individual countries in a number of categories. The "IDRM Regional Report of the Americas" (Center for International Rehabilitation 2004) reported on human rights issues within Canada that affect people with disabilities. While acknowledging Canada's significant historical discrimination against people with disabilities, the Report provides useful information about definitions of disability (inconsistent in Canada); estimated population (12.4 percent of Canadians); and legal protections and access to education, healthcare, housing and employment. This information gives a broad picture of a country with laws and protections in place for people with disabilities but also with significant barriers to accessing resources and services, particularly in regard to full inclusion and participation in Canadian society. Clearly, legal equality provisions at both the federal and provincial levels are not sufficient to provide substantive equality and inclusion for all persons with disabilities.

From Charity Models to the Charter

The evolution of disability policy and legal frameworks in the international arena was mirrored by the development of national and provincial legislation in Canada. Both internationally and nationally, there has been a significant change, starting in the 1970s, to place disability issues within the context of human rights. This shift signifies the change from the original charity models of disability, exemplified in Canada in the nineteenth-century push for industrialization by the categories of the "deserving poor," which included people with disabilities, and the "undeserving poor," which included the able-bodied unemployed (Roeher Institute 1996). This categorization flowed from the English Poor Laws of the sixteenth and seventeenth centuries and resulted in the nineteenth-century response: the development of a policy of institutionalization of "undesirables" in prisons, work houses or poor houses. This forced segregation became the predominant policy of containing people who did not conform to the norms of society through physical, mental or even moral "difference."

The early twentieth century saw a further shift towards the policy of institutionalization of persons with disabilities with large-scale institutions providing resources and services in most provinces, particularly after the 1940s. These institutions were supported by an underlying theoretical principle that persons with disabilities, both physical and mental, should be cared for in a safe and secure setting by being segregated and removed from society on the basis of their "incurable" disability (Roeher Institute 1996). The emphasis was on a biomedical/charity model that provided care to persons with disabilities within a hierarchy of needs focused on physical and mental limitations that left them dependent on a "benevolent" government that determined their needs based on budgetary considerations and policy requirements. Therefore, persons with disabilities were *administered to* as a result of an individual pathology approach rather than *involved in* decisions about their care within a human rights approach that would seek to provide entitlement to political and social resources.

The 1970s and 1980s saw a policy shift away from institutionalization towards community-based programs, including inclusion in public education (Roeher Institute 1996). The deinstitutionalization movement focused on a human rights framework for inclusion into society of those formerly labelled "different" or "deviant," for example, patients in psychiatric institutions (as referenced by Larson in Chapter 10); however, the two competing arguments for the elimination of institutional care focused on opposing ideologies: one on economic costs (neoliberalism) and the other on inclusivity (structuralism). While deinstitutionalization was gaining significant public approval, legal approaches to people with disabilities were fundamentally changed both by the major international U.N. conventions signed by Canada, as signatory nations undertake to develop national legislation that fits with the conventions, and by the repatriation of the Constitution and the drafting of the *Charter of Rights and Freedoms* in 1982, led by Prime Minister Pierre Trudeau (Regehr and Kanani 2010).

Draft versions of the Charter did not originally include disability in Section 15 (the nondiscrimination clause). The first version to be tabled in the House of Commons and Senate in 1980 stated, "Everyone has the right to equality before the law and to equal protection of the law without discrimination because of race, national or ethnic origin, colour, religion, age or sex" (Draft Charter 1980). The rationale for the exclusion of disabilities was explained by Justice Minister Jean Chrétien to the Coalition of Provincial Organizations of the Handicapped (COPOH) as necessary to limit nondiscrimination clauses to those areas that "have long been recognized and which do not require substantial qualification" (COPOH 1980: 8). This rejection of disability within the equality provisions of the Charter led to intense political lobbying by COPOH to pressure politicians to recognize the need to amend the draft Charter to include disabilities in Section 15 (Peters 2004). The argument put forward by COPOH was that to refuse to add disabilities to Section 15 was to entrench a stratified system of rights, in which some rights were more valuable and intrinsic than others, within the overarching legislation in Canada: the law that supersedes all others.

When the draft Charter went to the committee stage, a number of organizations supported amending Section 15 to reframe it from a nondiscrimination clause to one of equality rights, which was supported by Jean Chrétien, although he continued to resist adding disability to the section (Peters 2004). It was only after the all-party Parliamentary Special Committee on the Disabled and the Handicapped supported the inclusion of disability rights in the equality clause and gained considerable caucus interest in the area that Justice Minister Jean Chrétien, on January 28, 1981, agreed to amend the Charter to include both physical and mental disabilities in the equality clause. This significant victory for equality rights set the stage for subsequent litigation to define and develop the equality clause over the next twenty-five years.

Human Rights Legislation

In addition to the Charter, which is the supreme law of Canada, federal and provincial legislatures have enacted human rights codes to protect individuals from discrimination. While the Charter prescribes conduct by the state, including legislation, human rights legislation can affect both state and individual actions. Pothier (2006) describes a system in which the Supreme Court of Canada (scc) has ruled on disability issues under both Charter and human rights legislation, with both areas developing simultaneously and influencing rulings in a reciprocal fashion. Therefore, developing issues argued under the Charter may have an impact on rulings under human rights laws and vice versa.

There is a federal Canadian Human Rights Act (1985) in addition to provincial and territorial human rights laws. While each provincial or territorial Act encompasses many of the same principles, there are regional differences in approach, although each Act defines discrimination and specifies the prohibited grounds for discrimination (Regehr and Kanani 2010). An example of this is that all provincial and territorial laws prohibit discrimination on the basis of physical and mental disability, but only eight provinces and territories prohibit discrimination on the basis of a criminal conviction. Similarly, each province has separate and different mental health legislation, detailing involuntary admission to psychiatric care. The criteria for involuntary admission differ substantially: from "danger to self and others" in Alberta to an unspecified risk of "harm" in Newfoundland and Labrador (Regehr and Kanani 2010). As with all legislation in Canada, provincial laws are required to conform to the Charter; however, discriminatory legislation may remain in effect until challenged in the courts.

Human rights laws also distinguish between direct discrimination where an overt rule or policy discriminates against a person or group based on stereotypes — for example, refusal to hire women — and adverse effects discrimination. In this situation, the rule or policy appears on the surface to be neutral, but the effect of the policy is to discriminate — for example, a policy in a work setting that requires all employees to work on weekends regardless of their religious beliefs and practices (Regehr and Kanani 2010). The Supreme Court of Canada has ruled that employers must take "reasonable steps to accommodate ... short of undue hardship" (*Ontario Human Rights Commission v. Simpson-Sears,* at para. 18). The difficulty with the reasonable accommodation approach is that if the courts decide that an employer has made reasonable efforts to accommodate the complainant then a finding of liability against the employer will not be upheld. In other words, substantive equality may be overlooked in favour of balancing the rights of complainants and employers.

Chouinard (2009) also states that the complaints process itself under both the federal and provincial legislation gives wide powers to human rights commissions to determine whether to investigate complaints or refer them to a tribunal for adjudication, that is, to dismiss or ignore complaints and complainants. She argues that the powers granted to quasi-judicial bodies like human rights commissions are a reflection of the inequities in gaining access to justice for marginalized groups within an ableist dominant culture. Chouinard uses the term "shadow citizenship" (2009: 221) to describe the rights given to people with disabilities whereby they are theoretically empowered to overcome barriers and discrimination through enabling legislation but are, in reality, denied opportunities to participate fully in a society that recognizes and supports that inclusion. Even the ambitious legislation in Ontario, the 2005 Accessibility for Ontarians with Disabilities Act (AODA), which set a timeline of twenty years to fully dismantle barriers to inclusion for people with disabilities, has floundered in its mandate. Goals included the following:

> Developing, implementing and enforcing accessibility standards in order to achieve accessibility for Ontarians with disabilities with respect to goods, services, facilities, accommodation, employment, buildings, structures and premises on or before January 1, 2025. (Accessibility for Ontarians with Disabilities Act 2005, s.1 (a))

Mayo Moran's Second Legislative Review (2014) at the halfway point of the plan details the shortfalls of the Ontario provincial government in planning and implementing the standards necessary to fundamentally change Ontario society from an ableist culture to an inclusive structure in partnership with people living with disabilities. As the AODA Alliance (2015) reports, few Ontarians with disabilities have seen material changes in their living and working conditions in the past ten years, and they continue to face systemic barriers to inclusion.

The Impact of Case Law on Disability Rights

Over the last twenty-five years, a body of case law has gradually evolved to provide some definition and advancement for people with disabilities within the legal system, using the Section 15 equality provisions of the Charter and applying these provisions to existing legislation. While there have been a number of advances in the area, Pothier (2006) argues that there has not been a clear linear progress but rather a more complex mix of advancement and retreat. She delineates the areas where substantive progress has been made, for example, in language that moves from a charitable expression of concern to terminology involving discrimination and the need for equality. This change in language is accompanied by an understanding of the marginalization of people with disabilities within an able-bodied society. The Supreme Court of Canada has also acknowledged the marginalization that exists for people with mental health diagnoses, and in *R. v. Swain* (1991), the scc commented that "the mentally ill have historically been the subject of abuse, neglect and discrimination in our society. The stigma of mental illness can be very damaging" (*R. v. Swain* 1991, para.39).

The Supreme Court of Canada has also recognized the medical model of disability as an outdated construct and moved towards the recognition of a social model of disability, which recognizes that disability resides within society rather than the individual. However, limitations in understanding still persist, including in the area of comparative analysis that defines equality and inequality, as the comparators can be within various levels of disability or without. There are dangers in applying either comparator, particularly in using an ableist lens to evaluate and analyze disability.

Case law in the area of access to healthcare exemplifies this continuing struggle to overcome systemic and legal barriers to equality. The Section 15 equality provisions of the Charter came into effect on April 17, 1985, three years after the Charter became law. This three-year delay was to give all levels of government the opportunity to review and revise legislation that was not compliant with the new equality provisions. The aim was to provide formal legal equality to all Canadians under Section 15; however, subsequent Supreme Court of Canada rulings, along with lower court rulings, have provided some direction and advancement of the rights of people with disabilities without making the sweeping changes that disability rights advocates were hoping for with the inclusion of disability as a protected equality right. Pothier argues that instead of substantive action to promote equality within a human rights framework, the Supreme Court of Canada has remained "remedially timid" (2006: 316) in its decisions.

A review of two important Supreme Court of Canada decisions in the area of access to healthcare reveals a number of issues that challenged existing policy. In the first case, *Eldridge et al. v. British Columbia (Attorney General)* in 1997, the

Supreme Court of Canada overruled both B.C. Supreme Court and B.C. Court of Appeal decisions that held that the Medical Services Plan (MSP) did not have to provide sign language interpretation services for deaf patients to aid in communication with their health care providers. The argument advanced and accepted by the two lower courts was that the refusal of the B.C. government to provide these services was not discriminatory as everyone was treated equally: that is, no so-called ancillary services were provided free of charge under the provisions of the Medical Services Plan. The Supreme Court of Canada overturned these rulings and stated that the refusal to fund sign language interpreters met the standard of adverse effects discrimination against deaf people, which resulted in the ancillary services of sign language interpretation for deaf patients to be provided under the MSP. The *Eldridge* case decision stated that the Charter could be applied to legislation on two fronts: firstly, that a piece of legislation can be found to be discriminatory without justification for its discriminatory provisions; and secondly, that although a law may be found to be nondiscriminatory, the way in which the law is applied by a decision-making body may be discriminatory, as in this case.

Eldridge was an important early decision in advancing the rights of people with disabilities in the public health care system, and Rioux (2009) argues that a number of important concepts were clarified and defined in the ruling, including the entitlement of people with disabilities to government benefits and the obligation of governments to demonstrate equality in the distribution of those benefits by providing reasonable accommodation as the underlying principle of equality rights. Additionally, the case was important in its discussion of the social construction of disability and the separation of the functional aspects of disability that reside within the person, and the human rights violations and discrimination that reside within social structures.

The *Auton* case in 2004, however, limited the application of *Eldridge*, as the Supreme Court of Canada ruled that not all medically necessary services could be covered by the Medical Services Plan. The case involved a group of parents who argued that the B.C. government should be required to fund a particular treatment method for their children with autism. In rejecting this claim, Rioux (2009) argues that the Court did not consider adverse effects discrimination and lost an opportunity to further advance understanding of a social model of disability within an able-bodied society. Instead, barriers to inclusiveness remain firmly entrenched, as the Court also provided a comparison between children with autism and typical children in terms of funding core health services for both. As Pothier argues, when comparators are drawn from able-bodied dominant society, "inequality for the disabled is likely to go unrecognized" (2006: 314).

Current Issues and Ethical Considerations

One of the most important current issues, euthanasia, the right to die or assisted suicide, has provoked nuanced discussions about this complex issue within the disability rights movement and beyond. There are also, of course, ethical considerations that surround and permeate this issue, particularly given the history of discrimination against people with disabilities both nationally and globally. The social work profession has been involved in discussions around euthanasia and assisted suicide for many years, and it is a particularly important consideration for social workers working in the health care system. While Ogden and Young (1998) found that a majority of social workers in British Columbia (78 percent) believed that assisted suicide should be legalized, the research also found that 80 percent of respondents believed that social workers have an important role to play in the development of social policy around this issue, partly because they believe that this is a continuation of their experience and practice as counsellors within the health care system. However, Csikai (1999) and Himchak (2011), focusing their discussion of assisted suicide within the parameters of the National Association of Social Work Code of Ethics in the U.S., state that social workers are not permitted to actively participate in assisted suicide but should explore end-of-life decisions within individual, family and cultural contexts. The emphasis is on balancing the core values of social work to provide a voice for the marginalized poor and vulnerable elderly or at-risk clients and to work towards systemic change to eliminate poverty and inequality. The Canadian Association of Social Workers (2015) have also released a *Statement of Principles on Euthanasia and Assisted Suicide* that focuses on self-determination and informed consent within a context of protection for vulnerable people in a health care system under financial constraint. The CASW states that patient care should not be compromised by a consideration of cost reductions and "efficiencies" to be found within the health care system.

Within Canada, the Supreme Court of Canada has provided a significant shift in approach with its most recent decision, *Carter et al. v. Attorney General of Canada et al.* (February 2015). The decision provides new definitions and dialogue around the rights of people with disabilities to make decisions about ending their lives. Essentially, the debate around assisted suicide cannot be separated from the ethical issues and dilemmas that have arisen for people with disabilities in the past when they were prevented from exercising autonomy over their lives. Using a human rights framework to analyze the issue of assisted suicide, however, does not diminish the ethical difficulties inherent in choosing to end lives that have, in the not-very-distant past, been considered to be worthless in an ableist society.

The Supreme Court of Canada has previously ruled on this issue, in the Sue Rodriguez case in 1993 (*Rodriguez v. British Columbia, Attorney General* 1993). Sue

Rodriguez challenged the constitutionality of the *Criminal Code* ban on assisted suicide (Section 241), as she was suffering from ALS and wanted a physician-assisted death. She anticipated her progressively degenerative disease would prevent her from committing suicide herself once she had decided that she no longer wanted to continue living, and she wanted to die with dignity. By a five-to-four majority verdict, the SCC ruled that striking down the prohibition on assisted suicide would create a situation in which abuse could flourish. The SCC was concerned about a "slippery slope" (Pothier 2006: 316) that could result in deaths without real consent.

The most recent case, *Carter et al. v. Attorney General of Canada et al.* (2011) combines two cases, that of Gloria Taylor and Kay Carter, both of whom are now deceased, but who argued that the ban on assisted suicide was contrary to their Section 15 equality rights under the Charter. The British Columbia Civil Liberties Association argued the case in the B.C. Supreme Court, the B.C. Court of Appeal and before the Supreme Court of Canada. The original ruling in the B.C. Supreme Court in 2011 stated that the *Criminal Code* prohibition on assisted suicide violated the Section 15 rights of Gloria Taylor; the judge struck down the provision in the *Criminal Code,* but suspended the ruling for twelve months to give the federal government time to rewrite the law (BC Civil Liberties Association 2012). The judge also gave Taylor an immediate exemption from Section 241; however, Taylor died in October 2012 without invoking the exemption. The B.C. Court of Appeal upheld the original decision, and the case was argued in front of the Supreme Court of Canada in October 2014.

In February 2015, the Supreme Court of Canada rendered its decision in the *Carter* case. In a unanimous decision, the SCC upheld the original trial judge's decision that the criminal prohibition on assisted suicide violates the Section 7 Charter rights to life, liberty and security of the person. In its deliberations, the Court considered the *Rodriguez* decision, legislation permitting assisted suicide in other countries and U.S. states, and debates within Canadian legislatures. The decision was framed within arguments that the fundamental right to life does not create a "duty to live" (*Carter v. Canada* 2015 SCC 5 at para. 63) in circumstances where an individual makes a choice about ending their life. The SCC determined that assisted suicide is legal in the following circumstances:

> For a competent adult person who (1) clearly consents to the termination of life and (2) has a grievous and irremediable medical condition (including an illness, disease or disability) that causes enduring suffering that is intolerable to the individual in the circumstances of his or her condition. (*Carter v. Canada* 2015 SCC 5 at para. 147)

This definition includes both physical and mental medical conditions, and the

Supreme Court Justices framed issues of informed consent within the following paradigm:

> Concerns about decisional capacity and vulnerability arise in all end-of-life medical decision-making. Logically speaking, there is no reason to think that the injured, ill and disabled who have the option to refuse or to request withdrawal of lifesaving or life-sustaining treatment, or who seek palliative sedation, are less vulnerable or less susceptible to biased decision-making than those who might seek more active assistance in dying. (*Carter v. Canada* 2015 scc 5 at para. 115)

Concerns have already been raised about the impact this decision may have on people with disabilities in terms of their autonomy and self-determination, particularly as the facts of the cases argued in front of the scc involve individuals who were originally able-bodied and who became disabled as adults through the onset of debilitating physical illness. It could be argued that disability rights look somewhat different for people born with disabilities who have to navigate through an ableist society from birth, and that the decision around assisted suicide for adults disabled later in life may reflect an ableist bias inherent within Western society and culture. Similarly, the decision encompasses both physical *and* mental disabilities, which raises the question of informed consent from people diagnosed with mental health conditions. The scc categorically rejected the "slippery slope" argument in making its determination. However, the implications of this decision in terms of new government legislation to regulate assisted suicide have yet to be determined, and the federal government has one full year to either draft a new law or simply allow the section prohibiting assisted suicide in the *Criminal Code* to lapse.

Clearly, a large number of ethical concerns are embedded in this very difficult issue, not least whether the lives of people with disabilities would be seen as qualitatively different from that of able-bodied people now that assisted suicide is permitted. After a long struggle to gain the human rights accorded to the able-bodied, does the right to dying with dignity signal a step forward or backwards? The *Rodriguez* case, it could be argued, continued in the tradition of paternalistic decision-making for those deemed incapable of autonomy and self-determination by virtue of their disability. The *Carter* case makes substantial changes to the very idea of human rights within a right-to-die framework.

Chapter Summary

The history of the legislated mistreatment of people with disabilities is a long and shameful one in Canada and elsewhere. The pathologizing of people with disabilities through a discriminatory lens of forced sterilization, segregation, denial of access to education, healthcare and the full rights of citizenship — voting, marriage, ownership of property — has been difficult to fully eradicate through changes to laws and policies over the more than fifty years since the UN Declaration of Human Rights was first promulgated. The history of the eugenics movement, the Nazi atrocities of World War II, and conceptions of people with disabilities as deserving of pity rather than the human rights afforded to abled-bodied people have all contributed to the current understanding — and misunderstanding — that surrounds people with disabilities as they navigate through a legal system that still largely focuses on equality of opportunity and nondiscriminatory practice rather than substantive equality. A human rights approach is an essential component and foundation for developing a framework for real equality.

Further, although a transformative approach was developed in the 1990s in international regulatory bodies, actual equality for persons with disabilities has been slow to emerge in nation states. Instead, they continue to focus on the rehabilitative and medical models in legislation that enact, for example, the removal of physical barriers to access, the promotion of employment opportunities and the addition of "disability" to equality provisions in human rights codes. Rioux and Valentine (2006) argue that more substantive changes are necessary that would provide actual equality within the social, economic and political arenas: areas that to date have either resisted or ignored demands for full integration within a human rights framework.

In addition, while disability activists have successfully lobbied for physical and mental disability to be included in legislation, including the Charter and human rights codes, subsequent case law has not advanced the equality rights for people with disabilities to the extent that was anticipated in the 1980s and 1990s. The shift towards an understanding that disability resides within social structures rather than within individual "deficits" has been a slow process. New areas of contention, in particular the Death with Dignity movement to legalize assisted suicide, may open up discussions that have been largely avoided to date around autonomy and self-determination for people with disabilities who in the past were, of course, forcibly subjected to medical treatment without consent. Within this subject above all others, past history informs broader societal attitudes towards assisting people with disabilities to choose their own deaths, which adds to the necessity of placing this discussion within the context of a human rights framework. Essentially, substantive equality may be impossible to achieve without these vital and extremely difficult discourses.

Discussion Questions

1. Discuss the importance of placing disability rights within a human rights framework for analysis as opposed to a charity model. What are the implications for using the human rights framework for social work practice with people with disabilities?

2. The history of eugenics in Canada reveals medical, political, economic and social beliefs about disability that still resonate today in terms of inclusion and access to resources. What steps need to be taken to ensure substantive equality for people with disabilities, both physical and mental?

3. Signatory nations to United Nations Declarations pledge to develop laws that conform to the standards espoused in the Declarations, for example, the UN Declaration on Human Rights. How do you think equality for people with disabilities can be achieved globally?

4. Critics of the Supreme Court of Canada have argued that Section 15 Charter decisions on disability rights have been disappointing to date. From a social work perspective, what kind of leadership do you think the scc should take in this area?

5. The recent Supreme Court of Canada decision in the *Carter* case strikes down the *Criminal Code* prohibition on assisted suicide. Discuss the ethical concerns that flow from this decision, using a social work lens for analysis and evaluation. Is this decision a step towards substantive equality for people with disabilities or a retrograde decision that will further marginalize vulnerable individuals and groups?

References

Accessibility for Ontarians with Disabilities Act, 2005, S.O. 2005, c.11.

AODA Alliance. 2015. "Final Report of Mayo Moran's Independent Review of the Accessibility for Ontarians with Disabilities Act Just Made Public: Report Reveals Serious Problems." <http://www.aoda.ca>.

Auton v. British Columbia (Attorney General), [2004] 3 S.C.R. 657.

BC Civil Liberties Association. 2012. "Carter v. Canada: The Death with Dignity Case." <http://www.bccla.org/our-work/blog/death-with-dignity-case>.

Canadian Association of Social Workers. 2015. "Statement of Principles on Euthanasia and Assisted Suicide." <http://www.casw-acts.ca/en/statement-principles-euthanasia-and-assisted-suicide>.

Canadian Charter of Rights and Freedoms, Part I of the *Constitution Act,* 1982, Being Schedule B to the *Canada Act 1982* (U.K.) 1982, c. 11 [Charter].

Canadian Human Rights Act (R.S.C., 1985, c.H-6).

Carlson, Elof Axel. 2001. *The Unfit: A History of a Bad Idea.* Cold Spring Harbor, NY: Cold Spring Harbor Laboratory Press.

Carter et al. v. Canada (Attorney General), 2015 SCC 5.

Center for International Rehabilitation. 2004. "International Disability Rights Monitor 2004: Regional Report of the Americas." <bbi.syr.edu/publications/blanck_docs/2003-2004/IDRM_Americas_2004.pdf>.

Chouinard, Vera. 2009. "Legal Peripheries: Struggles over DisAbled Canadians' Places in Law, Society, and Space." In Tanya Titchkosky and Rod Michalko (eds.), *Rethinking Normalcy: A Disability Studies Reader*. Toronto: Canadian Scholars Press.

COPOH (Coalition of Provincial Organizations of the Handicapped). 1980. *Brief to the Special Joint Parliamentary Committee on the Constitution*. Toronto.

Criminal Code of Canada (R.S.C., 1985 c. C-46).

Csikai, Ellen L. 1999. "Euthanasia and Assisted Suicide: Issues for Social Work Practice." *Journal of Gerontological Social Work* 31, 3/4: 49–63.

Eldridge v. British Columbia (Attorney General), [1997] 3 S.C.R. 624.

Harris-Zsovan, Jane. 2010. *Eugenics and the Firewall: Canada's Nasty Little Secret*. Winnipeg, MB: J. Gordon Shillingford Publishing.

Himchak, Maureen V. 2011. "A Social Justice Value Approach Regarding Physician-Assisted Suicide and Euthanasia Among the Elderly." *Journal of Social Work Values & Ethics* 8, 1.

Largent, Mark A. 2008. *Breeding Contempt: The History of Coerced Sterilization in the United States*. New Jersey: Rutgers University Press.

Moran, Mayo. 2014. "Second Legislative Review of the Accessibility for Ontarians with Disabilities Act, 2005." <https://www.ontario.ca/document/legislative-review-accessibility-ontarians-disabilities-act>.

Ogden, Russel D., and Michael G. Young. 1998. "Euthanasia and Assisted Suicide: A Survey of Registered Social Workers in British Columbia." *British Journal of Social Work* 28: 161–175.

Ontario Human Rights Commission v. Simpson-Sears, [1985] 2 S.C.R. 536.

Peters, Yvonne. 2004. "Twenty Years of Litigating for Disability Equality Rights: Has It Made a Difference?" Council of Canadians with Disabilities. <http://www.ccdonline.ca/en/humanrights/promoting/20years>.

Pichot, Andre. 2009. *The Pure Society: From Darwin to Hitler*. London: Verso.

Pothier, Dianne. 2006. "Appendix: Legal Developments in the Supreme Court of Canada Regarding Disability." In Dianne Pothier and Richard Devlin (eds.), *Critical Disability Theory: Essays in Philosophy, Politics, Policy and Law*. Vancouver: University of British Columbia Press.

R. v. Swain [1991] 1 S.C.R. 933.

Regehr, Cheryl, and Karima Kanani. 2010. *Essential Law for Social Work Practice in Canada* 2nd edition. Don Mills, ON: Oxford University Press.

Rioux, Marcia H. 2009. "Bending Towards Justice." In Tanya Titchkosky and Rod Michalko (eds.), *Rethinking Normalcy: A Disability Studies Reader*. Toronto: Canadian Scholars Press.

Rioux, Marcia H., and Bonita Heath. 2014. "Human Rights in Context: Making Rights Count." In John Swain, Sally French, Colin Barnes and Carol Thomas (eds.), *Disabling Barriers: Enabling Environments*. London: Sage.

Rioux, Marcia H., and Fraser Valentine. 2006. "Does Theory Matter? Exploring the Nexus between Disability, Human Rights and Public Policy." In Dianne Pothier and Richard

Devlin (eds.), *Critical Disability Theory: Essays in Philosophy, Politics, Policy, and Law.* Vancouver: University of British Columbia Press.

Rodriguez v. British Columbia (Attorney General), [1993] 3 S.C.R. 519.

Roeher Institute. 1996. *Disability, Community and Society: Exploring the Links.* North York, ON: The Roeher Institute.

Sexual Sterilization Act (1933, c.59, s.1).

Sexual Sterilization Act (SA 1928, c. 37).

U.N. (United Nations). 1948. *Universal Declaration of Human Rights.* Geneva.

____. 1971. *Declaration on the Rights of Mentally Retarded Persons.* Geneva.

____. 1975. *Declaration on the Rights of Disabled Persons.* Geneva.

____. 1993. *Standard Rules for the Equalization of Opportunities for People with Disabilities.* Geneva.

____. 2000. *Human Rights Commission of Resolution 2000/51.* Geneva.

____. 2006. *Convention on Rights of Persons with Disabilities.* Geneva.

WHO (World Health Organization). 2011. *World Report on Disability.* Geneva.

Chapter 6

Disability Policy in Canada: Fragments of Inclusion and Exclusion

Michael J. Prince

> Disability policy is perceived by people with disabilities as being impenetrable and unnecessarily complex, with little in the way of a coherent underlying ideology or policy framework. We use the term "disability policy" as if it referred to an entity that was widely recognized and acknowledged as such. The reality however is quite different. (McColl and Stephenson 2008: 2)

This chapter explores from a Canadian perspective the question of what is meant by disability policy. Disability measures comprise an important part of social policy activities by the federal government and even more so by provincial governments and other public authorities within their jurisdictions. However, the shifting boundaries and eclectic content of disability policies are not always understood by students, practitioners or members of the general public; nor are the competing notions that underlie this policy field widely appreciated. Therefore, a high-level mapping of disability policy is presented here along with ways of understanding the scope and substantive content of Canadian disability policy. More specifically, the aims of this chapter are to indicate how various models or perspectives on disability relate to disability policy and practice; to discuss the politics of disability policy and the nature of the disability policy community; and to offer a brief assessment of the recent disability record in Canada. Ultimately, the aim is to encourage students to think about disability issues and policy making in new and more critical ways.

This exploration of disability policy is presented in four sections. The first section looks at different perspectives on disability. It discusses the scope and content of disability policy in terms of dominant ideas and program areas of activities. I suggest that a disjuncture exists between social understandings of disability and most public policies in practice. The second section examines the politics of disability policy in Canada drawing attention to disability interest groups, coalitions and policy networks, and social movement organization activities. The third section considers Canada's disability policy record, introducing the concept of a *déjà vu discourse on disability reform*. The fourth section offers a chapter summary.

Disability Perspectives and Public Policies

Disability is the subject of assorted perspectives, interests and debates. A functional view of disability — expressed in personal and professional assessments of having difficulty with daily living activities or having a physical or mental condition or a health problem that reduces the kind of activity that an individual can do — is a dominant perspective of disability. Such difficulties and limitations restrict a person's ability to participate fully in society. This is the conventional Canadian definition of who is a person with a disability and what makes him or her disabled. It is rooted in biological and medical ways of understanding disablements. The Canadian Human Rights Act, for example, defines disability as any previous or existing mental or physical disability and includes disfigurement. Previous or existing dependence on alcohol or a drug is also included in this statutory definition of disability. Other federal and provincial laws define disability in terms of a range of impairments: physical, sensory, neurological, learning, intellectual or developmental, psychiatric or mental disorder. In this context, disability is a thing — whether temporary or permanent, stable or episodic, mild or severe — that is located in the person.

A second perspective is the social rights or the socio-political model in the disability studies literature. Here, disability is part of the fabric of Canadian society, something that all individuals experience in one way or another and from which everyone can learn. Attention focuses especially to attitudes, beliefs, body identities and social values, as well as to issues of human rights, prejudice and stigma. Moreover, disability is an assemblage of socio-economic, cultural and political disadvantages resulting from an individual's exclusion by society. Disability exists or occurs when a person with an impairment encounters barriers to performing everyday activities of living, barriers to participating in the societal mainstream, and barriers to exercising his or her human rights and fundamental freedoms. Here, disability is understood as a social process more than as some individual condition.

A significant disjuncture exists between this socio-political perspective and much of Canadian public policy and service provision. Most programs and delivery systems embody aspects of other perspectives on disability: a biomedical, charitable and worthy poor welfare viewpoint (McCreath 2011; Rioux and Prince 2002). Traditionally, and still today, most public policy on disability focuses on a person's functional limitations due to disease, injury or chronic illness as the cause or a major explanation for relatively low levels of formal educational attainment, employment and income. An image of people with disabilities still common is of a person who suffers from an affliction, accidental or biological, thus to be pitied or feared. Disability politics is about choices over whether the priority in policy and practice should relate to body structures and functions, daily activities and social activities, or environmental and cultural factors requiring adaptation and transformation.

What, then, is disability policy? Various definitions are available in the Canadian literature (for examples, see Boyce, Tremblay, McColl, Bickenbach, Crichton, Andrews, Gerein and D'Aubin 2001; Cameron and Valentine 2001; Jongbloed 2003; Prince 2004). From a macro-sociological approach, William Boyce and his associates regard disability policy as an identifiable form of governance within a liberal democratic society:

> Disability policy embraces courses of action that affect the set of institutions, organizations, services, and funding arrangements of the disability system. It goes beyond formal services and includes actions or intended actions by public, private, and voluntary organizations that have an impact on disability. (Boyce et al. 2001: 5)

For David Cameron and Fraser Valentine (2001), the disability policy sector entails certain values, decisions, initiatives, services, processes and programs formulated by modern democratic states in response to particular needs of persons living with disabilities. Cameron and Valentine characterize disability policy in Canada as a rather incoherent field of services and programs. It is a fragmented field evident in the various definitions of disablement in effect and it is an uncoordinated field with a complicated array of organizations and programs. Compared to other policy domains — education, health care or criminal justice as cases in point — disability has a lower profile in Canadian politics and policy discourse. In recent years, however, activism by the disability rights movement and new developments in biotechnology have, in different ways, raised the salience of questions concerning disability in Canadian society (Doern and Prince 2012; Stienstra 2012).

Many authors describe disability policy as a subset of Canadian social policy. For example, Alan Puttee (2002: 1) refers to disability policy as "the bundle of public programs directed at people with disabilities" of which some are federal programs and others are the responsibility of provincial governments. Mary Ann McColl and Lyn Jongbloed (2006: 6) portray disability policy as a "web of services and programs concerning disability" and, in particular, as "a patchwork of legislation, regulations, programs, providers and entitlements that requires considerable probing to reveal, and considerable patience to understand" (2006: 5). Deborah Stienstra echoes this theme of obscurity and intricacy, from a political science perspective:

> The net of government responsibilities for programs and services related to disability is intertwined and complex. Not only do the federal and provincial governments have separate and overlapping responsibilities, the federal/provincial/territorial ministers and officials have become an additional layer of government involvement. (Stienstra 2012: 13)

In using terms such as bundle, web, patchwork and net to indicate the nature of disability policy, the lesson to draw is that disability policy, in a collective overall sense, is not so much a closely tied-together pattern or coordinated network as it is a jumble of activities and inactions. Although frequently presented within an overarching framework of ideas and policy talk, disability policies and services are actually experienced by individuals, families and social groups as a frustrating maze or bizarre labyrinth (McCreath 2011; Panitch 2007; Prince 2008).

Just as notions of ability and disability are cultural conceptions, so too disability programs are historical constructs, their meanings varying over time and within a given period and given political context. Elements of this policy field are comparatively old, predating the modern welfare state, while other parts are fairly recent (Boyce et al. 2001; Prince 2000, 2001a; Puttee 2002; Rioux and Prince 2002). Accordingly, the personal tragedy and deserving charity models of disability influence policy design in particular ways that differ from a model of disablement based on medical rehabilitation or a model based on equality rights. In regard to perspectives on the welfare state surveyed, the Canadian movement defended programs against cutbacks in recent decades, fully aware of the limitations and contradictory effects of many of these programs while, more recently, it has worked alone and with other social movements in renewing an active state in economic and social affairs. These are defining features of disability activism in Canada (Prince 2012).

Canadian disability policy making includes the governmental and related state machinery of the public sector, together with the structures and practices of the voluntary sector, families, and their informal support networks, plus the domain of Aboriginal governments and communities. Policies and programs nest in multiple environments — an assortment of policy fields, institutional sectors, and government jurisdictions and organizations — which interact in diverse and changing ways. In addition to the federally-based citizenship regime and territorially and provincially based citizenship regimes, other forms of collective membership are reviving or re-emerging in Canada, notably various indigenous citizenships through treaty settlements and land claims; and, in our urban political communities, city-based memberships combine the ancient idea of the city state with modernist notions of belonging to urban settlements. This multi-level, multi-sector focus reflects Canadian federalism and our increasingly pluralistic society and welfare provision (Rice and Prince 2013). Policies and practices operate at the local, provincial/territorial and national levels of government, across public and private sectors, Aboriginal communities, and family systems. The result is a country with complex political ideas and constitutional rules on shared-rule and self-rule in multiple communities, in which claims for citizenship must navigate.

Contending understandings of inclusion are a key feature of contemporary disability politics and policy. The concept of "social inclusion" is a rhetorical device of the movement to mobilize collective action; it is a desired state of community affairs suggesting the absence of barriers and discrimination, purportedly endorsed by governments; and it is an idea with which disability groups organize their mandates and represent their activities and tactics. For all these reasons, inclusion is an idea that merits critical reflection to illuminate assumptions and power relations.

Marcia Rioux and Fraser Valentine (2006) argue that a basic contradiction exists between the vision of inclusion as held by governments and the vision understood by disability groups. Canadian governments, Rioux and Valentine suggest, downplay a rights-based approach to inclusion and citizenship; instead, governments emphasize selective services, discretionary programs, and, through social insurance contributions, earned benefits. For some time now, governments have stressed spending limitations, viewing public programs as expensive responses to social needs. Their preference is to promote social partnerships, which means other sectors of society are to play a significant role in tackling obstacles to participation. Most government activities and programming emphasize biomedical and functional approaches to disability. Whereas governments interpret inclusion in terms of equality of opportunity, Rioux and Valentine argue that most Canadian disability groups emphasize equality of treatment and a human rights approach. This difference between disability groups and governments in interpreting what inclusion means "creates a circle of tension and confusion" (Rioux and Valentine 2006: 48), resulting in inconsistent messages, inadequate processes for dialogue, and an incoherent policy context. Murphy (Chapter 5) also emphasizes the discrepancies within the legal system, which still largely focuses on equality of opportunity and nondiscriminatory practice rather than substantive equality.

The Politics of Disability Policy

Canadian disability politics plays out through struggles over absences and actions constituted by cultural, economic and political structures (Prince 2009). The main contours of disability activism concern the pursuit of respectful inclusion, adequate social security and an authentic democratic voice. In contemporary Canada, issues of recognition and of redistribution are central features of activism by the disability movement and analysis by disability studies. Claims making by the movement includes a politics of representation that encompasses traditional concerns of citizen participation and voting, and, more recently, the practices of deliberative democracy and community dialogue. Overall, Canadian disability politics comprises three forms of struggle for social change and justice: the comparatively new politics of cultural recognition and identity interacting with the long-established politics of redistribution of material goods, and a politics of representation that combines conventional and alternative modes of decision making. Analytically, these three forms of political struggle correspond to distinct institutional domains: the politics of recognition to the cultural order of society, the politics of redistribution to the market economy and welfare state — including the role of social workers and other human service professionals as interpreters and implementers of public policies — and the politics of representation to the political system and civil society.

Fundamental obstacles to full participation by Canadians with disabilities include their nonrecognition as full persons in prevailing cultural value patterns; the maldistribution of resources in the form of income, employment, housing and other material resources; and their misrepresentation or marginal voice in elections, policy development and decision-making processes. Budget making and the allocation of public resources deeply matter to the disability community. Persons with disabilities face considerable barriers, including higher risks of unemployment, violence, discrimination and poverty than do other Canadians. With their authoritative allocation of resources and values, government budgets are central to supporting the principles of equity, inclusion and full citizenship for all.

Legislative and constitutional reforms are decisive developments in Canadian politics for persons with disabilities. Such reforms include amendments to federal and provincial human rights laws through the 1970s and 1980s, the entrenchment of the *Canadian Charter of Rights and Freedoms* in 1982 with a section providing for equality rights for persons with mental and physical disabilities, and the federal Employment Equity Act, passed in 1985 and extended in 1996. The Charter, in particular, bestows a highly significant constitutional status on persons with disabilities, encouraging disability groups to express their interests in the language of equality rights and to seek clarification of these rights and others through tribunals and the courts. By virtue of direct identification in the Charter, disability and persons with disabilities have constitutional status. Section 15 offers an officially authorized space for disability groups to legally defend and advance their material, procedural and cultural concerns. To define and enforce these fundamental rights and freedoms, such as mobility and equality, litigation has become an important strategy of individuals with disabilities and organizations representing their interests. This has raised the profile of the Canadian judiciary in the disability field and the wider social policy domain (Chivers 2008; Prince 2009).

Disability advocates, families and community groups have learned that judicial victories are not necessarily a case of winner-take-all. A rights-based approach to seeking equality through litigation can be lengthy, financially expensive and emotionally stressful for individuals involved, and risks fragmenting wider campaigns for obtaining services or supports for all groups. In addition to court rulings against disability claims, even victories can result in further delays due to appeals, discretion of public agencies in interpreting decisions, and then the frustratingly gradual, partial implementation of changes.

Like other disability movements, the Canadian community does emphasize a form of identity politics in reference to altering self-conceptions and societal conceptions of people with disabilities from passive, deviant and powerless to positive, self-created conceptions for themselves. However, struggles of the disability movement are not to the exclusion of material issues of employment, accessible education and income security or of governmental issues of public participation in policy making. A politics of socio-economic redistribution is at the core of disability activism in Canada, complemented by a politics of recognition and a democratic politics of representation, the latter of which involves claims for more accessible, empowering and accountable policy making structures and processes.

Countless associations populate the disability policy community. On behalf of a cluster of interest groups or service agencies, associations may represent a particular disability, a distinct client group, a specific provincial or regional area, or a functional activity such as legal advocacy. The community differentiates significantly by perspectives and structures. A number of umbrella associations — at national, provincial/territorial and urban levels — represent the relevant interests of a constellation of groups. Disability movement organizations in Canada do adopt interest group tactics and engage with political parties to advance disability policy objectives. Canada's disability community is state-focused in pursuing economic and social reforms, interacting with various state institutions and employing conventional tools of research, consultations, lobbying and litigation. Comparatively few disability groups pursue nonconventional politics of radical protests. Canada's disability community favours such terms as obstacles, inclusion, equality rights and citizenship, rather than oppression and domination, a language more common in British disability politics or the language of minority groups and civil rights in American disability politics.

As policy networks, associations serve as structural bridges between the disability community and the disability state. Canada's disability state encompasses legislative, executive, judicial and administrative agencies with a direct involvement in disability issues and with the disability community. Along with specific organizations and particular officials, the disability state includes the macro-institutions of parliamentary government, federalism, the inherent right of Aboriginal self-government, and the *Canadian Charter of Rights and Freedoms*. Policy networks are specific organizational relations between government and other state institutions, and community agencies and actors. These networks form around particular issue areas, reform processes, disabilities, jurisdictions and policy instruments of importance to the community. School testing, inclusive childcare, disability income benefits, accessible transportation and labour market programs are illustrations of particular policy networks.

The disability policy community also contains a multitude of organizations and associations with specialized spheres of responsibility. This differentiation provides the organizational means for expressing a diversity of specific interests and for providing specialized information on particular experiences across the country. The community is not integrated with one or two macro-associations coordinating the diversity of groups and broadly representing all the key interests. A potential drawback to this high level of organizational differentiation is that it limits the capacity of the community to interact, to formulate strategies for the whole community, or to plan the actions of members in public policy processes.

When facing the state, disability organizations encounter openings for engagement mottled with significant barriers and challenges. At provincial levels, disability groups face a service sector with a considerable contracting out of public services to nonprofit societies and for-profit enterprises. Social work and other human service professionals are often employed in these settings, and they encounter dilemmas that require balancing advocacy, service provision and service brokering, along with knowledge of policies, regulations, procedures and practices. At all levels, disability groups face financial restraint and political caution by governments in federal and provincial jurisdictions. Groups interact with government bureaucracies with policy and research capacities seriously diminished due to cutbacks. Disability organizations labour to fund advocacy, policy research and consultation work, infrequently getting funding for such activities from governments. Furthermore,

Carter (Chapter 11) also speaks to the restrictions placed on Canadian charities to engage in non-partisan political advocacy work.

Active in claiming a self-defined identity in place of that previously dominant in society, disability movement organizations question traditional state practices and professional controls. Challenging a purely biomedical perspective on disability, activists are promoting a socio-political model with a focus on the interaction between individuals and the larger environment. The psychiatric survivors' movement calls for drug-free treatments and greater use of peer counselling, while the "mad movement" is promoting dignity and self-respect around bipolar disorder and schizophrenia. The movement conveys strong interest in social reform and in public services and programs generally (LeFrançois, Menzies and Reaume 2013).

In Canada, the traditional representative institutions of parliamentary cabinet government and their younger sisters, executive federalism and the *Charter of Rights and Freedoms*, prevail in most engagement relationships with the disability community. Public servants in program departments and in central agencies, such as finance or treasury boards, and cabinet ministers determine when consultations will happen, under what terms and conditions, and timelines. At times, parliamentarians, the courts or community groups play a decisive role.

In many cases, public servants play the lead in gathering together and summing up community interests into policy recommendations and decisions. This is by no means a neutral or simple practical exercise. It is invariably predisposed in motivation and inevitably partial in result. It involves interpreting, filtering and ranking suggestions within a pre-existing set of assumed constraints and opportunities, as perceived by state officials. At times, such constraints appear upfront in consultation processes; many other times, these dominant assumptions are blandly implied in bureaucratic euphemisms. Although the vague words framing a consultation may give little offence in the short term, because of their imprecision, ultimately, they are insulting to groups that feel misled and manipulated by tokenistic exercises in citizen participation. An example in British Columbia can be briefly noted: parents and self-advocates have regularly complained about the lack of consultation and inclusion within the processes of Community Living BC (CLBC), the provincial crown agency responsible for services for adults with developmental disabilities, even though they have been included on CLBC community councils.

Canada's Disability Policy Record

The Canadian disability movement's record on mobilizing for social change, according to some observers, is impressive. On the impact of disability organizations on the political process, Laura Bonnett notes: "Not only have they influenced legislation in various parts of the country, they have also empowered and enabled many people with disabilities to re-envision what full citizenship looks like" (2003: 156). Significant features of the disability movement today include a solidarity expressed by honouring histories, leaving no one behind, coming together around shared reform priorities, and a belief in civic engagement as a crucial way for breathing life into the vision of access and inclusion. Another commentator, Sally Chivers, remarks that "the Canadian disability movement has made ... meaningful progress by working both against and within state systems to achieve recognition of disabled people's human rights" (2008: 307).

Public policies are mixed blessings for people with disabilities. Policies may offer people with disabilities eligibility to income programs, access to tax measures, and the legal benefit of protective employment standards and human rights laws. But, too often in practice, policies impose controls, are hard to claim, perpetuate stereotypes or reinforce dependencies. Health and social work professionals, educational personnel and program administrators frequently impose disabled identities on people, even while other professionals may be challenging these stereotypes. They do so by suppressing differences, downplaying capacities and fitting people into diagnostic categories. Despite some organizational reforms and consultative processes of democratic engagement, political systems remain ableist and exclusionary. People with disabilities are significantly underrepresented at all levels of politics and governing. Even with these contradictions, the Canadian disability movement regards the state as the sector with the most potential for advancing equality rights and social inclusion of people with disabilities.

In the everyday world of living with disabilities, the personal, the professional and the political all intertwine. Individuals and families struggle to gain official recognition of personal needs, to navigate the complexity of public, voluntary, and private agencies to secure essential services. They work to retain those services as a person passes from one life stage or age category to another; they lobby for improvements to supports, and perhaps, to resist cutbacks to programs. For many people with disabilities, politicizing citizenship centres on contested relationships with medical systems of knowledge and power. It may involve an individual or group grappling with and at times resisting an "illness label" given to them that jars with their own understanding. Conversely, it can entail struggling for medical recognition of a condition as a legitimate one (Moss and Teghtsoonian 2008). Contesting care involves locating the cause of or experience with an illness to outside forces and broader ideas of equity and injustice. People with particular health conditions, such as hepatitis C, join together for support and solidarity, as well as activism, forming collective identities. Personal and collective action can challenge medical science and may result in changes to diagnostic protocols and treatment practices.

Boundaries of the disability policy field do fluctuate. In some respects, policy has maintained the broad focus articulated by the Canadian disability movement and parliamentary committees in the 1980s, aided by constitutional reform and the entrenchment of the *Charter of Rights and Freedoms*. In other respects, policy focus has narrowed, as measured by inconsistent political attention, low priorities, and few substantive actions on major concerns. In a similar manner, policy conversation on disability has shifted over recent decades to a rights language of citizenship and equality (Stienstra 2012; United Nations 2006). Yet it is unclear that this discourse — preferred by many movement activists, used by public officials, and adopted in governmental statements — has widespread public acceptance or basic adoption in public-policy-making processes. If there is a shift in disability policy talk, it deals with employability as the dominant emphasis.

When reviewing the Canadian record on disability policy making, a *déjà vu discourse on disability reform* is clearly evident (Prince 2004). There is a strong sense that we have been here before in terms of the problems identified and the promises made by political parties, parliamentarians and public servants. This phenomenon involves the presentation of reform ideas by community groups to legislative committees, cabinet ministers or task forces; the official declaration of plans and promises by governments and other public authorities, followed by external reviews of the record; and then official responses with a reiteration of previously stated plans and promises. Some changes, to be sure, have taken place, but the overall pace of reform is slow and the scale of change is typically modest.

Along with being about words, déjà vu discourse includes a series of practices by governmental and political actors: actions, inaction and reactions. In disability policy, governmental practices of déjà vu discourse include the following strategies and tactics:

- stressing gains made on the surface while overlooking the structural gaps;
- consciously not taking action on further measures, an example of non-decision making;
- downplaying disability as a human rights issue and, at times, discrediting the use of litigation and the *Charter of Rights and Freedoms* to advance equality and equity claims; and
- promising additional actions, often in unspecified tomorrows, to be taken up, in accordance with the principles of limited government and shared social responsibility, by various institutions and groups.

Disability activist and scholar Michael Oliver provides a further example of déjà vu politics with respect to cabinet ministers responsible for disability issues in Britain:

I have lost count of the number of conferences and meetings on disability I have attended over the years where the Minister turns up (often late), ignores the other speakers, makes a short, patronizing speech, which only demonstrates their ignorance, announces a small grant or irrelevant government initiative and then leaves before they can be asked any questions. (Oliver 2009: 169)

Oliver describes these as "public relations exercises," a style of politics that has remained more or less the same in recent times. This style goes by other names too: the political management of public issues; symbolic gestures of public policy; and the containment of government interaction with community organizations. Whatever it is called and whenever it happens, it has disempowering consequences for disability activism and social change. Such ministerial behaviour takes little account of the real challenges and needs of people with disabilities and offers precious little in substantive policy and program reform.

Groups that participate in these processes no doubt become more cynical and also perhaps more tactical in the way they frame issues and interact with government organizations. They learn to recast issues and ideas in different ways, tailor analysis and advocacy styles to shifting political contexts, and to come equipped with data when available and where possible. Disability policy analysis, advocacy and evaluation seem to circle back to the beginning, time and again. In most jurisdictions in Canada we seem unable to break away from this déjà vu discourse to make significant advances in the policy vision for people living with disabilities.

All the while, people with disabilities across the country face high levels of unemployment and poverty; labour market programs are largely failing to provide appropriate employment supports and services in order for the disabled to search for, obtain and maintain gainful work; people with disabilities rely increasingly on provincial social assistance as a main source of income; and important gaps persist in unmet needs of basic services for children and adults with disabilities, often with dependence on charitable agencies for assistance with the activities of everyday living taken for granted by most Canadians (McCreath 2011; National Council of Welfare 2010; Prince 2009; Senate Report 2009; Stienstra 2012). As Cameron and Valentine (2001: 30) observe, "Canada does not have a comprehensive and integrated system to meet the needs of persons with disabilities. There is no national disability policy. Instead, disability policy is mediated through a complex federal reality where jurisdictional division, duplication and overlap, and policy fragmentation are common."

In this disjointed and convoluted system, the effects of disability policy on people range from supportive resources to restrictive laws, minimal interventions to oppressive conditions, and from experiencing a positive status to struggling with a spoiled identity of stigma. Social work and human service professionals may well participate in and confront these conditions depending on their formal training and mentorship, their own life experiences, and the organizational contexts of their practice.

Chapter Summary

Intellectual developments in Canadian disability policy studies are bubbling as seen in critical and feminist theory, case study research, historical analyses, comparative investigation and autobiographical work (Boyce et al. 2001; LeFrançois, Menzies and Reaume 2013; McColl and Jongbloed 2006; Moss and Teghtsoonian 2008; Panitch 2007; Prince 2010; Rioux and Valentine 2006; Vick 2012; Withers 2012). Substantial societal change, however, moves slowly in the way people think about disability and inclusion (Prince 2009), and in how policies and services enhance the lives of disabled individuals (McCreath 2011; Senate Report 2009; Stienstra 2012). Disability policy is an expression of values in a political community — prejudice and acceptance — toward various groups of people classified as disabled. Canadian disability policy is a codification of public and private power that positions individuals with disabilities and individuals without disabilities in relation to one another and within the structures of society.

At the core of disability policy in Canada, as in other countries, is a contradictory mix of social attitudes and working models of disablement. Public policy is many things. It can be a source of exclusion and discrimination for people with disabilities. It can be a tool for challenging prejudicial beliefs, tackling discriminatory actions and removing barriers. It can also, more ambitiously, be an instrument for creating positive social change by shifting attitudes and behaviours and by establishing social rights and obligations in a political community. Whatever its effects, public policy involves the social construction of ability-disability relations. In this process, policy and practice often construct people with disabilities as passive clients and program users in dependent relationships, rather than as workers, volunteers, caregivers, taxpayers and active citizens. Canada's disability policy community is inherently political because it includes interest groups, advocacy coalitions and court cases, and because groups of people, through various forms of social action, are raising issues of inequality, making decisions on service delivery, affirming differences of the human condition, and seeking to shape societal attitudes and practices.

Getting people with disabilities on the policy agendas of federal and provincial governments in the form of plans and strategies is one achievement. Receiving serious attention and sustained action by decision-makers and officials is quite another matter. A déjà vu discourse on disability policy issues has consequences for social change in Canadian affairs. This discourse naturalizes the limited scale and pace of reforms in disability policy and practice. More dangerously, the discourse not only perpetuates a pattern of relentless incremental changes but also conceals the erosion and decline in existing programs and benefits to persons with disabilities. The language of "shared social responsibility" for addressing disability issues further legitimates a limited role by governments and places heavy duties on individuals and families as well as other institutions, notably local nonprofit community agencies.

Discussion Questions

1. How would you describe the prevailing attitudes and way of talking about disability in your community? What is the character of political discourse in regard to the image of people with disabilities and their participation in various aspects of society?

2. Does the organization in which you work, learn or volunteer have a policy on disability issues? If so, what are the main elements and ideas in it? If not, why does the organization not have such a policy?

3. In your city or in your province, who are the main disability groups and coalitions active in policy advocacy and mobilization? What reform ideas and social changes are espoused by disability movement organizations?

4. Why are we seemingly trapped in a déjà vu cycle on disability issues in Canada?

5. With respect to improving the status of people living with disabilities in Canada, what do you think are the prospects for social change? How successful is the Canadian disability movement in effecting positive changes in public policy? Identify concrete examples.

References

Bonnett, Laura. 2003. "Citizenship and People with Disabilities: The Invisible Frontier." In Janine Brodie and Linda Trimble (eds.), *Reinventing Canada: Politics of the 21st Century*. Toronto: Pearson Education.

Boyce, William, Mary Tremblay, Mary Anne McColl, Jerome Bickenbach, Anne Crichton, Steven Andrews, Nancy Gerein and April D'Aubin. 2001. *A Seat at the Table: Persons with Disabilities and Policy Making*. Montreal and Kingston: McGill-Queen's University Press.

Cameron, David, and Fraser Valentine. 2001. "Comparing Policy-Making in Federal Systems: The Case of Disability Policy and Programs — An Introduction." In D. Cameron and F. Valentine (eds.), *Disability and Federalism: Comparing Different Approaches to Full Participation*. Montreal and Kingston: McGill-Queen's University Press.

Chivers, Sally. 2008. "Barrier by Barrier: The Canadian Disability Movement and the Fight for Equal Rights." In Miriam Smith (ed.), *Group Politics and Social Movements in Canada*. Peterborough: Broadview Press.

Doern, G. Bruce, and Michael J. Prince. 2012. *Three Bio-Realms: Biotechnology and the Governance of Food, Health, and Life in Canada*. Toronto: University of Toronto Press.

IRIS (Institute for Research and Development on Inclusion and Society). 2012. "Disability

and Inclusion Based Policy Analysis." North York. <irisinstitute.files.wordpress.
com/2012/01/is-five-190142-iris_disability_inclusive_lens_eng.pdf>.

Jongbloed, Lynn. 2003. "Disability Policy in Canada: An Overview." *Journal of Disability Policy Studies* 13, 4: 203–209.

LeFrançois, Brenda A., Robert Menzies and Geoffrey Reaume (eds.). 2013. *Mad Matters: A Critical Reader in Canadian Mad Studies*. Toronto: Canadian Scholars' Press.

McColl, Mary Ann, and Lyn Jongbloed. 2006. "Introduction." In Mary Ann McColl and Lyn Jongbloed (eds.), *Disability and Social Policy in Canada* 2nd edition. Concord, ON: Captus University Press.

McColl, Mary Ann, and Rachel Stephenson. 2008. "A Scoping Review of Disability Policy in Canada: Effects on Community Integration for People with Spinal Cord Injuries." Kingston: Queens's University, Report to SCI-Solutions Network. <chspr.queensu.ca/downloads/Reports/Disability%20Policy%20in%20Canada-final%20report-May09.pdf>.

McCreath, Graeme. 2011. *The Politics of Blindness: From Charity to Parity*. Vancouver: Granville Island.

Moss, Pamela, and Katherine Teghtsoonian (eds.). 2008. *Contesting Illness: Processes and Practices*. Toronto: University of Toronto Press.

National Council of Welfare. 2010. *Welfare Incomes 2009*. Ottawa: Her Majesty the Queen in Right of Canada.

Oliver, Michael. 2009. *Understanding Disability: From Theory to Practice*. Basingstoke: Palgrave Macmillan.

Panitch, Melanie. 2007. *Disability, Mothers, and Organization: Accidental Activists*. London: Routledge.

Prince, Michael J. 2000. "Battling for Remembrance: The Politics of Veterans Affairs Canada." In Leslie A. Pal (ed.), *How Ottawa Spends 2000–2001: Reassessing the Federal Role*. Toronto: Oxford University Press.

____. 2001a. "Canadian Federalism and Disability Policy Making." *Canadian Journal of Political Science* 34, 4:791–817.

____. 2001b. "Tax Policy as Social Policy: Canadian Tax Assistance for People with Disabilities." *Canadian Public Policy* 27, 4: 487–501.

____. 2002a. "The Governance of Children with Disabilities and Their Families: Charting the Public-Sector Regime in Canada." *Canadian Public Administration* 45, 3: 389–409.

____. 2002b. "Designing Disability Policy in Canada: The Nature and Impact of Federalism on Policy Development." In A. Puttee (ed.), *Federalism, Democracy and Disability in Canada*. Montreal and Kingston: McGill-Queen's University Press.

____. 2004. "Canadian Disability Policy: Still a Hit-and-Miss Affair." *Canadian Journal of Sociology* 29, 1: 59–82.

____. 2008. "Claiming a Disability Benefit as Contesting Social Citizenship." In Pamela Moss and Katherine Teghtsoonian (eds.), *Contesting Illness: Processes and Practices*. Toronto: University of Toronto Press.

____. 2009. *Absent Citizens: Disability Politics and Policy in Canada*. Toronto: University of Toronto Press.

____. 2010. "What about a Disability Rights Act for Canada? Practices and Lessons from America, Australia, and the United Kingdom," *Canadian Public Policy* 36, 2: 199–214.

____. 2012. "Canadian Disability Activism and Political Ideas: In and Between Neo-Liberalism and Social Liberalism." *Canadian Journal of Disability Studies* 1, 1: 1–34.

Puttee, Alan. 2002. "Federalism, Democracy and Disability in Canada: An Introduction." In Alan Puttee (ed.), *Federalism, Democracy and Disability Policy in Canada*. Montreal and Kingston: McGill-Queen's University Press.

Rice, James J., and Michael J. Prince. 2013. *Changing Politics of Canadian Social Policy* 2nd edition. Toronto: University of Toronto Press.

Rioux, Marcia H., and Michael J. Prince. 2002. "The Canadian Political Landscape of Disability: Policy Perspectives, Social Status, Interest Groups and the Rights Movement." In Alan Puttee (ed.), *Federalism, Democracy and Disability Policy in Canada*. Montreal and Kingston: McGill-Queen's University Press.

Rioux, Marcia H., and Fraser Valentine. 2006. "Does Theory Matter? Exploring the Nexus between Disability, Human Rights, and Public Policy." In Dianne Pothier and Richard Devlin (eds.), *Critical Disability Theory: Essays in Philosophy, Politics, Policy, and Law*. Vancouver: University of British Columbia Press.

Schalock, Robert L. 2004. "The Emerging Disability Paradigm and its Implications for Policy and Practice," *Journal of Disability Policy Studies* 14, 4: 204–215.

Senate Report. 2009. *In from the Margins: A Call to Action on Poverty, Housing, and Homelessness*. Ottawa: Standing Senate Committee on Social Affairs, Science, and Technology.

Stienstra, Deborah. 2012. *About Canada: Disability Rights*. Halifax and Winnipeg: Fernwood Publishing.

United Nations. 2006. *Convention on the Rights of Persons with Disabilities and Optional Protocol*. Geneva: Author.

Vick, Andrea. 2012. "Theorizing Episodic Disabilities: The Case for an Embodied Politics." *Canadian Social Work Review* 29, 1: 41–60.

Withers, A.J. 2012. *Disability Politics and Theory*. Halifax and Winnipeg: Fernwood Publishing.

Chapter 7

Experiences and Perspectives of Families who Have Children with Disabilities

Kevin Lusignan

In this chapter, I provide a mere glimpse into the experiences of families who have children with disabilities, the transitions that occur throughout a family life cycle, and identify some of the common issues that many families face. My perspective as a parent who has two adult children with intellectual disabilities and another adult child who has an acquired brain injury influences the writing of this chapter. At the time of writing this chapter, I am serving as the president of the Family Support Institute (FSI) of British Columbia, an organization with a parent-to-parent model that supports other families who have loved ones with a disability. I also serve as the executive director of the Community Ventures Society, a nonprofit agency that serves people of all abilities, and have been involved as an activist and an advocate in the Community Living movement in British Columbia over the past twenty years.

The Family Experience

This chapter focuses on the family — not to exclude or problematize family members with disabilities, but to gain important insights into the experiences of family members. Such insights inevitably enhance practice with families to better assist them in meeting the needs of family members with a disability. Families play a powerful role in shaping the experience and the development of the self-perception of their sons or daughters, sisters or brothers, grandchildren, nieces or nephews.

Social workers often work closely with families to ensure adequate support and care for their children.

Each family goes through a series of developmental stages of life, from birth to death. This process is unique to each family and the stages may not necessarily occur or will not occur in a linear fashion. The family life cycle stages may include children leaving home as single adults, becoming a common-law couple, or entering into marriage, securing employment, having children as a couple or a single person, children attending school, raising adolescents, launching children from the home into adulthood, aging, retirement and later life. Families also come in all permutations and sizes, including same-sex parents, single parents, and blended families. The notion of the nuclear family is changing and is being replaced with a view of the family that involves much diversity (Becvar and Becvar 1999: 16).

Each family is made up of individuals who are unique and have characteristics that combined together give rise to unique family systems, that is, the "whole is more than the sum of its parts" (Bertalanffy 1969: 18). Families are also influenced by the family's socioeconomic status, parenting styles or parent wellness. Conversely, the family could also be influenced by substance misuse issues, neglect and violence. In terms of roles, each family fulfills functions related to affection, self-esteem, spirituality, finances, caregiving, socializing, recreation and education. (Turnbull et al. 2011). Furthermore, each family has its own unique culture, and when two people come together in a common-law relationship or marriage they are also entering into a relationship with the other people in their partner's family along with all associated family rules and patterns (Becvar and Becvar 1999; Seligman and Darling 2007). Over time, couples negotiate the rules of engagement that they bring from their own extended families, and if they are to stay together as a couple, then they will need to arrive at a mutually satisfactory arrangement of the rules and form consistent and stable patterns of interaction (Becvar and Becvar 1999: 18). Further, the rules need to be renegotiated at each stage of the developmental process, as each stage involves changing family culture. Changing family culture often involves conflict (Avruch 2006: 29).

When a child is born or is adopted into a family or acquires a disability, and the family learns — immediately or later — that their child has a disability, most families find it a very difficult or traumatizing event (Brown 2009; Dale 1995; Gronenburg 2008; Naseef 1997; Seligman and Darling 2007; Thomson 2010; Turnbull et al. 2011; Zimmermann 1996). Although this will depend on the severity of the disability, and their general coping skills and support, parents of newborns with disabilities often experience feelings of meaninglessness and powerlessness called *anomie* (Seligman and Darling 2007: 103). Some parents might perceive their child's disability in alignment with society's predominantly deficit-based notion that a child born with a disability is a tragedy (Harvey 2002; Oliver 2009). First reactions to their children with disabilities are often negative, but parents, despite the difficulties, form an attachment to their children that turns into love (Addison 2003; Batshaw 1991; Seligman and Darling 2007; Zimmermann 1996).

Over time, most families come to terms with their child's disability and accept them as any other child in their family or society and readjust their dreams for their children. Families may be waiting for a diagnosis so they know what to do or plan an intervention only to find out later down the road that, for the most part, the diagnosis does not matter because it does not change anything (Zimmermann 1996: 122) and they love their child regardless. For some children the diagnosis might not be timely because the doctor may not know what to look for or may be unfamiliar with the condition. Timely diagnosis is important because often the social service and school systems require a diagnosis to obtain service or funding. Once a diagnosis has been confirmed, then families engage in learning about their child's disability. Some families ardently look for a "cure." Parents and even extended family may feel guilty because they feel responsible in some way, while some families try to make sense of the situation, or rationalize and look at a child with a disability as a gift from God. Other parents may see a child with a disability as punishment from God, depending on their outlook and culture (Turnbull et al. 2011). There may be points throughout their child's development when parents see other children doing activities that very much remind them that their child is not reaching developmental milestones, and the grief reappears for a short time (Batshaw 1991; Seligman and Darling 2007; Zimmermann 1996).

I think that every parent has dreams for their children, even before they are born. An expecting parent imagines the wonderful experiences they will have with the child who is yet to arrive. I remember dreams of what the future might look like before my daughter Angela was born. However, the experience that should have been a celebration, instead involved my wife in one hospital and my newly born daughter in another. Angela had a difficult birth resulting in a lack of oxygen to Angela's brain that caused seizures, many weeks in intensive care, and the possibility that Angela might not make it. It was an emotionally traumatizing time for our young and unsophisticated family. Fortunately, over the course of several weeks Angela grew stronger and we were able to bring her home. We were initially told that Angela would probably have cerebral palsy and epilepsy to some degree. At a year old, my mother noticed that Angela was not progressing as she should and we went to visit the doctor who gave us a diagnosis that she would be "mentally retarded" and suggested that we would have to put her in an institution. The pain, anger and fear about the future were overwhelming. I remember being at home and throwing a full jar of instant coffee against the wall in a fit of rage. I was worried about having a daughter with an intellectual disability in the society that we lived in. At the same time, it was hard to imagine for us that our little baby that we love could ever be sent to an institution and of course we disagreed with the doctor and raised Angela in a loving home. I know that for a while there was a vacuum where dreams of the future should have been.

At the early childhood stage, parents want to begin to get some control back in their lives and parents eventually start to work on creating a normalized life by getting out into the community with their family, by focusing on employment, enjoying social relationships and making room for leisure time. How successful a family is at normalizing their lives depends upon their access to formal and informal resources such as familial and community supports, funding, housing, transportation and personal finances. Equally important is the nature and severity of the child's disability, especially if the family does not have adequate formal and informal supports and resources (Seligman and Darling 2007; Statistics Canada 2008). Families also start to turn their attention to early intervention programs for their children such as infant development programs, early childhood education, preschool and integrated childcare. Social workers and professionals start to get involved with many families and help guide them through the process of learning about resources and navigating the system in the best interests of their child. Early intervention is considered a critical asset for setting the stage for a child's future development (Dunlap and Fox 2006; Turnbull et al. 2011). Infant Development Programs (IDP) start from birth until three years of age, and professionals usually connect with families in the home. For many families this is the start of regular contact with professionals and the experience of having a professional presence in the home.

IDP professionals work as generalists with families to understand more about the child's disability or condition, how to access resources in the community, look for ways to enhance parent-child attachment, help with parenting skills and with finding peer support for the family. Families may also involve children in Early Childhood Education that connects children to inclusive childcare centres and later preschool programs intended to help children prepare for kindergarten. However, there are often waitlists, and a diagnosis may be required to access the services. In Canada, families report that finding appropriate childcare is often difficult and their children have often been refused entry into a childcare centre because of their disability, especially with children who have severe disabilities (Statistics Canada 2008: 19).

Many families also begin to think about interventions such as Applied Behaviour Analysis (ABA), speech therapy and physical therapy because they want to do everything they can to enhance their child's development and ameliorate the situation for their loved one (Seligman and Darling 2007: 49). Families might also be facing their child's life-limiting condition and need the emotional support and guidance of a social worker, IDP consultant or other human service professional. Families may have hopes and dreams that need expression and thoughtful exploration given their limited experience with their child's particular disability and the myriad of emotions they may encounter. At this stage, families may have some learning to do, and I have often heard parents say, "No one gives you the manual." So, professionals will want to be gentle with families when providing support and guidance because families need time to process, learn and adjust. Interactions with professionals in the early childhood stage are important because these early experiences greatly influence a family's perspective, receptiveness and trust in accepting help from social services agencies in the future (Seligman and Darling 2007: 50).

Disability and Family Life

Stigma

For centuries, people with disabilities have often faced stigma and have sometimes been thought of as less than human (Roeher Institute 1996: 1). Stigma is a mark of difference that distinguishes someone from "normal" and is evidenced by a reaction to meeting a person with a disability that evokes fear, repulsion, surprise, anxiety and uncertainty of how to act (Garland-Thomson 2009: 68). Families also face stigma (Seligman and Darling 2007; Turnbull 1985; Turnbull et al. 2011) and even before their children are born, families are influenced by society's deficit-based mental model (Block 2009; Cooperrider and Whitney 2005; Lord and Hutchison 2007; McKnight 1995; Prince 2009; Whitney and Trosten-Bloom 2003). Mental models "are deeply ingrained assumptions, generalizations, or even pictures or images that influence how we understand the world and how we take action" (Senge 2006: 8).

Society has a mental model that an unborn child will be *typical*. Once a child is born with a disability, friends, relatives and community contacts may act differently and distance themselves because they do not know what to say (Kappes 1995; Adams 1995). As children get older, the differences are seen as greater, especially when a child has difficulty communicating. Sometimes children are not invited to birthday parties, school plays or field trips, nor are the families (Clancy 2013). Even worse, families may face the stigma directly. One example in Canada was a family facing eviction because their son with autism was too noisy (*Vancouver Sun*, October 12, 2013) and another instance of direct stigma was a mom receiving a vitriolic message inviting her to "euthanize" her child with autism because the sender felt that people who are not "normal" do not belong in society. In this instance, the community rallied around and supported the family because they found the action of the sender of the letter reprehensible (*Vancouver Sun*, August 20, 2013).

Stigma is even more pervasive for racialized populations, women, and people living in poverty. Through a narrative ethnographic study of Canadian Muslim women, in *Racialized Bodies, Disabling Worlds,* Dossa (2009) explores how racialized Muslim women with disabilities are rendered socially invisible. Their stories highlight the social marginalization and disenfranchisement they experience in a disabling world. Dossa makes a case for positive acknowledgement of perceived differences of nationality, religion, multiple abilities, and gendered and race-based identities, and argues for the need to bridge two disparate bodies of work: disability studies and anti-racist feminism.

Likewise, as illustrated by Durst in Chapter 9, Indigenous families and individuals may not be eligible for services and funding that non-Indigenous children are entitled to; therefore, some parents, grandparents and extended family are solely responsible for the care of their loved ones with no formal support (Turpel-Lafond 2013: 5). Subsequently, many families experience great unease when facing stigma and try to manage appearances in order to hide their child's disability by taking extra precautions to minimize the level of stigma directed at their family. Also in an effort to hide from stigma, parents of children with disabilities will often befriend other families in similar situations because they have something in common. Families might also take their family member out in the community less because of prevailing negative attitudes (Seligman and Darling 2007: 139). This runs contrary to the earlier discussion pertaining to "normalizing" family life. There may be times in a family's life where they need to withdraw and maintain their own unique routines.

> *I disliked going to restaurants when Angela was younger because she was a messy eater, she did not have social graces and sometimes had problem behaviour in the community. People would stare. I was embarrassed and defensive. Over time I grew a thicker skin and she learned more about socially appropriate behaviour in the community. It is amazing to look back over thirty-two years and see the progress that she has made and how our family has learned. Going to restaurants now is a breeze compared to when she was younger. Now, she even orders her own dinner with an iPad using the app Proloquo2Go. The community has made progress in terms of inclusive attitudes and I notice that places of business are becoming more disability-friendly and inclusive. However, we still have a long way to go before people with developmental disabilities are truly welcomed in the community.*

Family Quality of Life

In Statistics Canada's analytical paper, *Participation and Activity Limitation Survey 2006: Families of Children with Disabilities in Canada,* it outlines that families feel the effects more strongly when their child's disability is more severe.

Overall, the majority of parents with disabilities reported high levels of satisfaction with their health and lives in general. However, in comparison to parents of children who had mild to moderate disabilities, parents of children whose disabilities were severe to very severe were less likely to evaluate their own health and life satisfaction as good to excellent, and were more likely to indicate that they had high levels of stress. In addition, parents of children with severe to very severe disabilities were more likely to indicate that their child's disability had an impact on their employment, finances, leisure, and personal time, and their ability to find help and childcare. (Statistics Canada 2008: 20)

Obviously, there is a need for increased support for families who have children with significant disabilities. When there is a child who has additional needs in the family and services and sufficient supports are not provided, there are many stressors that influence the family system (Brown 2009: 45). Stress is incurred at — and waiting for — a diagnosis (Turnbull et al. 2011), when there are medical concerns (Statistics Canada 2008: 9), when there is problem behaviour (Binnendyk et al. 2009), when children begin school and through each school transition (Targett and Wehman 2013), and moving out of the family home (Seligman and Darling 2007: 157). Parents may also be further affected when they have a negative perception of their child's disability because they are deeply affected by a deficit-based mental model. Some advocate for "optimism training" to shift the perception of families towards a more positive view of a loved one (Durand et al. 2009).

Families are also further impacted and stressed when they have financial difficulties. In 2006, 20 percent of families felt that there are financial difficulties related to having a child with a disability (Statistics Canada 2008: 11). Families who have a child with a disability have a greater predisposition to living in poverty, and especially in a single parent household. In two-parent families, often only one parent can work, and there are extra costs associated with having a child with a disability such as medical costs, alternative diets, transport and renovations to the home. In addition, there are barriers to the workforce like finding care for children, having to work shorter hours due to caregiving responsibilities, and having to turn down opportunities for advancement at work. The burden for single parents is even greater, and some are unable to work and may require social assistance (Harvey 2002: 8–13).

Caregiving can be a major undertaking for some families, and depending on the nature and severity of their loved one's disability, the caregiving requirements can be considerable. Most families with nondisabled children reduce the direct giving of care as the child becomes independent. However, when one has a child with a disability, there is sometimes a difficulty adjusting to the transition from adolescence into adulthood, and this may truncate the typical family pattern and cycle. As a result, many families experience more years of active parenting, advocacy, medical and school appointments, with the extra responsibilities sometimes lasting until the parents pass away. Stress is cumulative, and "living with a child with a disability over many years can take its toll psychologically, physically, and financially and can contribute to feelings of exhaustion, despair, and resignation" (Seligman and Darling 2007: 191). Often stress is caused by a lack of support from the government and could be made manageable with some resources in place. The lack of support may affect families by having to place their child in foster care, or result in family breakdown, or create deleterious effects on the parent's emotional and physical health. In the case of family breakdown, single-parent families who have children with disabilities in Canada often live in poverty (Harvey 2002: 9). One example in British Columbia is when a stressed-out mother in Prince Rupert committed murder/suicide with her son with autism, ostensibly because she did not have the support to manage getting through the day. The tragedy may have been preventable had she had the proper supports (*Prince Rupert Northern View* 2014).

The caregiving impact is often more severe for the mother — or mothers — of the family, given that women are often considered the primary caregiver although gender roles are evolving. The impact is felt financially and impinges on personal time and added stress. However, when caregiving responsibilities are shared in the family, then it can be made more manageable (Statistics Canada 2008: 11). On the other hand, sometimes when the needs of a child are considerable, the family is unable to fulfill all the child's needs and must allow the boundaries of the family to be permeable and be open to others helping raise the child (Seligman and Darling 2007; Turnbull et al. 2011). Even though families deliver more than the average amount of care, in Canada, two-thirds of mothers feel guilty and think they should be doing more (Statistics Canada 2008: 10). Social workers and other human service professionals can be instrumental in providing support and assisting mothers to reframe this guilt, as well as accept and ask for assistance from their partner, extended family or specific service providers.

Fathers are also important elements of the family system and their involvement is related to their child's development and to the cohesion of the family. However, within the context of heterosexual families, society has often viewed the mother as the primary caregiver, and as a result, often men have been intentionally or unintentionally excluded by mothers and professionals. Some men are exposed to cultural beliefs that men should be strong, silent, tough guy, "fix-it types" and that caregiving is women's work. The greater a man's traditional gender socialization that he should be strong and silent, the more difficult it is when a child with a disability comes into the family, and it has been reported that men may have more difficulty if the child with a disability is a boy. Men who have adopted the strong-and-silent gender role may have more difficulty with communicating openly, dealing with emotions and processing grief. In response, fathers may withdraw, bury themselves in work and avoid caring for their child with a disability (Seligman and Darling 2007: 222–225). Social workers and other human service professionals can be instrumental in providing support and assisting fathers to recognize and attempt to reframe these emotions, developing alternate responses to their role within the family.

At the same time, many fathers are involved with their children who have disabilities and find ways to adjust, reframe and develop coping strategies to help maintain their personal well-being and contribute to the family unit (Brown 2009; Shapell 1995). They share parenting responsibilities and take an interest in their child's development and are often involved with the medical issues, school and with advocacy (Dale 1995: 4–5). Fathers need support and would benefit from peer-to-peer support from other men who have a child with a disability (Meyer 1995; Naseef 1997; Seligman and Darling 2007). Further research and exploration is needed with respect to understanding the experiences and dynamics of LGTBQ couples in parenting children with disabilities.

Aside from the importance of parental roles, relationships between siblings are often the most enduring, and sustained interactions take on a life cycle of their own. In some instances, sisters and brothers often resent siblings with disabilities, because they get less attention from their parents. Concurrently, siblings may also be resentful because they are expected to help out with caregiving of their sibling in order to help out the family unit and support their parents, especially if the family has limited financial resources. The increased expectations of care especially relate to female siblings because they are often expected to take on more responsibility with respect to caring for their sibling with a disability. Siblings are also impacted by stigma and may be teased in school about their sibling with a disability. When siblings look to the future, they may often fear that they will be responsible for looking after their brother or sister with a disability and wonder how they will manage (Seligman and Darling 2007: 239–240). In *Invisible No More: A Photographic Chronicle of the Lives of People with Intellectual Disabilities,* the author writes under the heading of *Apprehension*:

> The [22-year-old] sat on the bed with her back against the headboard, one arm around her [10-year-old] baby brother, as she read him a bedtime story, carefully pausing at the right places to show him the simple pictures in the book. It was a struggle to keep David's attention focused on the story, but her pictures and perseverance won out. Just as she knew it would. David let himself be tucked in, one more hug, and with a tender look, mother-in-waiting dimmed the lights. Most people who don't have a sibling with a disability cannot know how it feels to live with someone

like David. The future is worrisome: What will happen to David when the parents can no longer look after him? What will befall them as siblings? (Pietropaolo 2010: 42)

Consequently, the experience of siblings may also be positive, and brothers and sisters may have more influence on their sibling with a disability than their parents (Shapell 1995: 65–66), and often children with disabilities will want to emulate their siblings (Turnbull et al. 2011). Siblings also may benefit from the experiences with their sisters or brothers with a disability and may benefit from "enhanced maturity, self-esteem, social competence, insight, tolerance, pride, vocational opportunities, advocacy and loyalty" (Turnbull et al. 2011: 38). Professionals can support siblings by including them and helping to find resources that will connect them with other siblings who have brothers and sisters with disabilities.

A strong parental subsystem (same-sex, common-law, or married) is perhaps the most important stabilizer of the family system, but that does not prevent a single parent from having a strong family (Turnbull et al. 2011: 17). Despite the common belief that having a child with a disability in the family causes higher rates of family breakdown, the research shows that it does not cause higher rates of divorce, but it does create the potential for more conflict and stress in some families (Statistics Canada 2008: 12). However, some families felt that the presence of a child with a disability in the family made them stronger and more cohesive as a family (Seligman and Darling 2007; Turnbull et al. 2011).

The role of the family and parents is particularly critical during the thirteen years of attendance within the school system as this period often impacts the quality of life of families in significant ways. People with disabilities have been excluded from the school system, and since the 1950s, many parents have had to fight to see their children included in schools (Turnbull et al. 2011: 97–101). In elementary school, students with disabilities are more included in the classroom and when they get into high school the system often pushes the child towards a segregated resource room due to a concept called mainstreaming. Mainstreaming is distinguished from inclusion because there is a working assumption that children with disabilities are part of the "special education department" and should be included in a regular classroom only when they can keep up with the rest of the students in the class (Spence-Cochran, Pearl and Walker 2013: 179–181). In contrast, inclusive education involves the full participation of special needs students into regular classrooms (Sailor 2006: 168).

Families often experience difficulty with the school system due to the lack of inclusion and the differential treatment of their children with disabilities. In some schools there are seclusion rooms that involve locking a child behind closed doors. In British Columbia, there has been a great deal of concern expressed about the use of seclusion rooms in schools (Inclusion BC 2014). Another heartbreaking example of differential and exclusionary treatment was in New Westminster, B.C., where class photos of a group of elementary students were taken with a 7-year-old boy in a wheelchair situated way off to the side of the risers from where his peers were sitting (Fletcher 2013).

As a result of such exclusionary practices, parents have to be ardent advocates for their children's inclusion in the school system (Turnbull et al. 2011). Parents also soon realize that they must learn to advocate for their children, know about Individual Education Plans (IEP), know the education system rules, and be involved with the schools to create success and inclusion for their child (Targett and Wehman 2013: 72). Professionals can also help families prepare for the school experience by providing advice, being part of the planning process, working with the schools, and pointing families to support and advocacy groups (as discussed by Carter in Chapter 11).

> I remember Angela starting school. She was the first child with a disability included in her school. Even though we knew that she needed full-time attention from a teacher's aide, the school only provided her with a half-time teacher's aide. We expressed concern and they promised us it would be fine. I showed up on the second day of school to pick her up only to find her wandering about in front of the school. Here was a child with no notion of traffic safety wandering around unsupervised. I pulled her from school due to safety concerns until they provided a full-time aide — which they did within a few days. Thankfully the rest of the elementary experience was better. She was fully included in elementary school, but when she progressed to high school, she was segregated away from her peers and into a "resource room" with other children who had intellectual disabilities, rather than being included in typical classrooms. Even so, because the teachers were so great, school was a positive experience for her.

It often gets harder for parent caregivers as children move into their teen years, as parents get older, and their children generally get bigger and stronger. The teen years bring issues to the forefront like puberty and sexuality. Often families do not know how to address these issues and this creates added stress for the families (Turnbull et al. 2011). In addition, looming large in the future are issues such as deciding on appropriate residential arrangements, getting funding and looking for vocational opportunities. Families also worry about the loss of service as their child transitions from child to adult services. There are often concerns about the lack of socialization now that their child is leaving school; families worry about how much longer they can provide care, and families worry about increased dealings with the government and care providers (Seligman and Darling 2007: 53–54).

This is another critical point in time where social workers and other human service professionals can be instrumental in providing support and assisting families to access the necessary resources.

It is often the case that adult children continue to live with their parents, sometimes into their senior years. So why do some parents have difficulty or resist the transition of adult children leaving home? The first of several reasons is that transitions are challenging and there may be an uncertainty about the future because of lack of knowledge (Turnbull et al. 2011). Lack of funding and suitable arrangements may cause parents to choose to keep their adult children at home. Families also have to make decisions about housing and models of care. In addition, families of children with disabilities face the fear of letting go, fear of dreaming, fear of change, fear of asking for help and fear of death (Etmanski 2000: 22–26).

Families can overcome these fears and build a vision for the future with the assistance of a social worker, or on their own, or with another professional by developing a plan for the future through person-centred planning (Lord, Leavitt and Dingwall 2012: 101–107). Person-centred planning is a planning process that emerged in the 1970s (O'Brien and O'Brien 2002: 25–29) where the "central theme ... is inclusion" (Holburn 2002: 79). It is focused on the person with a disability rather than on the needs of a program or service (Lord and Hutchison 2007; Ritchie 2002). Person-centred planning is infused within Positive Behaviour Supports (Carr et al. 2002; Eber et al. 2009; Kincaid 2006), within customized employment approaches (Callahan and Condon 2007; Griffin, Hammis and Geary 2007; Inge, Targett and Armstrong 2007; McLean 2002; O'Bryan 2002), and is important in fostering relationships in the community (O'Brien and Mount 2007; Wetherow and Wetherow 2002). Person-centred planning is guided by values that require a person with an intellectual disability to be involved in the planning process, to be given choices and to be encouraged toward self-determination (Lord and Hutchison 2007; O'Brien and O'Brien 2002; Ritchie 2002). The focus is on a person's strengths and gifts rather than on his or her perceived deficits (Cooperrider, Whitney, and Stavros 2008; DiLeo 2007; Murphy and Rogan 1995).

Person-centred planning should give rise to "five essential outcomes." These include being a part of the community, having quality relationships, having choices and preferences honoured, living with dignity, fulfilling respected roles, and "continuing to develop personal competencies" (Kincaid 2006: 440–441). The process of planning can involve using a graphic illustration approach that is not unlike a systemic strategic plan for a person, called a PATH (Wetherow and Wetherow 2002: 63–64). A person-centred planning process is important for people with disabilities because seeking inclusion in the community requires intentionality, and just the act of planning alone provides a glimpse into the future that families move towards naturally (Cooperrider, Whitney and Stavros 2008; Turnbull and Turnbull 2006).

Families Need to Know

It is important to connect families with other families in similar situations (Dunlap and Fox 2006; Lord and Hutchinson 2007). The Family Support Institute of British Columbia is one such example of an organization that provides parent-to-parent counselling and support. Other sources of help are support groups, extended family, and faith-based activities. Families say that one of their greatest needs was for timely information to help guide the path of decisions (Harvey 2002: 23).

> I became a single parent when Angela was ten. We then shared our three children for two weeks on, two weeks off. Very quickly, the demands of single parenting were significant and sometimes overwhelming due to behavioural issues with my daughter. As a result of the behaviour and the demands that arise, even to this day, I often feel that I shortchange my other children by giving more attention to Angela.
>
> Shortly after the breakup of my first marriage, I joined a parent group supported by the Burnaby Association for Community Inclusion. Through that group, I have made many good lifelong friends who are also parents who have children with disabilities. Although we come from diverse backgrounds and have different experiences with our children, we understand each other and the effort that is required. Through this group of friends, I learned a great deal from people who had walked before me.
>
> I also met my second wife in that parent support group. In the ten years that I was a single parent I had several relationships that did not last. When I met Sharon she understood the commitment, as did I — we blended our families and, suddenly, we each had two children with disabilities. In our twelve years together, we have become a strong and resilient family.

What is also important to a child with a disability is whether or not the parents or the family culture perceive the glass as half empty or as half full. In other words, do parents think with a deficit-based viewpoint or do they see the strengths and abilities of their child? A strength-based perspective is of importance to individuals with disabilities because the best chance of success is working from people's strengths. Shifting to a positive view will enhance the perspective and in turn better equip families to deal with the vicissitudes of life (Lord and Hutchison 2007: 136–139). There are many aspects that influence a family's perspectives in this regard, thus it is important for human service professionals to listen closely to develop an understanding of the particular aspects such as family and individual capacity, health, and cultural distinctions.

In terms of what families need to know, it is also important for families to provide opportunities for their children to learn about social interactions (Dunlap and

Fox 2006: 38–41). When providing opportunities for socialization, teach in natural contexts, rather than in artificial contexts, with the aim being that the learning will generalize to other contexts (Risley 2006: 428). Wherever possible, parents should have expectations for their children with respect to being employed in the future and make the expectations known to their children. Ensure that children have some responsibility for chores around the house. Early expectations for fulfilling chores are important because it builds momentum that over years increase the chances of paid employment. It is also important to promote self-determination with children and encourage them to make decisions about choices, goal setting and solving problems (Targett and Wehman 2013; Wehmeyer, Gragoudas and Shogren 2006).

Another important point for some families is learning to deal with problem behaviour. Positive Behaviour Supports (PBS) are "about using our understanding of human behavioral science to organize supports that result in more productive, preferred, and healthy lives" (Dunlap et al. 2009: 4). PBS are important to fostering inclusion, because "widespread inclusionary practices … are unlikely to occur unless positive behavioral supports" (Sailor 2006: 164) become commonplace in our communities. People with intellectual disabilities who struggle with social skills or have problem behaviour may encounter barriers to forming relationships, working, and belonging in the community (Dunlap and Fox 2009; Dunlap, Sailor, Horner, and Sugai 2009). Problem behaviour such as screaming, hitting out, self-injury or any other behaviour that does not conform to social norms in the community is concerning for people with intellectual disabilities, because it has been "observed that social connectedness is the essential feature of being human" (Dunlap 2006: 373).

Working with Families

In the past, the rule was that professionals acted as experts (Singer and Wang 2009; Turnbull et al. 2011). An alternative approach is for professionals to involve families in decision making, identify their strengths and work with them in a collaborative way. To create a trusting relationship with families, professionals should be nonjudgmental, honest, positive, flexible and accessible (Singer and Wang 2009: 40–41).

> I remember when Angela's behaviour was considerable and I had been assigned a social worker who had previously been a protection worker. In my view, her previous protection experience influenced her view of our family. We had a meeting at my house and I was asking for more support to help deal with Angela's behaviour and she said that there were no funds and that "maybe my house didn't have to be so clean?" I was offended by her suggestion that I was somehow not supporting my daughter and that the trade-off was a

clean house. Besides, who would not clean their house before a social worker arrives? After that negative experience, the presence of a social worker in my home caused added stress.

Chapter Summary

This chapter on the journey and experience of families who have children with disabilities canvasses the life cycle of families from birth to death, comments on how families cope and support their children, and the ongoing *dreams* they have for their children. Moreover, the chapter describes how families are affected by stigma, and how having a child with a disability may affect the quality of life of the family with respect to the demands of caregiving. Further, the chapter describes the impact of having a family member with a disability on mothers, fathers, siblings and extended family members. The chapter also outlines the impact on the family related to the severity of the child's disability, financial stressors, perspectives about their child's disability, lack of funding and services, and the approximately thirteen-year experience with the school system. Finally, the chapter described important aspects that families might need to know from their professional supports and the importance of how professionals work with families.

It is important to acknowledge that much of the chapter emphasizes the challenging experiences of families. Families do have difficulties, greater stress and face stigma in the community; however, this is not the whole story. Families are strong, resilient and they love their children, with or without disabilities. There is a burgeoning *new story* of a good and inclusive side of the community (Lord and Hutchison 2007). Indeed, I have seen the community be more inclusive, and people can be very respectful, understanding and welcoming. There are many leaders, advocates and authors who believe that inclusion for people with disabilities requires a strengths and an asset-based perspective of the community. They believe that people in the community have the capacity to respond positively to people with disabilities and their families. In their considerable experiences, people and communities step forward if they are extended an invitation to help (Etmanski 2000; Hutchison, Lord and Lord 2010; Lord, Leavitt and Dingwall 2012; McKnight and Block 2010; Wetherow and Wetherow 2002).

In terms of what professionals can do to help families, it is imperative that they keep in mind the capacity of the family; adjust interventions to be congruent with the coping skills and stage of the family life cycle; look to influence patterns and interactions that may not be serving families and children with disabilities, and highlight their strengths; connect families with others so they are supported; help families to find resources and information; assist them in addressing aspects of stigma and discrimination; and respect where the family is at in their process of acceptance or grief at various stages and milestones, and ask them how you can support them best.

Often the first goals for families involves quality of life, health, safety and happiness for their loved one, with employment and relationship goals as the next steps. In my experience, happiness, health and safety are preconditions for moving on to the elusive, but possible, next stage of inclusion and belonging. Adequate funding and support are a must for families to remain resilient; therefore, often advocacy is required. In British Columbia and many other Canadian provinces, we have seen the power of families to move people from institutions to community, to advance inclusion in our schools, in our workplaces and in our communities. As a result of the work of others and what we have learned, I have seen our family go through the transition towards bigger dreams for our children. Our higher expectations of Angela and Trevor have resulted in more inclusive lives; they are engaged in paid work and they have plans for their lives that have surfaced through person-centred planning processes.

I now know that as parents, we need to raise expectations, work from our strengths, learn from best practices and involve others in a collaborative process. We also need to let go sometimes. We need to have trust in our children, the people that work with them, and the communities and organizations that support them. At the same time, we must hold all of the systems accountable and aim toward continuous quality improvement measured by the actual quality of life of our children. Finally, I know that our family has had lots of help along the way from professionals such as social workers, and they have made a profound difference in supporting our family, but only when they have worked as partners rather than as experts.

Discussion Questions

1. How do we understand the role of family members given the diversity of family composition?
2. How can we support families throughout the lifespan and plan for the transitions?
3. How can we assess the strengths of a family in order to ensure a contextually appropriate intervention?
4. How can we connect families to others to provide support, learning and advocacy?
5. How can we advocate for systemic changes in society that will better support families?

References

Adams, Ben. 1995. "Our Brave New World." In Donald J. Meyer (ed.), *Uncommon Fathers: Reflections on Raising a Child with a Disability*. Bethesda, MD: Woodbine House Inc.

Addison, Anne. 2003. *One Small Starfish: A Mother's Everyday Advice, Survival Tactics & Wisdom for Raising a Special Needs Child*. Arlington, TX: Future Horizons.

Avruch, Kevin. 2006. *Culture and Conflict Resolution*. Washington, DC: United States Institute of Peace.

Batshaw, Mark L. 1991. *Your Child Has a Disability: A Complete Sourcebook of Daily and Medical Care*. Baltimore, MD: Paul H. Brookes Publishing Co.

Becvar, Dorothy Stroh, and Raphael Becvar. 1999. *Systems Theory and Family Therapy: A Primer*. MD: University Press of America.

Bertalanffy, Ludwig von. 1969. *General Systems Theory: Foundations, Development, Applications*. New York: George Braziller.

Binnendyk, Lauren, Brenda Fossett, Christy Cheremshyski, Sharon Lohrman, Lauren Elkinson and Lynn Miller. 2009. "Toward an Ecological Unit of Analysis in Behavioral Assessment and Intervention with Families of Children with Developmental Disabilities." In Wayne Sailor, Glen Dunlap, George Sugai, and Rob Horner (eds.), *Handbook of Positive Behavior Support*. New York: Springer Science and Business Media.

Block, Peter. 2009. *Community: The Structure of Belonging*. San Francisco: Berrett-Koehler.

Brown, Ian. 2009. *The Boy in the Moon: A Father's Search for His Disabled Son*. Toronto: Random House.

Callahan, Michael, and Ellen Condon. 2007. "Discovery: The Foundation of Job Development." In Cary Griffin, David Hammis, and Tamara Geary, *The Job Developer's Handbook: Practical Tactics for Customized Employment*. Baltimore, MD: Paul H. Brookes.

Carr, Edward G., Glen Dunlap, Rob Horner, Robert L. Koegel, Ann P. Turnbull, Wayne Sailor, et al. 2002. "Positive Behavior Support: Evolution of an Applied Science." *Journal of Positive Behavior Interventions* 4.

Clancy, A. 2013. Personal communication, June 25.

Cooperrider, David L., and Diana Whitney. 2005. *Appreciative Inquiry: A Positive Revolution in Change*. San Francisco: Berrett-Koehler.

Cooperrider, David L., Diana Whitney and Jacqueline M. Stavros. 2008. *Appreciative Inquiry Handbook: For Leaders of Change*. San Francisco: Berrett-Koehler.

Dale, Bob. 1995. "Creating Answers." In Donald J. Meyer (eds.), *Uncommon Fathers: Reflections on Raising a Child with a Disability*. Bethesda, MD: Woodbine House Inc.

DiLeo, Dale. 2007. *Raymond's Room: Ending the Segregation of People with Disabilities*. St. Augustine, FL: Training Resource Network.

Dossa, Parin. 2009. "Disability, Marginality, and the Nation-State — Negotiating Social Markers of Difference: Fahimeh's Story." In Tanya Titchkosky and Rod Michalko (eds.), *Rethinking Normalcy: A Disabilities Studies Reader*. Toronto: Canadian Scholars' Press Inc.

Dunlap, Glen. 2006. "Discussion: Social Inclusion." In Lynn Kern Koegal, Robert L. Koegal, and Glen Dunlap (eds.), *Positive Behavioral Support: Including People with Difficult Behavior in the Community*. Baltimore; MD: Paul H. Brookes.

Dunlap, Glen, and Lise Fox. 2006. "Early Intervention and Serious Problem Behaviors." In Lynn Kern Koegal, Robert L. Koegal, and Glen Dunlap (eds.), *Positive Behavioral Support: Including People with Difficult Behavior in the Community*. Baltimore; MD: Paul H. Brookes.

____. 2009. "Positive Behavior Support and Early Intervention." In Wayne Sailor, Glen Dunlap, George Sugai and Rob Horner (eds.), *Handbook of Positive Behavior Support*. New York: Springer Science and Business Media.

Dunlap, Glen, Wayne Sailor, Rob Horner and George Sugai. 2009. "Overview and History of Positive Behavior Support." In Wayne Sailor, Glen Dunlap, George Sugai and Rob Horner (eds.), *Handbook of Positive Behavior Support*. New York: Springer Science and Business Media.

Durand, V. Mark, Meme Heineman, Shelley Clarke and Melissa Zona. 2009. "Optimistic Parenting." In Wayne Sailor, Glen Dunlap, George Sugai and Rob Horner (eds.), *Handbook of Positive Behavior Support*. New York: Springer Science and Business Media.

Eber, Lucille, Kelly Hyde, Jennifer Rose, Kimberli Breen, Diane McDonald and Holly Lewandowksi. 2009. "Completing the Continuum of Schoolwide Positive Behavior Support: Wraparound as a Tertiary-Level Intervention." In Wayne Sailor, Glen Dunlap, George Sugai, and Rob Horner (eds.), *Handbook of Positive Behavior Support*. New York: Springer Science and Business Media.

Etmanski, Al. 2000. *A Good Life: For You and Your Relative with a Disability*. Vancouver, BC: Planned Lifetime Advocacy Network.

Fletcher, Thandi. 2013. "The Photo that Broke a Mother's Heart." *The Province Online*. June 13. <theprovince.com/news/photo+that+broke+mother+heart/8523150/story.html>.

Garland-Thomson, Rosemary. 2009. "Disability, Identity and Representation: An Introduction." In Tanya Titchkosky and Rod Michalko (eds.), *Rethinking Normalcy: A Disabilities Studies Reader*. Toronto: Canadian Scholars' Press Inc.

Global News. 2014. "Mother-Son Murder-Suicide Highlights Lack of Autism Funding in Canada." April 25. <globalnews.ca/news/1292113/mother-son-murder-suicide-highlights-lack-of-autism-funding-in-canada/>.

Griffin, Cary, David Hammis and Tamara Geary. 2007. *The Job Developer's Handbook: Practical Tactics for Customized Employment*. Baltimore, MD: Paul H. Brookes.

Gronenburg, Jennifer Graf. 2008. *Road Map to Holland: How I Found My Way Through My Son's First Two Years with Down Syndrome*. New York: New American Library.

Harvey, Louise. 2002. "Children with Disabilities and Their Families in Canada: A Discussion Paper." Commissioned by the National Children's Alliance for the First National Roundtable on Children with Disabilities.

Holburn, Steve. 2002. "The Value of Measuring Person-Centered Planning." In Connie Lynn O'Brien and John O'Brien (eds.), *Implementing Person-Centered Planning: Voices of Experience*. Toronto, ON: Inclusion Press.

Hutchinson, Peggy, John Lord and Karen Lord. 2010. *Friends and Inclusion: Five Approaches to Building Relationships*. Toronto: Inclusion Press.

Inclusion BC. 2014. "Stop Hurting Kids: Restraint and Seclusion in BC Schools." <inclusionbc.org/stophurtingkids>.

Inge, Katherine, Pamela Sherron Targett and Amy Armstrong. 2007. "Person-Centered

Planning: Facilitating Inclusive Employment Outcomes." In Paul Wehman, Katherine Inge, W. Grant Revell, and Valerie Brooke (eds.), *Real Work for Real Pay: Inclusive Employment for People with Disabilities*. Baltimore, MD: Paul H. Brookes.

Kappes, Nicholas. 1995 "Matrix." In Donald J. Meyer (ed.), *Uncommon Fathers: Reflections on Raising a Child with a Disability*. Bethesda, MD: Woodbine House.

Kincaid, Don. 2006. "Person-Centered Planning." In Lynn Kern Koegal, Robert L. Koegal, and Glen Dunlap (eds.), *Positive Behavioral Support: Including People with Difficult Behavior in the Community*. Baltimore, MD: Paul H. Brookes.

Lord, John, and Peggy Hutchison. 2007. *Pathways to Inclusion: Building a New Story with People and Communities*. Concord, ON: Captus Press.

Lord, John, Barbara Leavitt and Charlotte Dingwall. 2012. *Facilitating an Everyday Life: Independent Facilitation and What Really Matters in a New Story*. Toronto: Inclusion Press.

McKnight, John. 1995. *The Careless Society: Community and its Counterfeits*. New York: Basic Books.

McKnight, John, and Peter Block. 2010. *The Abundant Community: Awakening the Power of Families and Neighorhoods*. San Francisco, CA: Berrett-Koehler Publishers, Inc.

McLean, Debra. 2002. "A Simple Half-hitch." In Connie Lyle O'Brien and John O'Brien (eds.), *Implementing Person-Centered Planning: Voices of Experience*. Toronto, ON: Inclusion Press.

Meyer, Donald J. 1995. *Uncommon Fathers: Reflections on Raising a Child with a Disability*. Bethesda, MD: Woodbine House Inc.

Murphy, Stephen T., and Patricia M Rogan. 1995. *Closing the Shop: Conversion from Sheltered to Integrated Work*. Baltimore, MD: Paul H. Brookes.

Naseef, Robert A. 1997. *Special Children, Challenged Parents: The Struggles and Rewards of Raising a Child with a Disability*. Toronto: Carol Publishing Group.

O'Brien, Connie Lyle and John O'Brien (eds.). 2002. *Implementing Person-Centered Planning: Voices of Experience*. Toronto, ON: Inclusion Press.

O'Brien, John, and Beth Mount. 2007. *Make a Difference: A Guidebook for Person-Centered Direct Support*. Toronto, ON: Inclusion Press.

O'Bryan, Anne. 2002. "Vocational Profiles." In Connie Lyle O'Brien and John O'Brien (eds.), *Implementing Person-Centered Planning: Voices of Experience*. Toronto, ON: Inclusion Press.

Oliver, Michael. 2009. "The Social Model in Context." In Tanya Titchkosky and Rod Michalko (eds.), *Rethinking Normalcy: A Disabilities Studies Reader*. Toronto: Canadian Scholars' Press Inc.

Pietropaolo, Vincenzo. 2010. *Invisible No More: A Photographic Chronicle of the Lives of People with Intellectual Disabilities*. Piscataway, NJ: Rutgers University Press.

Prince, Michael J. 2009. *Absent Citizens: Disability Politics and Policy in Canada*. Toronto, ON: University of Toronto Press.

Prince Rupert Northern View e Edition. 2014. "Social Services for Families with Autistic Children Called into Question Following Murder-Suicide Involving Mother and Son." April 16. <thenorthernview.com/news/255411211.html>.

Risley, Todd. 2006. "Get a Life! Positive Behavioral Intervention for Challenging Behavior through Life Arrangement and Life Coaching." In Lynn Kern Koegal, Robert L. Koegal, and Glen Dunlap (eds.), *Positive Behavioral Support: Including People with Difficult*

Behavior in the Community. Baltimore; MD: Paul H. Brookes.

Ritchie, Pete. 2002. "A Turn for the Better." In Connie Lyle O'Brien and John O'Brien (eds.), *Implementing Person-Centered Planning: Voices of Experience.* Toronto, ON: Inclusion Press.

Roeher Institute. 1996. *Disability Community and Society: Exploring the Links.* North York, ON: Author.

Sailor, Wayne. 2006. "New Structures and Systems Change for Comprehensive Positive Behavioral Support." In Lynn Kern Koegal, Robert L. Koegal, and Glen Dunlap (eds.), *Positive Behavioral Support: Including People with Difficult Behavior in the Community.* Baltimore, MD: Paul H. Brookes.

Seligman, Milton, and Rosalyn Benjamin Darling. 2007. *Ordinary Families, Special Children: A Systems Approach to Childhood Disability.* New York: Guildford Press

Senge, Peter. 2006. *The Fifth Discipline: The Art and Practice of the Learning Organization* rev. edition. New York: Doubleday.

Shapell, Irvin. 1995. "The Bike." In Donald J. Meyer (ed.), *Uncommon Fathers: Reflections on Raising a Child with a Disability.* Bethesda, MD: Woodbine House Inc.

Singer, George H., and Mian Wang. 2009. "The Intellectual Roots of Positive Behavior Support and Their Implications for its Development." In Wayne Sailor, Glen Dunlap, George Sugai and Rob Horner (eds.), *Handbook of Positive Behavior Support.* New York: Springer Science and Business Media.

Spence-Cochran, Kim, Cynthia E. Pearl and Zachary Walker. 2013. "Full Inclusion into Schools: Strategies for Collaborative Instruction." In Paul Wehman (eds.), *Life Beyond the Classroom: Transition Strategies for Young People with Disabilities.* Baltimore, MD: Paul H. Brookes Publishing Co.

Statistics Canada. 2008. *Participation and Activity Limitation Survey 2006: Families of Children with Disabilities in Canada.* Ottawa, Ontario: Social and Aboriginal Statistics Division.

Targett, Pamela, and Paul Wehman. 2013. "Families and Young People with Disabilities: Listening to Their Voices." In Paul Wehman (ed.), *Life Beyond the Classroom: Transition Strategies for Young People with Disabilities.* Baltimore, MD: Paul H. Brookes Publishing.

Thomson, Donna. 2010. *The Four Walls of My Freedom.* Toronto: McArthur & Company.

Turnbull, Ann P. 1985. "From Professional to Parent: A Startling Experience." In H. Rutherford Turnbull and Ann P. Turnbull (eds.), *Parents Speak Out: Then and Now.* Columbus, OH: Charles E. Merrill.

Turnbull, Ann P., and H. Rutherford Turnbull. 2006. "Group Action Planning as a Strategy for Providing Comprehensive Family Support." In Lynn Kern Koegal, Robert L. Koegal and Glen Dunlap (eds.), *Positive Behavioral Support: Including People with Difficult Behavior in the Community.* Baltimore, MD: Paul H. Brookes.

Turnbull, Ann P., H. Rutherford Turnbull, Elizabeth J. Erwin, Leslie C. Soodak and Karrie A. Shogren. 2011. *Families, Professionals, and Exceptionality: Positive Outcomes Through Partnerships and Trust.* New Jersey: Person Education Inc.

Turpel-Lafond, Mary Ellen. 2013. "When Talk Trumped Service: A Decade of Lost Opportunity for Aboriginal Children and Youth in B.C." Special Report from the Representative for Children and Youth.

Wehmeyer, Michael L., Stelios Gragoudas and Karrie A. Shogren. 2006. "Self-Determination, Student Involvement, and Leadership Development." In Paul Wehman (ed.), *Life Beyond the Classroom: Transition Strategies for Young People with Disabilities*. Baltimore, MD: Paul H. Brookes Publishing Co.

Wetherow, David, and Faye Wetherow. 2002. "Community-Building and Commitment-Building." In Connie Lyle O'Brien and John O'Brien (eds.), *Implementing Person-Centered Planning: Voices of Experience*. Toronto, ON: Inclusion Press.

Whitney, Diana, and Amanda Trosten-Bloom. 2003. *The Power of Appreciative Inquiry: A Practical Guide to Positive Change*. San Francisco: Berrett-Koehler.

Zimmermann, Susan. 1996. *Grief Dancers: A Journey into the Depths of the Soul*. Golden, CO: Nemo Press.

Chapter 8

Intersectionality
and Disability

Judy E. MacDonald

(Dis)Ability[1] is complex and multilayered, with diverse experiences of ableism. Understanding the conditions under which people with disabilities navigate their environments is an important element of social work practice, from the historical gaze of oppression to current-day barriers, through self-identification, to societal labelling. How one comes to disability is varied; through genetic makeup in intellectual disabilities like Down syndrome, to birthing complications, illness, or an accident, or through mental health struggles. Adding to this complexity is the severity of the disability and the person's degree of independence and subsequent level of care. Attendant care can also heighten the person's vulnerability to misuse and abuse (Barriga 2013; DAA 1996). Further, intersecting identities cross the person's experience, be it identities of race, class, gender, age or sexual orientation. Within this chapter, the complexities involved in disability formation will be exposed, beginning with a historical gaze into oppression, examples of current-day injustices, an exploration into the social construction of identity and finally, the role of intersectionality, as illustrated through gender, race and sexual orientation.

Oppression

"I find it tiring to always have to explain my realities" (Myers, MacDonald, Jacquard and Macneil 2014: 76), recalls a student with a disability, who is an electric wheelchair user within postsecondary education. Hughes (2012: 68) suggests "disability is a life lived before a looking glass that is cracked and distorted by the vandalism of normality." People with disabilities have been misunderstood, ignored, patholo-gized and abused in the guise of maintaining a preconceived notion of normalcy (MacDonald 2008; Titchkosky and Michalko 2009; Withers 2012). Historically, people with disabilities have been hidden away from society in institutions, family attics, garages and backyard makeshift jails (MacDonald and Friars 2009). Hitler's T4 eugenics program during World War II saw the execution of 250,000 to 500,000 persons with disabilities because they were considered genetically faulty specimens of the human race (Chadwick 2003). The program was referenced as "'life unworthy of life" (Binding and Hoche 2012; Chadwick 2003; Morris 1989). As depicted earlier in the text by Dunn and Langdon in Chapter 2 and Murphy in Chapter 5, scientific debates on forced sterilization and eugenics were taking place in both the United States and Canada as early as the 1920s as a means to eliminate "mental defects" and physical abnormalities (Chadwick 2003; Morris 1989).

In North America, forced sterilization was performed on people with devel-opmental and mental health disabilities until the mid-1970s (Begos 2002; Wight-Felske 2003). "They were wives and daughters. Sisters. Unwed mothers. Children ... Some were blind or mentally retarded [sic]. Toward the end they were mostly black and poor" (Begos 2002). This illustrates the intersection of ability, gender, race and class.

Modern-day eugenics are exhibited through more subtle practices, such as patients with disabilities being denied the right to have their names put on trans-plant lists (MacDonald and Friars 2009). MacDonald and Friars (2009) write about a hospital referral for a 17-year-old woman with an intellectual disability diagnosed with congestive heart failure who required a lung-heart transplant. The transplant team assessment classified her as a high risk, believing that neither she nor her family had the intellectual or financial means to handle the post-operative protocols critical to transplant success. Karla, single mother to 7-year-old Anthony who requires 24-hour care due to multiple disabilities, also speaks about her experi-ence with the children's hospital.

> They've asked me many times what kind of treatment did I want, even for things like pneumonia. So basically ... I could choose to let him die, no questions asked ... The next time he got sick he'd pass away and it would be that simple. (Beagan, Stadnyk, Loppie, MacDonald, Hamilton-Hinch and MacDonald 2005: 45)

Karla had to fight with the hospital to have a "Please Resuscitate" note put on her son's chart. Passive euthanasia is another form of modern-day eugenics.

Within Canada, the lived experiences of Betty Anne Gagnon and her subse-quent death on November 20, 2009, is a clear example of how human degradation of a person with a disability morphs from historical practices into present-day oppression ("Justice for Betty Anne Gagnon" n.d.). Reported within the *Edmonton Journal* (2013), "Gagnon was locked up in various 'jail cells' on the Scrivens' rural property, including the garage, basement, a chain-link fence enclosure for dogs and a derelict school bus without water or heat." Betty Anne was a woman with a disability caused from oxygen deprivation at birth. She needed assistance with daily functions, such as cooking and financial matters, in order to live as independently as possible. Before moving in with her sister and brother-in-law, she lived for eighteen years with two women as supportive roommates, who considered her part of their family. Through social action, these women ran the Justice for Betty Anne campaign and put pressure on the government to critically examine what went wrong in this situation, so that no other person with a disability will have to endure the abuse Betty Anne suffered.

> At the time of her death, the five-foot two inch mentally disabled woman weighed only 65 pounds. She had bruises on her body, two black eyes and blood in her nose ... she had a fecal stone in her intestine and feces in her ears. (Warnica 2013)

Her sister and brother-in-law were originally charged with manslaughter, assault, criminal negligence causing death, and conspiracy to commit extortion, yet through a plea bargain the couple pleaded guilty to a significantly lesser charge of failure to provide the necessities of life. On October 31, 2013, Denise Scriven and Michael Scriven were sentenced to twenty months incarceration ("Justice for Betty Anne" n.d.). Horrific abuse and mistreatment, along with grievous system failures, describe the essence of this case.

People living on the margins are constantly being measured up against the defined norms of society; white is the norm for skin colour, able-bodied for ability, and heterosexual relations for sexual expression (Wilmot 2005). Anyone venturing outside the defined lines of normalcy is viewed as different. Difference has been equated with "othering"; if you walk differently, learn differently, experience the world from a different physical, mental or cognitive location, then you are regarded as "other." People with disabilities have fought hard to have their voices heard and to be recognized as an identified group within society (Enns and Neufeldt 2003; Stienstra and Wight-Felske 2003). Coming out from behind the walls of family homes, the brick and mortar of institutions, and societal discourses that place them as "other" has challenged society to become more accessible and inclusive. Legislation such as the *Charter of Rights and Freedoms* in Canada prevent discrimination against people with disabilities, as the United Nations Convention on the Rights of Persons with Disabilities brings global recognition to the barriers faced by those with disabilities. Yet, people with disabilities continue to experience oppression in overt and covert ways. Social workers need to understand those experiences of oppression and work with people with disabilities as allies (Bishop 1994) by challenging the socially imposed category of "other." Social workers need to be able to identify the intersecting layers of oppression; and how stereotypes of ability, class, gender and race can impact upon one's experiences.

For example, Leilani Muir was born into poverty — class. She was not allowed to eat at the family table with her brothers and was later discarded by her mother because she was a girl — gender (Wahlsten 1997). She was wrongfully labelled as a "moron" upon admission to the Alberta Provincial Training School — ability (Wahlsten 1997). All of these factors ultimately lead to her involuntary sterilization, which was a grievous violation of her rights. Involuntary sexual sterilization was targeted toward the most vulnerable, as "single mothers, First Nations and Métis people, eastern European, and poor people were disproportionately represented amongst those subjected to eugenics ideas" (Wilson and Lang 2010).

Identity

"My body may be disabled, but I am not! Whatever it is that makes me a human being, special to myself, there is nothing disabled … about it!" (Matthews 1983). Identity is fluid, it is not a stagnant, fixed entity (James and Shadd 2001). Galarneau and Radulescu's (2009) research found that disability was not a constant; over a six-year period, only 13 percent of the participants experienced disability in each of the six years. Disabilities can fluctuate in a number of ways; severity of symptoms can change. For example, someone living with chronic pain can have one day defined as a three on the pain scale — zero being no pain, whereas ten is the worst pain ever experienced — and the next day they experience an eight. The environment can impact one's disability as well, as in the case of an asthma sufferer being exposed to cigarette smoke. Finally, circumstances can impact disability. For example, someone with a hearing disability may frequently experience their hearing aid batteries losing power very suddenly or there will be a distracting beeping noise to signal when the power is low (Vick 2012).

How one comes and when one comes to disability varies. As a person with a disability, I might identify as being disabled in one context, and yet in another context I might choose to identify as a woman, a parent or a scholar. Within each of us, there are multiple elements that define who we are and what we stand for. Many people who live with impairments politically and purposely choose not to identify as being disabled. Some people within the Deaf culture outwardly reject the disability label for its normative positioning, claiming their linguistic minority status (Scully 2012). Beresford (2000: 169) shares that "many psychiatric system survivors are unwilling to see themselves as disabled. They associate disability with the medicalization of their distress and experience. They reject the biological and genetic explanation of their distress imposed by medical experts." Disability is an identity that has been denied voice and subsequently silenced: an identity that has witnessed much abuse and oppression. According to Scully (2012: 110), "the common feature of a disability identity is not the nature or extent of the impairment, but the political experience of oppression." Some people living with disabilities reclaim their power through identifying with the disability rights movement in a shared sense of common experience, while others gain strength through outwardly resisting the movement (Watson 2002).

Coming to this identity is not an easy process; people get harassed, and even bullied, they get cast into the category of "other" where they are forgotten, pushed aside, and denied participation, or they are pitied and treated like children. Knowing that these experiences await, it is understandable that claiming to be disabled is a difficult process. Some don't have the option of "hiding" their disability, as their physical or behavioural presentation immediately sanctions them to the category of "other." Coming to identity is often a process in itself, involving levels of social and political awareness. Socially constructed notions of disability restrict one's own understanding of ability. If you are not a wheelchair user or exhibit obvious physical impairments then you cannot possibly be perceived as disabled. Vick (2012) challenges the Canadian government to think beyond these narrow limiting definitions of disability as they restrict access to disability benefits for people who come to disability in a fluid, ever-changing manner. An attempt to secure disability benefits, be it through insurance or government pensions, notoriously meets with prejudice and barriers.

MacDonald's (2006) narratives of women in the helping professions living with chronic pain and working with pain sufferers reveals the story of a client carrying their dying child into the children's hospital while being filmed by the insurance company. That film was then used by the insurance company to deny the mother's disability benefits claim; the company stated that if the mother was able to carry their child into the hospital then they were not disabled enough to be off work. Threats to take the story to the front pages of the local newspaper had to be made before the insurance company would agree to support the claim. People with disabilities have been treated as liars and cheats, they have been filmed within the privacy of their own homes, and followed around in the community; these are all attempts to "catch" them doing an activity that is deemed to be "normal" so that the insurance company can deny their benefit claims (Kagan and Cain 2005; MacDonald 2006).

Living with a disability does not mean you stop living, it means that you struggle with societal barriers, face the prejudices and biases of the ill-informed, and push for a more inclusive and accessible society. Being disabled does not mean that I always experience my body or mind in one particular way. For example, in living with chronic pain, one day I might be able to garden for thirty minutes, but the next day I might not be able to garden at all. Being held to an embodied experience captured in a moment is not the definition of being disabled. Living with a disability in any particular moment depends on a variety of factors, the embodied experience, the social and environmental supports at one's disposal, financial means, degree of community accessibility, and attitudinal reflections within society. Living with a disability is not solely an individual experience, it is a personal experience within a societal context (Oliver 1990, 1996).

People with disabilities have experienced multiple forms of oppression historically and within present day. "Ableism needs to be acknowledged as part of the anti-oppressive discourse" (Carter, Hanes and MacDonald 2012: 127) so that social workers understand the multiple and layered experiences of oppression witnessed by people with disabilities. As social workers we need to destabilize, take apart and challenge dominant ways of knowing disability. Through the process of coming to understand the different ways of knowing by those on the margins, we begin to redefine normalcy and "remake the centre's norms" (Titchkosky and Michalko 2009: 6).

In summary, identity is a complex concept, whereby an individual could identify as disabled in one incident and not in another. Identity is fluid, ever changing, influenced by social, political and economic variables. A person might identify as disabled to secure economic benefits, such as with Canada Revenue Agency to access the tax exemption, while at the same time not disclose to an employer for fear of being labelled or discriminated against. Self-identification is the best approach to understanding one's identity; a process of respecting the individual's own interpretation of identity. This process is often used in affirmative action admission policies within schools of social work.

Intersectionality

Intersecting experiences of race, class, gender or sexual orientation add yet another layer of oppression and marginalization to the experiences of people with disabilities (Baines 2011; Carniol 2010; Mullaly 2010). Marsiglia and Kulis (2009: 43–54) identify intersectionality as the interconnection of "different systems of inequality" and "the meeting point of multiple identities." According to Collins (1998), intersectionality is a matrix of domination where experiences of privilege or oppression can be encountered through the combination of identities. Intersectional theory respects both experiences of oppression and locations of privilege; those on the margins are called to examine their own internalized dominance (Pease 2010). As a woman with a disability, I would acknowledge my experiences of oppression, including my struggle for accommodations in a doctoral program; at the same time, I would challenge my own privilege, including my heterosexual position, by being cognizant of my heteronormative language. Mollow (2006: 284) claims "disability studies has been slow to theorize intersectionality, particularly when it comes to race." She further explains that when race and disability have been explored, it has been predominantly in a hierarchal manner where "like race" illustrations have been used to push for disability to be recognized. Bishop (1994) asserts that hierarchal ordering of oppression is kept alive through such intended competitions, where one marginalized group is pitted against another.

Mullaly (2010: 201) proposes the following formula to reveal the complexity of intersecting oppression: oppression = a + b + c + (ab) + (ac) + (bc) + (abc). If you were a woman with a disability living in poverty, you would have ability, gender and class as intersecting identities. Your experience of oppression could have emanated from ability + gender + class + (ability x gender) + (ability x class) + (gender x class) + (ability x gender x class).

Considering Betty Anne Gagnon and her intersecting oppressions, Betty's developmental disability, her female gender and her economic status of lower class were all mitigating factors in her lived experiences of oppression. Betty needed some assistance with living due to her developmental disability, which was caused by the lack of oxygen at birth (ability). Women throughout history have been marginalized, subject to abuse and denied access to equitable employment (Status of Women Canada 2013), and Betty Anne was female (gender). Betty Anne's economic status left her vulnerable to be taken advantage of by her sister and brother-in-law (class), as they took her money to pay for their drug habit ("Justice for Betty Anne" n.d.). Betty Anne being female heightens her risk of abuse, coupled with the intersection of ability and class putting her at even greater risk, as women with disabilities are both the poorest of the poor (HRSDC 2006) and are at greatest risk for physical and sexual violence (Nova Scotia Advisory Council on the Status of Women 2006; DAWN Canada 2010).

Within this chapter, intersecting experiences of disability oppression will be explored through the identities of gender, sexual orientation and race, recognizing that other identities could have been selected, such as age, class and religion. One of the reasons for selecting gender and race is due to their historical exclusion in progressive social work that was predominately class-based (Mullaly 2010), whereas sexual orientation is one of the more recent acknowledged areas of oppression. When exploring the intricacies of these oppressions, specific areas of commonality emerged: violence, poverty — emanating from class oppression — and embodiment — both in terms of disease pathology and treatment within the health system. Hence, these three areas will be addressed within each of the intersecting oppressions of gender, sexual orientation and race.

Gender and Disability

Women who live with disabilities have felt outside the women's movement (Dominelli 2002; Riessman 2003), be it through inaccessible events or by not having their needs addressed as legitimate concerns. Likewise, women with disabilities have experienced this same level of exclusion within the disability movement, as images of Rick Hansen, Christopher Reeve or Terry Fox craft the societal metaphors of disability (Ghai 2009). This is not intended to discredit the work and legacy of these men, but to push us to realize that disability encompasses many social locations of gender, class, race, sexual orientation and other aspects, and social workers need to acknowledge those differences. An image reflects on a 9-year-old girl climbing the steps of the U.S. Congress, crawling one step at a time, proclaiming that she will make it to the top if it takes her all night (Neudel 2011). Through determination and will, this young woman wanted to bring change to the experiences of people with disabilities. The experiences of women in a patriarchal world order, coupled with the marginalization of disability, creates double jeopardy, whereby they face discrimination on two intersecting planes.

Violence

Eighty-three percent of women with disabilities will be sexually assaulted at some point in their life (Nova Scotia Advisory Council on the Status of Women 2006), which is a difficult statistic to conceptualize. In other words, only 17 percent of women with disabilities will not experience sexual assault. The Office of the High Commissioner for Human Rights (United Nations 2012: 15) reported to the United Nations General Assembly that "violence experienced by women and girls with disabilities remains largely invisible." A key recommendation from the report acknowledged that services and programs for women and girls experiencing violence need to be accessible. On the other hand, the DisAbled Women's Network of Canada (DAWN Canada 2010) found that only one out of ten women with disabilities got the services and supports they needed when dealing with a shelter, specifically as it related to accessibility. Only 25 percent of the shelters had TDD/TTY (Text Telephone for the Deaf), 17 percent provided sign language interpretation services, while only 5 percent had Braille. Yet, 40 percent of married women with disabilities will be assaulted by their partners (Nova Scotia Department of Community Services 2002), indicating a critical need for accessible shelters. Further, women with developmental disabilities have at least a 20 percent greater risk of abuse, as do women from the Deaf community (DAWN Canada 2010). Social work has the opportunity to be leaders in this field, as a full, comprehensive strategy is needed to address violence against women with disabilities.

Internationally, the United Nations Committee on the Rights of Persons with Disabilities (United Nations 2013) suggest little is known about the actual numbers of women and girls with disabilities who have experienced violence, especially in developing countries. Under-reporting is believed to be linked to the lack of health services, accessible equipment — such as mobility aids and telecommunication devices — and support services, in addition to isolation experienced through rural geography and caregiver interference, and cultural assumptions pertaining to disability and woman abuse. The Disability Rights Fund, under the auspices of the UN Convention on the Rights of Persons with Disabilities, funds community projects promoting the rights of people with disabilities, including the focus on women with disabilities. Uganda, the first country to sign the convention in 2008, has had a number of successful projects reaching out to women and girls with disabilities, including the development of the Disabled Women's Network and Resource Organization. This network provides accessible housing, a forum for the voices of women with disabilities to be heard, group activity and employment strategies. One woman comments on the significance of communal space: "Talking with other disabled women ... can mean the opening up of a whole range of ways of accepting myself. The most empathetic person I can talk to about being a disabled woman is another disabled woman!" (Smith n.d.).

Poverty
Violence against women with disabilities can take the form of economic violence through unemployment, underemployment and poverty. DAWN (n.d.) reports the unemployment rate of women in Canada with disabilities is 74 percent, with developing countries being close to 100 percent. These high rates of unemployment indicate social exclusion and isolation for many women living with disabilities, yet Galarneau and Radulescu (2009) believe maintaining a solid connection to the workforce not only facilitates the acquisition of needed resources, but it also builds self-esteem and enables community linkages. Further, the longer a woman lived with a disability, the greater her risk for low income, as women living with a disability for six years were four times more likely to be in the low-income bracket than nondisabled women. Stereotypes about people with disabilities, coupled with the fear of accommodation costs, get in the way of employers hiring people with disabilities. WorkBC (2008) reported 90 percent of employees with disabilities rated "average or better" on their job performance evaluations when compared to their colleagues who were not disabled. And, "according to the Job Accommodation Network, employers can accommodate most adaptive needs for $500 or less — all the more reasonable when it's amortized over the duration of the employment" (WorkBC 2008: 19). Plus, people with disabilities stay in their jobs, as staff retention is 72 percent higher for these employees, thus saving the employer money in training, relocation costs, hiring and other costs. Yet, given these

statistics, DAWN Canada (n.d.) still reports "the most inescapable reality for women with disabilities is poverty."

Globally, less than 5 percent of girls living with disabilities have access to education (United Nations 2011). Within Canada, 12 percent of people with disabilities have a university or college degree, in comparison to more than double the population for nondisabled persons (Statistics Canada 2006). Women with disabilities have a slightly higher percentage of degree completion compared to men with disabilities, 13 to 10 percent, respectively. In the profession of social work, similar discrepancies exist. Dunn, Hanes, Hardie and MacDonald (2006: 9) in a survey of schools of social work in Canada found that only 5.5 percent of Bachelor of Social Work students identified as having a disability, and 4.1 percent of Master of Social Work students and 1.3 percent of Social Work PhD students identified as having a disability. Students with disabilities were more likely to be found in bachelor level social work programs, which leaves one to question if enough is being done to recruit and support students with disabilities in graduate programs. The literature focuses on students with disabilities transitioning from high school to college/university, completion rates for high school, college diplomas and bachelor level degrees, and employability (McCloy and DeClou 2013; Woods, Cook, DeClou, and McCloy 2013), instead of students with disabilities at the higher levels within postsecondary education. The Higher Education Quality Council of Ontario conducted a study in 2011 finding students with disabilities were only 6 to 7 percent of the student population on campuses across the country (Stienstra 2012), yet people with disabilities represent between 14 and 20 percent of provincial populations (Statistics Canada 2006). Lightman, Herd, Um and Mitchell (2009) identify linkages between post-secondary education completion, employability and living beyond poverty. For people with disabilities to have a chance of living outside of poverty, they need access to post-secondary education, accommodations to facilitate success, and linkages to employment post-degree completion (Dunn et al. 2006; Dunn, Hanes, Hardie, Leslie and MacDonald 2008). Social workers can advocate for access and accommodations for students with disabilities to help facilitate this engagement.

Embodiment

Women's bodies have been pathologized through the colonization and hierarchal positioning of patriarchy (Garland-Thomson 2006; Wendell 1996). Since the rise of the women's movement, women have championed the call to be understood as more than "boobs and tubes," pushing health care to experience women beyond female bodily parts and reproductive functioning (Boston Women's Health Collective 2011). For women with disabilities, issues of reproduction, including pregnancy and birthing, are often complicated. Physicians are often not versed in best practices, and women are left on their own to figure out what might work for them. For example, how is a woman with spinal complications going to give birth? How is a mom with one functioning arm going to hold a baby to breastfeed? In the National Film Board documentary *Toward Intimacy*, women with disabilities talk with each other about the barriers they face in wanting to conceive and parent a child (McGee and Hubert 1992). From the risks of passing their disabling genetic profile onto their perspective children, to the judgments cast on their ability to parent, a blunt and heartfelt conversation unfolds.

Weitz (2004) believes that society views women with disabilities as asexual, in that they are both incapable and not wanting to have sexual relations. Women with disabilities are in contraposition to the sexualized stereotypes laden upon women. Women's bodies have been made up, sexualized, coloured and painted, all under the parameters of a heterosexual gaze. The ideal is unattainable, as women can never be thin enough, or proportioned in all the right places. Subsequently, feminists have redefined and repositioned women's bodies as both receivers and producers of pleasure, where women's bodies are embraced and celebrated. However, coming into a relationship with one's own body can challenge women with disabilities, for disabled bodies are often the point of frustration and struggle (Garland-Thomson 2006; Wendell 1996). This is evident in the struggle of living with chronic pain, where the sufferer is in battle against oneself, and the body is the battle zone. One woman living with chronic pain wrote: "The pain invading my body had become all encompassing, capturing elements of my emotional and spiritual self ... I knew if I succumbed to the pain it would engulf me" (MacDonald 2004: 21). Feminism and disability studies together challenge the understandings of the hierarchal ordering of modern medicine, whereby medicine holds the distinct authority in becoming the legitimized source of knowledge. In chronic pain, Greenhalgh suggests:

> The medicalization of pain is detrimental to women, specifically because it places them within a masculine biomedical order in which the patient's knowledge of her body and life is silenced in discourses of objectification that make the doctor the expert on the patient's body. (2001: 320)

When the etiology of one's medical condition is unknown, the blame for the condition gets passed on to the sufferer; for example, chronic pain with no known causation becomes psychologized, and women are left to believe that the etiology of their pain is psychological, not physiological. Women's experiences and knowledge of their own bodies are pushed to the sidelines by medical expertise. Wendell (1996: 99) questions the current practices of displacing women's self-knowledge: "Psychosomatic illness was not being diagnosed on the basis of positive evidence of psychological problems; it was a *default* diagnosis for physical symptoms. Why do physicians burden their patients with self-doubt?" Women with disabilities need to be listened to and respected for their self-knowledge pertaining to their bodies, for it is only through collaborative engagement that social workers and health professionals will be able to work with women with disabilities in an anti-oppressive manner — in a manner that will not reinforce their experiences of oppression (MacDonald 2008).

Queerness and Disability

Queer people have been historically marginalized, discriminated against and oppressed (Hylton 2006; Kitts 2010). Brown, Richard and Wichman (2010) believe it is critical to unpack heterosexism and homophobia as a beginning point to develop an understanding of the lived experiences of queer persons. "Heterosexism is based on societal values and personal belief systems, which dictate that everyone is, or should be, heterosexual" (The McGill Equity Subcommittee on Queer People 2010 as cited in Carniol 2010: 31). Relationships constituting male/female dyads is the predominate assumption, with cultural standards and processes guided by this belief. Homophobia is discrimination, prejudice, hatred and even violence directed at those who identify as queer (Carniol 2010). Shapiro (2015: 55) defines homo-ableism as "a new lexical item into the dialogue of social prejudice … a set of attitudes and actions whose end result is the subjugation of gays and lesbians with disabilities by gays and lesbians without disabilities."

People with disabilities and those who identify as queer have a common history, as both have been pathologized by the medical establishment, discriminated against in education and employment, and denied voice and location in social and politi-cal realms (McRuer 2006; Wendell 1996). A queer person in a health crisis who has their same-sex partner denied access to their care by the health care system is an example of applied homophobia, whereby institutional policies are crafted on heterosexist assumptions (O'Toole 1996). Imagine having a health care crisis, or being in the dying process, and not having your loved one at your side for comfort. The HIV/AIDS epidemic, particularly in its early days, produced lived experiences of "patients" being treated as foreign contaminated objects, with nurses and other health professionals refusing to touch patients, and some even refusing to provide care. The isolation and rejection experienced by the "patient" was as detrimental as the disease itself. MacIntosh (2007) believes that HIV/AIDS is both stigmatized and demonized within Canada, and often results in acts of avoidance, hostility or even ostracism. Reaching out and physically touching a "patient" was the most effective and meaningful therapeutic intervention a social worker could offer, as that gesture of human kindness broke down the barriers crafted by homophobia and conveyed a message of compassion.

Isolation, not fitting in and being perceived as "other" has been experienced by queer people living with disabilities within the disability community. They have spoken about the isolation and rejection they have experienced within the disability movement.

> I have heard some pretty homophobic personal remarks by disability rights leaders, remarks which were not challenged. I do not particularly want to get involved with such groups, not because I am a separatist, but because I feel wounded by such comments. (Doucette 1990: 66)

Disability advocates and leaders need to challenge themselves and their organizations on their heterosexist assumptions and homophobic acts. Likewise, Shapiro (2015) challenges the queer community to conduct an ableist scan of their practices, such as holding a World Pride cultural event, in the city of Toronto, in a physically inaccessible venue. Both disability communities and queer communities need to examine their own biases and exclusive practices.

Violence

In 2011, hate crimes committed toward lesbian, gay, bisexual or transgender persons accounted for 18 percent of all hate crimes in Canada, and were the third leading motivation for such crimes (Statistics Canada 2011). Crimes related to sexual orientation and mental/physical disabilities were the only groups experiencing an increase from the previous year. According to Kitts (2010), queer adolescents attempted suicide at two times the rate of their heterosexual peers, and D'Augelli, Pilkington, and Hershberger (2002) found that one quarter (25 percent) of lesbians had contemplated suicide. Contributing risk factors included increased rates of depression, homelessness, substance abuse, dropping out of school, and familial and societal rejection. Doucette (1990: 64) writes: "Disabled lesbians are harassed because we are women, because we are disabled, and because we are lesbian."

Rothman, Exner and Baughman (2011) completed an extensive review of seventy-five studies that explored gay, lesbian, and/or bisexual prevalence of sexual assault where gay or bisexual men had experienced sexual assault at some point during their lifetime at a rate of 12 to 54 percent, whereas lesbian or bisexual women experienced sexual assault ranging from 16 to 85 percent. The median lifetime sexual assault for gay/bisexual men was 30 percent, with lesbian/bisexual women at 43 percent. The prevalence of sexual assault amongst the general population in the U.S. ranges from 2 to 3 percent for men, and 11 to 17 percent for women. Within Canada, prevalence of sexual assault amongst males is less than 1 percent, and for women it is 4.6 percent (Statistics Canada 2008). Due to different laws and interpretations of sexual assault, comparisons between countries have to be done with caution. In a study done involving Canada and the U.S., lesbian and bisexual girls reported the highest prevalence of sexual assault, ranging from 25 to 50 percent of the population, compared to heterosexual girls reporting between 10 and 25 percent. Heterosexual boys were well under 10 percent, while gay or bisexual boys were similar to lesbian and bisexual girls with close to 25 to 50 percent of the population reporting an experience of sexual assault (Saewyc, Skay, Pettingell, Reis, Bearinger, Resnick, Murphy and Combs 2006). The highest percentage of sexual assault for lesbian and bisexual women is 85 percent (Rothman et al. 2011), while the percentage of women with a disability who will experience sexual assault within their lifetime is 83 percent (Nova Scotia Advisory Council on the Status of Women 2006). Thus, women with disabilities, along with lesbian and bisexual women, are at a high risk for experiencing sexual assault.

Barrett and St. Pierre (2013: 1) conducted a study of lesbian, bisexual and gay individuals experiencing intimate partner violence (IPV) in Canada. They found that "individuals who were bisexual" (sexual orientation), "younger" (age), "currently single, less educated" (class), "and who experienced physical/mental limitations" (ability) "were more likely to experience IPV." Bisexual individuals experienced increased frequency of IPV as well as heightened severity of the abuse, as 28.8 percent experienced physical injuries, compared to 15.5 percent of gay or lesbian victims. A marked limitation of the study was that the gender of the perpetrator could not be ascertained.

Sexual orientation coupled with disability needs to be explored in more depth, with targeted research addressing the complexities of this intersectionality. Eli Clare writes about Larry, a junior high school youth who was shot dead by a classmate in 2008 while they were sitting in a grade eight classroom.

> Larry wasn't just a gay kid, a gender-exploring kid. He was also a kid of color living in the foster care system, a 15-year-old in eighth grade, dealing with a learning disability ... why was he first bullied: was it because he was disabled or because he was Latino or because he was gay or because he was poor and gender variant? We lose so much if we turn Larry's life and death into a story simply about homophobia. If we don't understand how ableism, racism, poverty, sexism, homophobia, and transphobia tangle together to motivate violence. (2009)

The oppression, abuse and subsequent trauma queer persons experience is linked to cultural heterosexism (Hyman 2008). Couple these experiences of trauma with additional intersecting oppressions, such as living with a disability (ability), being an elder (age), and/or an African Canadian (race), the traumatization becomes more complex and chances of victimization heighten exponentially. Social workers need to recognize violence in its variant forms and be able to assess the impact of trauma associated with living on the margins.

Poverty

Billies, Johnson, Murungi and Pugh (2009: 377) found the intersection of class and sexual identity are not well researched, as "low-income LGBTGNC (lesbian, gay, bisexual, trans, gender nonconforming) adults are mostly invisible." The work that has been done is primarily associated with low-income queer youth and their high risk for suicide, substance abuse and sexually transmitted infections. Suicide attempts in LGBT youth range from 20 to 53 percent (Mustanski and Liu 2013), with no attention to class distinctions. McDermott (2011: 75), when exploring the connection between British LGBT youths' educational projection and their social class, found that middle-class LGBT youth had resources and supports, and a strong enough "self-assured relation to the world," and that their sexual or gender identity did not derail their educational pursuits, in contrast with working-class LGBT youth.

The intersection of adult queer persons and class predominately remain at a theoretical and analytical level. Drucker (2011) argues the overconsumption displayed in the commercial gay scene has alienated many queer persons, with the mode of production within capitalism impacting class structure within gay communities. Queer identities are nonconformist, challenge gay universalism, and promote diversity across difference, be it class, gender, sexual orientation, race, and other aspects of social location. According to Drucker (2011), this challenge is coming from queer youth in the low-income bracket who are outwardly resisting the white middle-class persona traditionally associated with the gay community. Research needs to be done to fully explore the intersecting experiences of queer persons who live in poverty, be it experiences of homelessness, unemployment, lack of access to post-secondary education, resistance to capitalism or other mitigating factors. Social workers need to challenge their unified perception of the gay community, as identities are variant and emerging through multiple communities. They also need to understand how being disabled and queer might increase one's vulnerability to poverty, moving beyond the heterosexual normative of identity entrenched in understandings of ability (Oliver, Sapey and Thomas 2012).

Embodiment

One of the more significant commonalities between queer and disabled identities is their passion and commitment to challenging normative standards within society, as "they both argue adamantly against the compulsion to observe norms" (Sandahl 2003: 26). Both "queer" and "crip" — a term used as an identifier by people with disabilities — are pejorative terms, once used to discriminate against, that have now been reclaimed, redirecting the power away from the abuser toward the marginalized. "Queering of crip/crippling of queer" (Price 2007: 80) relates to the intersecting identity and commonalities shared by people with disabilities and queer alike. Race/gender are linked through their struggles against oppression, while sexual identity/disability are tied to a liberation process of self-actualization (Price 2007).

Queer persons have either been invisible within the medical system or their entire embodied experience is viewed through their sexual expressions. In their clinical guide to caring for queer persons, Peterkin and Risdon (2003: 274) have only one page dedicated to working with queer persons with disabilities. Within the section they highlight conducting a proper sexual history, including dissemination of safer sex information, exploring how loss of function impacts sexual attractiveness, highlighting the confidentiality of sexual orientation, and offering to speak to their partner about the impact of disability. Imagine the application of this advice if the disabled queer person is going to the physician for an abscessed toe or the common cold. People with disabilities are tired of everything being about their "limitation," as Mackelprang and Salsgiver (2015: 229) acknowledge that "people assume that disability is the centre of life for people with disabilities." Likewise, why would you need a complete sexual history or need to focus on safe sex if the person is seeking clinical services for a common cold? Care providers need to extend beyond the person's disability and/or sexual orientation, not to forget about those aspects of their being but to envision them in their entirety.

Due to experiences of alienation within the health care system, lesbian and gay groups have created their own networks for assisting friends and family through ill health and disability. The most recognized interventions were when LGBT communities rallied around gay men dying of AIDS (Walden 2009). Another example is a group of lesbians who have been together for fifteen years helping care for their sisters when dealing with chronic illnesses. This group occupies the social space between family/friends and the formal system of care (Walden 2009). They work to breakdown isolation, provide physical and emotional care, and a safe place that validates their sexual orientation. Unfortunately, this group is not available in every community, so health care workers need to be challenged to provide inclusive practices in order to work toward the elimination of dual oppressions of ability and sexual orientation.

Social workers need to continue to challenge societal stereotypes of embodied assumptions about disabled and queer persons. Fowles (2014) reports on Kaleigh Trace's new book, *Hot, Wet, and Shaking*. Trace defines herself as a disabled, queer, feminist sex educator who does not hide her sexuality and disability, nor the expression of either. She writes about her sexual experiences as a disabled lesbian, challenging the asexual assumptions formed around ableism, as she pushes back on the outrageous and defiant:

I swallowed that shame down and left it to rot in my guts. I have always looked different. I will always be different. This will never change, and even though there are times when it will be difficult, I have made it my own personal project to never be ashamed of myself. (2014)

Social workers need to be allies to people living on the margins by listening to their stories, recognizing their expertise, and utilizing their knowledge to assist others in similar lived experiences. Social workers need to recognize that families come in various forms, defined according to the client in naming those who are significant in their life. Far too often loved ones have been kept from the bedside of a dying client because they don't meet the "traditional" definition of a family member. There is no greater injustice than denying interpersonal connection during this transitional life moment. As identity is based upon self-identification, the same follows for the identification of family, and this must be acknowledged by the helping professions.

Race and Disability

Canada is a country that is recognized internationally for its peacekeeping efforts and as an advocate of human rights, yet people with disabilities had to fight for recognition under the *Canadian Charter of Rights and Freedoms* (Stienstra and Wight-Felske 2003), and many Indigenous peoples both on and off reserve live in sub-standard and impoverished conditions (Kendall 2001; Manual and Posluns 1974). Hanes (2009: 92) argues Canada's immigration policy is being implemented under the belief that "none is too many" when it comes to the applications from people with disabilities. He explicitly states, "Canada's immigration history is steeped in anti-Semitism, racism, homophobia and sexism" (Hanes 2009: 92). Children with intellectual and developmental disabilities, along with adults with chronic health issues and disabilities, have been denied entry or deported based on the belief they will put undue stress on Canada's health and social service systems. Hanes (2009: 122) concludes "there has never been anything in Canadian immigration legislation that has placed value on people with disabilities." Soldatic and Fiske (2009) found similar patterns when examining Australia's immigration policy in a "locked up" and "locked out" approach to people with disabilities. People with disabilities are either "locked out" of the country in not being granted immigration status, or they are "locked up" if they are refugees or asylum seekers, a parallel process to the high rates of institutionalization for Australian-born persons with disabilities. Given the ethnic and cultural diversity amongst immigrant applicants, traditions of racism and ableism continue to craft policies and practices.

Barnes, Mercer and Shakespeare (1999: 90) acknowledge that Black people with disabilities "often face exclusion and marginalization even within disabled communities and the disability movement." As noted by O'Donnell and Wallace (2011), 31 percent of Indigenous people live with disabilities in Canada, compared to 15 percent of non-Indigenous Canadians. Durst (Chapter 9) also asserts that "Indigenous persons with disabilities are virtually invisible in Canada … a hidden and forgotten population." He supports the voice of Indigenous people, championing self-determination and self-governance, while storying the hope and resiliency of those living with disabilities. He also addresses the question of why Indigenous people have such high rates of disability.

According to Gionet and Roshanafshar (2013), Indigenous people living off-reserve were more likely to report poor health when compared to non-Indigenous people. This was primarily due to living with one or more chronic health conditions. Diabetes, asthma, obesity and health behaviours are all areas were Indigenous rated higher than non-Indigenous people. Furthermore, Indigenous people with disabilities relying on informal care networks, such as friends and family, for their health and disability needs may limit their access to expertise and specialized services (Newbold 1999).

Race is primarily left out of disability studies (Annamma, Connor and Ferri 2013); social work needs to bring the focus onto "race," given the high rates of intersection between "race" and ability.

Violence

Statistics Canada's (2011) report on hate crimes identifies 52 percent of crimes that year being motivated by race and ethnicity. Statistics Canada also found that persons with activity limitations — a term that's interchangeable with persons with disabilities — were twice as likely to experience a physical or sexual assault, compared to those without activity limitations. Persons living with "mental or behavioural disorders" were four times more likely to be victims of abuse (Perreault 2009). Violence against racially visible people with disabilities needs to be investigated.

In examining risk factors of partner violence against women with disabilities, Brownridge (2006: 818) found significant increased risk for women with disabilities who were "less likely to be well educated, and more likely to be unemployed, older, and of Aboriginal ancestry." Brownridge (2003: 65–66) states "estimates of the prevalence of violence against Aboriginal women range widely, from 25 percent to 100 percent." Aboriginal women are eight times more likely to be murdered through intimate partner violence than non-Aboriginal women (Brownridge 2003). Violence within Aboriginal communities is in part due to learned behaviour associated with the residential school experience and colonization (Brownridge 2003). Higher rates of violence, relying on informal care networks, and the increased risk of people with disabilities due to lack of mobility and isolation (Martin et al. 2006) creates the perfect storm for abuse of Aboriginal women with disabilities.

Shantha Barriga (2013), senior advocate for the Human Rights Watch, outlines major concerns about the safety of women and girls with disabilities, particularly highlighting the lack of reporting and inadequate services for victims of rape and physical abuse. The Human Rights Watch in northern Uganda found that one-third of the women with disabilities they interviewed had "experienced some form of sexual and gender-based violence, including rape" (Article 13 para. 4). Women with disabilities in developing countries have the intersection of gender, ability and race complicating their experiences of oppression. Living in rural, remote areas increases their risk of abuse, coupled with limited modes of transportation to access police or social services. Further complicating reporting, often the abusers are family members and/or caregivers. In northern Uganda, women with disabilities who have been victims of violence have been encouraged to report their experiences to local counsellors, which often results in mediation instead of charges being laid (Barriga 2013).

In Canada, advocacy groups and opposition parties within the House of Commons have been rallying for a national inquiry into missing and murdered Aboriginal women, with no avail from the federal Conservatives (Mas 2014). Over one thousand missing or murdered Aboriginal girls or women are the known cases, with a conviction rate of 53 percent compared to 75 percent for homicides in general (Ambler 2014: Chapter 2 – b). Although disability was not specifically addressed within the government report on missing and murdered Aboriginal women, given the rates of disability within Canada and within Aboriginal communities, the intersection is evident. Social workers need to inform themselves of the issues associated with violence against women, including the intersection of race and disability.

Poverty

Education has a direct correlation with income levels; those with less than a high school education have the greatest rates of poverty (Zeman, McMullen and de Broucker 2010). People with disabilities' access to education has been an ongoing concern, be it at the level of public school or post-secondary education (Dunn et al. 2006, 2008). In the United States, poor children and children of African American heritage are the largest group of students in "special education" classrooms (Oswald, Coutinho, Best and Singh 1999; U.S. Department of Education 1998). African American children represent 16 percent of the total school enrolment, yet they constitute 21 percent of enrolment in "special education" (U.S. Department of Education 1998). African American children living in poverty are 2.3 times more likely to be labelled by their teachers as having learning disabilities. Native American children are 1.1 times more likely to be in special education programs and make up 16.8 percent, compared to 11 percent, of the general school population (Allison and Vining 1999). Within Canada, "Aboriginal people with disabilities have an even higher rate of poverty" (Stienstra 2002: 7), and children with disabilities have a greater chance of being poorer than children without disabilities (Stienstra 2002).

Basically, the higher the minority representation in a community, the greater the number of minority students in "special education" (Harry 1992). Meyer and Patton (2001) believe this representation is not primarily indicative of higher rates of learning or developmental disabilities, but rather in large part due to the stereotypes of teachers and school board members toward students who are not white. Schools within communities with high diversity rates had less resources, older equipment, less qualified teachers, more substitute teachers, lacked culturally responsive curriculum, had restrictive professional development allowances, and had staff, including teachers, who were not culturally competent. Public education prepares students for post-secondary education, be it university or college, which is then believed to lead to gainful employment. If we are segregating students with disabilities and students living on the margins due to race and income, then what chance do we have of altering the current neoliberal economic agenda based upon white, able-bodied, heterosexual people being at the top of the economic scale?

Embodiment

In examining chronic health conditions, which lead to disabling effects, significant differences emerge; one-fifth of non-Aboriginal women living in Canada experience arthritis or rheumatism, in comparison to one-third of Aboriginal women (O'Donnell and Wallace 2011). Aboriginal women are at risk for stomach problems or intestinal ulcers (15.6 percent), compared to 3.3 percent for non-Aboriginal women (O'Donnell and Wallace 2011: 46). Australian research indicates that Aboriginal peoples are 4.1 times more likely to have chronic conditions than non-Aboriginals (Zhao, Guthridge, Magnus and Vos 2004). Statistics clearly indicate that Aboriginal peoples have high rates of disabilities within Canada and beyond.

Within Canada, African Canadians and Aboriginal peoples have been purposefully and directly located away from the urban centres and into remote and isolated geographical locations. For example, in Halifax, African Nova Scotians were forced off their land in Africville, as it became prime real estate, first by the city relocating sewage disposal pits and a garbage dump to the edge of their community, and when that did not work, the city expropriated the land, relocating Black families and bulldozing their homes (McGibbon and Etowa 2009). Aboriginal reserves are often located in remote geographical areas, leaving access to health and social services, along with employment opportunities, at a distance (Centre for Social Justice 2013). Lack of access to health and social resources can have a grave impact on one's health outcomes. Aboriginal people in Canada have a 2 percent higher rate of heart disease than the general population, with 20.4 percent of Aboriginals diagnosed with high blood pressure (McGibbon and Etowa 2009). For both breast and cervical cancer, ethnic minority women have more advanced disease at the time of diagnosis. Not surprisingly, they also have higher rates of morbidity and mortality (McGibbon and Etowa 2009).

Likewise, African American men have a greater risk of prostate cancer, and heightened chances of dying from the disease, than white American men (McGibbon and Etowa 2009). In considering mental health conditions, "racial profiling, racist assumptions, and stereotyping" (McGibbon and Etowa 2009: 58) have a significant impact on psychiatric diagnosis, assessment and intervention. Stress prompted by racism has been recognized as a major health issue (James, Bernard, Este, Benjamin, Lloyd and Turner 2010). In 1981, the Special Committee on the Disabled and the Handicapped recognized that Aboriginal people with disabilities had more obstacles in their way, including isolation, lack of services and prejudice (Ng 1996). To address the issues of ableism, racism must be on the agenda. Ableist and racist assumptions need to be unpacked, meaning they need to be thoroughly examined so that it is understood where the assumptions have come from, what perpetuates them within our social order, and how they can be challenged with the ultimate goal of elimination. Ostrander (2008) interviewed young African American and Hispanic men who had become disabled through gun violence. One of his participants purposely wore a camouflage jacket so that people would equate his injury and subsequent wheelchair usage with military war service instead of believing it was the consequence of gang wars.

Canadian researchers need to investigate the intersections of race, health and disability. According to McGibbon and Etowa (2009), few studies have been done linking racism and health or access to health services. Aboriginal and African Canadians identified racial profiling, lack of cultural literacy, insensitivity and lack of communication as barriers associated with access to health services (McGibbon and Etowa 2009). We need to do a better job of meeting and understanding the needs of racialized people with disabilities.

Implications for Social Work

Social work, whether a practice profession or academic discipline, has historically been ill-prepared to deal with the needs of people with disabilities in Canada (Carter et al. 2012; Dunn et al. 2006, 2008). Under the guise of disability, to deal with the intersections of race, sexual orientation, gender and other aspects of social location such as class and age, social work needs to work toward full inclusion. Here are suggestions:

- Understand identity related to individuals with disabilities as a process

— "disabilities are multiple, fluid, and evolving and, therefore, cannot be categorized into a single defining entity for the purpose of medicine or social organization" (MacDonald and Friars 2009: 141).

- Challenge the medicalization of disability, moving beyond the 20-year-old white male as the established norm to an understanding of disability with all its potential intersections — that is, women with disabilities, racialized individuals with disabilities, elders living with disabilities.

- Challenge stereotypical images — displace medical authority and social elitism, providing for accessible and inclusive health care. Displace medical model's "fix" or tragedy mentality where the ultimate goal in working with the person with a disability is a return to "normalcy."

- View disability as a political issue — challenge individual values based on economic productivity, neoliberal agendas and colonialism. We cannot have the number-one tip for better health for disabled persons to be "don't be poor" (Raphael 2006: 119).

- Identify systemic barriers and work toward a new definition of contribution that would incorporate a creative and progressive understanding of work and community life.

- Become familiar with disability programs and policies, both nationally and internationally. Develop a critical lens to existing services — identify barriers and accessible options. Advocate for appropriate resources, be it in health, income, or citizenship.

- People with disabilities intersecting with race, gender or sexual orientation deserve to be listened to, shown respect, accommodated within their work and living spaces, and, most of all, valued as persons.

- Become aware and actively involved in the disability movements globally, working within the organizations to push for a fuller inclusion of identities and inter-relationships with other social justice movements, be it the women's movement, LGTBQ Pride, or Idle No More (Aboriginal).

- Contribute to disability rights on a national and international platform, and with rights group associated with intersecting identities. Work with disability rights organizations, such as Disability Rights Fund.

Chapter Summary

This chapter began by exploring some of the marginalized experiences of people with disabilities. Historical and present-day oppressions exhibited through ableism were exposed. Various identities linked to living with a disability were touched upon, with the primary notion of identity being flexible, evolving and ever changing. Recognition was given to the process of coming into an identity as a person with a disability. From a postmodern perspective, intersectionality was investigated, looking at the interwoven, complex nature of positionality, as it evolves and changes through circumstances, time and location. This was followed by specific intersections with disability, beginning with Gender and Disability, followed by Queerness and Disability, and finally, Race and Disability. Each of these intersections were explored through three areas: violence, poverty and embodiment. The final section outlined the implications for social work, highlighting specific interventions, practices and knowledge that can be embraced for an inclusive practice. The chapter ends with discussion questions to help promote knowledge acquisition of intersecting identities of disability. A point to ponder as you leave this chapter is that some Indigenous tribes do not have a specific word for disability in their traditional languages, as in the Cree and Dine people of Manitoba. Rather, they embrace disability as part of their community, believing people that normative society would label as "disabled" have something to teach other members of the community (Stienstra and Ashcroft 2010).

Discussion Questions

1. Identify the intersecting oppressions of an Aboriginal girl living with a learning disability on a reserve
   i. Use Mullaly's (2010) formula of a + b + c + (ab) + (ac) + (bc) + (abc).
   ii. Given what you have learned in this chapter, identify the barriers this young woman will most likely be facing.
   iii. Using the "Implications for Practice" section, identify how you might intervene as a social worker. What plans could you put in place? How might you advocate for this young woman's rights, and how might you support her self-advocacy?
2. Think of your own experiences of oppression and privilege. What identities do you claim, and what barriers have you had to address? How do your own experiences inform what it might be like living with a disability in an ableist world? Finally, how do your own experiences inform your social work practice?

Note

1   This author often writes disability as (dis)Ability; (dis) to respect the person's identity as a person with a disability, and Ability to acknowledge the creative and innovative ways they have found to deal with our ableist, inaccessible society. For the purpose of consistency within the book, "disability" will be used throughout this chapter.

References

Allison, Sherry, and Christine Vining. 1999. "Native American Culture and Language: Considerations in Service Delivery." In T.V. Fletcher and C.S. Bos (eds.), *Helping Children with Disabilities and Their Families*. Tempe, AZ: Bilingual Press.

Ambler, Stella. 2014. "Invisible Women: A Call to Action. A Report on Missing and Murdered Indigenous Women in Canada." March. Report of the Special Committee on Violence Against Indigenous Women. Ottawa, ON: Parliament of Canada. <http://www.parl.gc.ca/HousePublications/Publication.aspx?DocId=6469851&Language=E&Mode=1&Parl=41&Ses=2&File=5>.

Annamma, Subini, David Connor and Beth Ferri. 2013. "Dis/Ability Critical Race Studies (Discrit): Theorizing at the Intersections of Race and Dis/Ability." *Race, Ethnicity and Education* 16, 1: 1–13.

Baines, Donna (eds.). 2011. *Doing Anti-Oppressive Practice: Social Justice Social Work* 2nd edition. Halifax, NS: Fernwood Publishing.

Barnes, Colin, Geof Mercer and Tom Shakespeare. 1999. *Exploring Disability: A Sociological Introduction*. Cambridge, UK: Polity Press.

Barrett, Betty, and Melissa St. Pierre. 2013. "Intimate Partner Violence Reported by Lesbian-, Gay-, and Bisexual-Identified Individuals Living in Canada: An Exploration of Within-Group Variations." *Journal of Gay & Lesbian Social Services* 25: 1–23. DOI: 10.1080/10538720.2013.751887.

Barriga, Shantha. 2013. "Letter to United Nations CRPD on Half Day of General Discussion on Women and Girls with Disabilities." *Human Rights Watch*. April 3. <http://www.hrw.org/news/2013/04/03/letter-united-nations-crpd-half-day-general-discussion-women-and-girls-disabilities>.

Beagan, Brenda, Robin Stadnyk, Charlotte Loppie, Nancy MacDonald, Barb Hamilton-Hinch, and Judy MacDonald. 2005. *I Do It Because I Love Her and I Care: Snapshots of the Lives of Caregivers*. Halifax, NS: The Healthy Balance Research Program.

Begos, Kevin. 2002. "Lifting the Curtain on a Shameful Era: Thousands Were Sentenced yo Sterilization During Rubber-Stamp Hearings in Raleigh." *Winston-Salem Journal*. December 9. <http://www.journalnow.com/news/local/article_fa19404e-8fdf-11e2-8fba-0019bb30f31a.html>.

Beresford, Peter. 2000. "What Have Madness and Psychiatric System Survivors Got to Do with Disability and Disability Studies?" *Disability & Society* 15, 1: 167–172. DOI: 10.1080/09687590025838.

Billies, Michelle, Juliet Johnson, Kagendo Murungi and Rachel Pugh. 2009. "Naming Our Reality: Low-Income LGBT People Documenting Violence, Discrimination and Assertions of Justice." *Feminism Psychology* 19, 3: 375–380. DOI: 10.1177/0959353509105628.

Binding, Karl, and Alfred Hoche. 2012. *Allowing the Destruction of Life Unworthy of Life*. (Christina Modak translator.) Holmen, WI: Policy Intersections Research Center.

Bishop, Anne. 1994. *Becoming an Ally: Breaking the Cycle of Oppression*. Halifax, NS: Fernwood Publishing.

Boston Women's Health Collective. 2011. *Our Bodies, Ourselves*. New York: Simon & Schuster.

Brown, Marion, Brenda Richard, and Leighann Wichman. 2010. "The Promise and Relevance of Structural Social Work and Practice with Queer People and Communities." In Steven Hick, Heather Peters, Tammy Corner and Tracy London (eds.), *Structural Social Work in Action*. Toronto: ON: Canadian Scholars Press.

Brownridge, Douglas. 2003. "Male Partner Violence Against Aboriginal Women in Canada: An Empirical Analysis." *Journal of Interpersonal Violence* 18, 1: 65–83. DOI: 10.1177/0886260502238541.

____. 2006. "Partner Violence Against Women with Disabilities; Prevalence, Risk and Explanations." *Violence Against Women* 12, 9: 805–822.

Carniol, Ben. 2010. *Case Critical: Social Services and Social Justice in Canada* sixth edition. Toronto, ON: Between the Lines.

Carter, Irene, Roy Hanes and Judy MacDonald. 2012. "Trials and Tribulations of the Persons with Disability Caucus of the Canadian Association for Social Work Education." *Canadian Disabilities Studies Journal* 1, 1: 109–142.

Centre for Social Justice. 2013. "Aboriginal Issues." <http://www.socialjustice.org/index.php?page=aboriginal-issues>.

Chadwick, Patricia. 2003. "Disability Social History Project." <http://www.disabilityhistory.org/timeline_new.html>.

Clare, Eli. 2009. "Excerpt from 'Hate Violence, Fierce Love: Histories of Grief, Rage & Resistance.'" <http://eliclare.com/what-eli-offers/lectures/hate-violence>.

Collins, Patricia Hill. 1998. *Fighting Words: Black Women and the Search for Justice*. Minneapolis: University of Minnesota Press.

D'Augelli, Anthony, Neil Pilkington, and Scott Hershberger. 2002. "Incidence and Mental Health Impact of Sexual Orientation Victimization of Lesbian, Gay, and Bisexual Youths in High School." *School Psychology Quarterly* 17, 2: 148–167.

DAA (Disability Awareness in Action). 1996. "Disabled Women." Disability Awareness in Action Resource Kit No. 6. Independent Living Institute. <http://www.independentliving.org/docs2/daakit61.html>.

DAWN (DisAbled Women's Network). (n.d.). "Fact Sheets on Women with Disabilities." <http://dawn.thot.net/fact.html>.

____. 2010. "Women with Disabilities and Violence Factsheet." <http://www.womensequality.ca/Imagespercent20PDFspercent202011/Womenpercent20withpercent20Disabilitiespercent20andpercent20Violence,percent20Factsheetpercent202010.pdf>.

Disability Rights Fund. n.d. "Grantees." Boston, MA. <http://www.disabilityrightsfund.org/>.

Dominelli, Lena. 2002. *Anti-Oppressive Social Work Theory and Practice*. Hampshire, UK; Palgrave MacMillan.

Doucette, Joanne. 1990. "Rethinking Difference: Disabled Lesbians Resist." In S. Dale Stone (ed.), *Lesbians in Canada*. Toronto, ON: Between the Lines.

Drucker, Peter. 2011. "The Fracturing of LGBT Identities under Neoliberal Capitalism." *Historical Materialism* 19, 4: 3–32. DOI: 10.1163/156920611X606412.

Dunn, Peter, Roy Hanes, Susan Hardie, Donald Leslie and Judy MacDonald. 2008. "Best Practices in Promoting Disability Inclusion within Canadian Schools of Social Work." *Disability Studies Quarterly* 28, 1.

Dunn, Peter, Roy Hanes, Susan Hardie, and Judy MacDonald. 2006. "Creating Disability Inclusion within Canadian Schools of Social Work." *Journal of Social Work in Disability and Rehabilitation* 5, 1: 1–19.

Edmonton Journal. 2013. "Sentencing Date Set for Betty Anne Gagnon Abuse Case." July 5. <http://www.edmontonjournal.com/news/edmonton/Sentencing+date+Betty+Anne+Gagnon+abuse+case/8621597/story.html>.

Enns, Henry, and Aldred Neufeldt (eds.). 2003. *In Pursuit of Equal Participation: Canada and Disability at Home and Abroad*. Concord, ON: Captus Press.

Fairtlough, Anna, Claudia Bernard, Joan Fletcher and Ahmet Ahmet. 2013. "Experiences of Lesbian, Gay and Bisexual Students on Social Work Programmes: Developing a Framework for Educational Practice." *British Journal of Social Work* 43, 3: 467–485. Dio: 10.1093/bjsw/bcs001.

Fowles, Stacey May. 2014. "Book Reviews: *Hot, Wet and Shaking* by Kaleigh Trace." *National Post*. <http://news.nationalpost.com/afterword/hot-wet-and-shaking-by-kaleigh-trace-review>.

Galarneau, Diane, and Marian Radulescu. 2009. "Employment among the Disabled." Ottawa, ON: Statistics Canada. <http://www.statcan.gc.ca/pub/75-001-x/2009105/pdf/10865-eng.pdf>.

Garland-Thomson, Rosemarie. 2006. "Integrating Disability, Transforming Feminist Theory." In L. Davis (ed.), *The Disability Studies Reader* 2nd edition. New York: Routledge Publishing.

Ghai, Anita. 2009. "The Women's Movement Must Do More for Disabled Women." Infochange Disabilities. <http://infochangeindia.org/disabilities/analysis/the-womens-movement-must-do-more-for-disabled-women.html>.

Gionet, Linda, and Shirin Roshanafshar. 2013. *Select Health Indicators of First Nations People Living Off Reserve, Metis and Inuit*. Ottawa, ON: Statistics Canada, Health Statistics Division.

Greenhalgh, Susan. 2001. *Under the Medical Gaze: Facts and Fictions of Chronic Pain*. Berkeley, CA: University of California Press.

Group for the Advancement of Psychiatry. 2012. "LGBT Mental Health Syllabus." <http://www.aglp.org/gap/1_history/>.

Hanes, Roy. 2009. "None Is Still Too Many: An Historical Exploration of Canadian Immigration Legislation as It Pertains to People with Disabilities." *Developmental Disabilities Bulletin* 37, 1–2: 91–126.

Harry, Beth. 1992. *Cultural Diversity, Families and the Special Education System*. New York: Teachers College Press.

HRSDC. 2006. *Disability in Canada: A 2006 Profile*. Ottawa, ON: Government of Canada.

Hughes, Bill. 2012. "Fear, Pity and Disgust: Emotions and the Non-Disabled Imaginary." In Nick Watson, Alan Roulstone and Carol Thomas (eds.), *Routledge Handbook of Disability Studies*. Abingdon, Oxon: Routledge Publishing.

Human Rights Watch. 2013. "Letter to United Nations CRPD on Half Day of General Discussion on Women and Girls with Disability." <http://www.hrw.org/news/2013/04/03/letter-united-nations-crpd-half-day-general-discussion-women-and-girls-disabilities>.

Hylton, Mary. 2006. "Queer in Southern MSW Programs: Lesbian and Bisexual Women Discuss Stigma Management." *Journal of Social Psychology* 146, 5: 611–628.

Hyman, Batya. 2008. "Violence in the Lives of Lesbian Women: Implications for Mental Health." *Social Work in Mental Health* 7, 1–3: 204–225. DOI: 10.1080/15332980802072553.

James, Carl, Wanda Thomas Bernard, David Este, Akua Benjamin, Bethan Lloyd, and Tana Turner. 2010. *Race and Well-Being: The Lives, Hopes and Activism of African Canadians.* Black Point, NS: Fernwood Publishing.

James, Carl, and Adrienne Shadd (eds.). 2001. *Talking about Identity: Encounters in Race, Ethnicity, and Language* 2nd edition. Toronto, ON: Between the Lines.

"Justice for Betty Anne Gagnon." <http://www.justiceforbettyannegagnon.com/http://www.justiceforbettyannegagnon.com/>.

Kagan, Gerald, and Jeffrey Cain. 2005. "Dealing with Disability Insurance Companies: How to Advocate Successfully to Obtain Your Benefits." *In Motion* 15, 3. <www.amputeecoalition.org/inmontion/may_jun_05/disabilityinsurancecompanies.html>.

Kendall, Joan. 2001. "Circles of Disadvantage: Aboriginal Poverty and Underdevelopment in Canada." *American Review of Canadian Studies* 31, 1–2: 43–59. DOI: 10.1080/02722010109481581.

Kitts, Robert. 2010. "Barriers to Optimal Care Between Physicians and Lesbian, Gay, Bisexual, Transgender, and Questioning Adolescent Patients." *Journal of Homosexuality* 57: 730–747. DOI: 10.1080/00918369.2010.485872.

Lightman, Ernie, Dean Herd, Seong-gee Um and Andrew Mitchell. 2009. "Post-Secondary Education and Social Assistance in Ontario." *Canadian Social Work Review* 26, 1: 97–113.

MacDonald, Judy. 2004. "One Woman's Experience of Living with Chronic Pain: The Proclamation of Voice." *Journal of Social Work in Disability & Rehabilitation* 3, 2: 17–35.

____. 2006. "Untold Stories: Women, in the Helping Professions as Sufferers of Chronic Pain (Re)Storying (dis)Abilities." <http://www.collectionscanada.gc.ca/thesescanada/AMICUS No. 33872393>.

____. 2008. "Anti-Oppressive Practices with Chronic Pain Sufferers." *Social Work in Health Care* 47, 2: 135–156.

MacDonald, Judy, and Gaila Friars. 2009. "Structural Social Work from a (dis)Ability Perspective." In S. Hicks, H. Peters, T. Corner and T. London (eds.), *Structural Social Work in Action.* Toronto: ON: Canadian Scholars Press.

MacIntosh, Josephine. 2007. "HIV/AIDS Stigma and Discrimination: A Canadian Perspective and Call to Action." *Interamerican Journal of Psychology* 41, 1: 93–102.

Mackelprang, Romel, and Richard Salsgiver. 2015. *Disability: A Diversity Model Approach in Human Service Practice* 3rd edition. Chicago, IL: Lyceum Books Inc.

Manual, George, and Michael Posluns. 1974. *The Fourth World: An Indian Reality.* Don Mills, ON: Collier-MacMillan Canada.

Marsiglia, Flavio Francisco, and Stephen Stanley Kulis. 2009. *Diversity, Oppression, and Change: Culturally Grounded Social Work.* Chicago, IL: Lyceum Books.

Martin, Sandra, Neepa Ray, Daniela Sotres-Alvarez, Lawrence Kupper, Kathryn Moracco, Pamela A. Dickens, Donna Scandlin and Ziya Gizlice. 2006. "Physical and Sexual Assault of Women with Disabilities." *Violence Against Women* 12, 9: 823–837. DOI: 10.1177/1077801206292672.

Mas, Susana. 2014. "No Call for National Inquiry in MPs' Report on Aboriginal Women." *CBC News.* March 7. <http://www.cbc.ca/news/politics/no-call-for-national-inquiry-in-mps-report-on-aboriginal-women-1.2563854>.

Matthews, Gwyneth Ferguson. 1983. *Voices from the Shadows: Women with Disabilities Speak Out.* Toronto, ON: Women's Educational Press.

McCloy, Ursula, and Lindsay DeClou. 2013. *Disability in Ontario: Postsecondary Education Participation Rates, Student Experience and Labour Market Outcomes.* Toronto, ON: Higher Education Quality Council of Ontario.

McDermott, Elizabeth. 2011. "The World Some Have Won: Sexuality, Class and Inequality." *Sexualities* 14, 1: 63–78. DOI: 10.1177/1363460710390566.

McGee, Debbie (Director) and Nicole Hubert (Producer). 1992. *Toward Intimacy.* National Film Board of Canada. <http://www.nfb.ca/film/toward_intimacy/>.

McGibbon, Elizabeth A., and Josephine B. Etowa. 2009. *Anti-Racist Health Care Practice.* Toronto, ON: Canadian Scholars Press.

McRuer, Robert. 2006. "Compulsory Able-Bodiedness and Queer/Disabled Existence." In L. Davis (ed.), *The Disability Studies Reader* 2nd edition. New York: Routledge.

Meyer, Gwen, and James Patton. 2001. "On Point: On the Nexus of Race, Disability, and Overrepresentation: What Do We Know? Where Do We Go?" Office of Special Education Programs, U.S. Department of Education. <http://www.urbanschools.org/pdf/race.pdf>.

Mollow, Anna. 2006. "'When Black Women Start Going on Prozac ...' The Politics of Race, Gender, and Emotional Distress in Meri Nana-Ama Danquah's *Willow Weep for Me.*" In Lennard Davis (ed.), *The Disability Studies Reader* 2nd edition. Abingdon, Oxon: Routledge.

Morris, Jenny. 1989. *Pride Against Prejudice: Transforming Attitudes to Disability, Celebrate the Difference.* London, UK: Women's Press.

Mullaly, Bob. 2010. *Challenging Oppression and Confronting Privilege* 2nd edition. Don Mills, ON: Oxford Press.

Mustanski, Brian, and Richard Liu. 2013. "A Longitudinal Study on Predictors of Suicide Attempts among Lesbian, Gay, Bisexual, and Transgender Youth." *Archives of Sexual Behavior* 42, 3: 437–448. DOI: 10.1007/s10508-012-0013-9.

Myers, Melissa, Judy MacDonald, Sarah Jacquard, and Matthew Macneil. 2014. "(Dis) Ability and Education: One Woman's Experience." *Journal of Postsecondary Education and Disability* 27, 1: 73–86.

Neudel, Eric. 2011. *Lives Worth Living: The Greatest Fight for Disability Rights.* Natick, MA: Story Line Motion Picture.

Newbold, Bruce. 1999. "Disability and Use of Support Services within the Canadian Aboriginal Population." *Health & Social Care in the Community* 7, 4: 291–296.

Ng, Edward. 1996. "Disability among Canada's Aboriginal Peoples in 1991." *Health Reports* 8, 1: 25–32.

Nova Scotia Advisory Council on the Status of Women. 2006. "Women with Disabilities in Nova Scotia: A Statistical Profile." <http://women.gov.ns.ca/pubs2006_07/WomenDisabilitiesApril06.pdf>.

Nova Scotia Department of Community Services. 2002. "Fact Sheet on Women with Disabilities." Halifax, NS: Government of Nova Scotia.

O'Donnell, Vivian, and Susan Wallace. 2011. *Women in Canada: A Gender-Based Statistical Report: First Nations, Métis and Inuit Women.* Ottawa, ON: Statistics Canada. <www.statcan.gc.ca/pub/89-503-x/2010001/article/11442-eng.pdf>.

O'Toole, Corbett Joan. 1996. "Disabled Lesbians: Challenging Monocultural Constructs." *Sexuality and Disability* 14, 3: 221–236.

Oliver, Michael. 1990. *The Politics of Disablement: A Sociological Approach*. New York: St. Martin's Press.

____. 1996. *Understanding Disability: From Theory to Practice*. London, UK: MacMillan Press.

Oliver, Michael, Bob Sapey and Pam Thomas. 2012. *Social Work with Disabled People* 4th edition. United Kingdom: Palgrave MacMillan.

Ostrander, R. Noam. 2008. "When Identities Collide: Masculinity, Disability and Race." *Disability & Society* 23, 6: 585–597.

Oswald, Donald, Martha Coutinho, Al Best and Nirbhay Singh. 1999. "Ethnic Representation in Special Education: The Influence of School-Related Economic and Demographic Variables." *Journal of Special Education* 32, 4: 194–206.

Pease, Bob. 2010. *Undoing Privilege: Unearned Advantage in a Divided World*. London, UK: Zed Books.

Perreault, Samuel. 2009. "Criminal Victimization and Health: A Profile of Victimization among Persons with Activity Limitations or Other Health Problems." *Canadian Centre for Justice Statistics Profile Series*. Statistics Canada.

Peterkin, Allan, and Cathy Risdon. 2003. *Caring for Lesbian and Gay People: A Clinical Guide*. Toronto, ON: University of Toronto Press.

Price, Janet. 2007. "Engaging Disability." *Feminist Theory* 8, 1: 77–89. DOI: 10.1177/1464700107074199.

Raphael, Dennis. 2006. "Social Determinants of Health: Present Status, Unanswered Questions, and Future Directions." *International Journal of Health Services* 36, 4: 651–677. DOI: 10.2190/3MW4-1EK3-DGRQ-2CRF.

Riessman, Catherine. 2003. "Women and Medicalization: A New Perspective." In Rose Weitz (ed.), *The Politics of Women's Bodies: Sexuality, Appearance, and Behavior*. New York: Oxford University Press.

Rothman, Emily Faith, Deinera Exner and Allyson Baughman. 2011. "The Prevalence of Sexual Assault against People Who Identify as Gay, Lesbian, or Bisexual in the United States: A Systematic Review." *Trauma, Violence, & Abuse* 12, 2: 55–66. DOI: 10.1177/1524838010390707.

Saewyc, Elizabeth, Carol Skay, Sandra Pettingell, Elizabeth Reis, Linda Bearinger, Michael Resnick, Aileen Murphy and Leigh Combs. 2006. "Hazards of Stigma: The Sexual and Physical Abuse of Gay, Lesbian, and Bisexual Adolescents in the United States and Canada." *Child Welfare* LXXXV, 2: 195–213.

Sandahl, Carrie. 2003. "Queering the Crip or Cripping the Queer? Intersections of Queer and Crip Identities in Solo Autobiographical Performance." GLQ: *A Journal of Lesbian and Gay Studies* 9, 1–2: 25–56.

Scully, Jackie. 2012. "Deaf Identities in Disability Studies: With Us or Without Us?" In Nick Watson, Alan Roulstone and Carol Thomas (eds.), *Routledge Handbook of Disability Studies*. Abingdon, Oxon: Routledge.

Shapiro, Lawrence. 2015. "Queer Disability and the Reality of Homo-Ableism." In Brian O'Neill, Tracy Swan and Nick Mulé (eds.), LGBTQ *People and Social Work: Intersectional Perspectives*. Toronto, ON: Canadian Scholars' Press.

Smith, Jane. n.d. "Trying to Be Normal." Melbourne, Australia: The Women with Disabilities

Collective. <http://www.wwda.org.au/womdis2.htm>.

Soldatic, Karen, and Lucy Fiske. 2009. "Bodies 'Locked Up': Intersections of Disability and Race in Australian Immigration." *Disability & Society* 24, 3: 289–301.

Special Committee on the Disabled and the Handicapped. 1981. "Obstacles." Ottawa, ON: House of Commons. <http://www.cndd.ca/assets/researchpercent20documents/ Canadianpercent20Government/Obstaclespercent20-percent20Canpercent20Govt. pdf>.

Statistics Canada. 2006. "Population With and Without Disabilities, and Disability Rate, by Province, Canada and Provinces (table)." Participation and Activity Limitation Survey 2006 (tables). <http://www.statcan.gc.ca /pub/89-628-x/2007002/t/4125013-eng. htm>.

____. 2008. "Gender Differences in Reported Violent Crimes in Canada, 2008." <http:// www.statcan.gc.ca/pub/85f0033m/2010024/part-partie1-eng.htm#h2_9>.

____. 2011. "Police-Reported Hate Crimes, 2011." <http://www.statcan.gc.ca/daily-quotidien/130711/dq130711a-eng.htm>.

____. 2015. "Annual Estimates for Population of Canada, Provinces and Territories, July 1, 1971 to July 1, 2015. <http://www.stats.gov.nl.ca/Statistics/Population/PDF/ Annual_Pop_Prov.PDF>.

Status of Women Canada. 2013. "International Day of the Girl." <http://www.swc-cfc. gc.ca/commemoration/idg-jif/facts-faits-eng.html>.

Stienstra, Deborah. 2002. "Intersection of Disability and Race/Ethnicity/Official Language/Religion." Prepared for the 'Intersections of Diversity' Seminar. <http:// disabilitystudies.ca/wp-content/uploads/2010/08/Intersection-of-disability.pdf>.

____. 2012. *About Canada: Disability Rights*. Halifax, NS: Fernwood Publishing.

Stienstra, Deborah, and Terri Ashcroft. 2010. "Voyaging on the Seas of Spirit: An Ongoing Journey Towards Understanding Disability and Humanity." *Disability & Society* 25, 2: 191–203.

Stienstra, Deborah, and Aileen Wight-Felske (eds.). 2003. *Making Equality: History of Advocacy and Persons with Disabilities in Canada*. Concord, ON: Captus Press.

Titchkosky, Tanya, and Rod Michalko (eds.). 2009. *Rethinking Normalcy: A Disability Studies Reader*. Toronto, ON: Canadian Scholars' Press.

U.S. Department of Education. 1998. Archived information, section II, student characteristics. <www2.ed.gov/offices/OSERS/OSEP/Research/OSEP98AnlRpt/ WPD_Files/Section2.doc>.

United Nations. 2011. "Women Watch Fact Sheet." Secretary-General. <http://www. un.org/womenwatch/enable/index.html#factsheet>.

____. 2012. "Annual Report of the United Nations High Commissioner for Human Rights. 'Thematic Study on the Issue of Violence against Women and Girls and Disability.'" <http://www.ohchr.org/Documents/Issues/Disability/ ThematicStudyViolenceAgainstWomenGirls.pdf>.

____. 2013. "Committee on the Rights of Persons with Disabilities." <http://www.ohchr. org/en/hrbodies/crpd/pages/crpdindex.aspx>.

Vick, Andrea. 2012. "Theorizing Episodic Disabilities: The Case for an Embodied Politics." *Canadian Social Work Review* 29, 1: 41–60.

Wahlsten, Douglas. 1997. "Leilani Muir Versus the Philosopher King: Eugenics on Trial in

Alberta." *Genetics* 99, 2–3: 185–198.

Walden, Elizabeth. 2009. "An Exploration of the Experience of Lesbians with Chronic Illness." *Journal of Homosexuality* 56: 548–574. DOI: 10.1080/00918360903005220.

Warnica, Marion. 2013. "Whatever Happened to Betty Anne Gagnon?" cbc News Edmonton. <http://www.cbc.ca/edmonton/interactive/betty-anne-gagnon/index.html>.

Watson, Nick. 2002. "Well, I Know This Is Going to Sound Very Strange to You, But I Don't See Myself as a Disabled Person: Identity and Disability." *Disability & Society* 17, 5: 509–527. DOI: 10.1080/09687590220148496.

Weitz, Rose. 2004. *Rapunzel's Daughters: What Women's Hair Tells Us about Women's Lives.* New York: Farrar, Staus, and Giroux.

Wendell, Susan. 1996. *The Rejected Body: Feminist Philosophical Reflections on Disability.* New York: Routledge.

Wight-Felske, Aileen. 2003. "History of Advocacy Tool Kit." In Deborah Stienstra and Aileen Wight-Felske (eds.), *Making Equality: History of Advocacy and Persons with Disabilities in Canada.* Concord, ON: Captus Press.

Wilmot, Sheila Jane. 2005. *Taking Responsibility, Taking Direction: White Anti-Racism in Canada.* Winnipeg, MB: Arbeiter Ring.

Wilson, Rob, and Moyra Lang. 2010. "Living Archives on Eugenics in western Canada." Community University Research Alliance (cura), funded by Social Science and Humanities Research Canada. <http://eugenicsarchive.ca>.

Withers, A.J. 2012. *Disability Politics & Theory.* Halifax, NS: Fernwood Publishing.

Woods, Kelly, Marjorie Cook, Lindsay DeClou and Ursula McCloy. 2013. "Succeeding with Disabilities: Graduates with Disabilities and the Factors Affecting Time-to-Completion." Toronto, ON: Higher Education Quality Council of Ontario. <http://www.heqco.ca/SiteCollectionDocuments/Succeeding_with_disabilities_ENG.pdf>.

WorkBC. 2008. "The WorkBC Employers' Tool Kit: A Resource for British Columbia Businesses. Booklet 3: Under the Labour Radar – Aboriginal People, Youth, Women and Persons with Disabilities." Kamloops, BC: The Ministry of Economic Development. <http://www.workbc.ca/Documents/Docs/toolKit_Book3.pdf>.

Zeman, Klarka, Kathryn McMullen and Patrice de Broucker. 2010. "The High Education/Low Income Paradox: College and University Graduates with Low Earnings, Ontario 2006." Government of Canada, Statistics Canada. <http://www.statcan.gc.ca/pub/81-595-m/81-595-m2010081-eng.htm>.

Zhao, Yuejen, Steve Guthridge, Anne Magnus and Theo Vos. 2004. "Burden of Disease and Injury in Aboriginal and Non-Aboriginal Populations in the Northern Territory." *Medical Journal of Australia* 180, 10: 498–502.

Chapter 9

Indigenous People with Disabilities: Stories of Resilience and Strength

Douglas Durst

Whether on reserves or in the cities, Indigenous peoples with disabilities are virtually invisible in Canada. They are a hidden and forgotten population lost in the busyness of people around them and the racism, ableism and discrimination inherent in Canadian society. Unfortunately, few social researchers in Canada have taken an interest in these marginalized peoples. For over twenty years, I have been researching this topic, and this chapter draws upon my research, including a project with the National Association of Friendship Centres (Durst 2006). This study found that Indigenous peoples with disabilities experience multiple oppressions: they are Indigenous, they have disabilities, they are often urban (off-reserve), and women are even further disadvantaged (Demas 1993; Durst and Bluechardt 2001). Indigenous peoples with disabilities have experienced racism, oppression and discrimination from the larger society and, sadly, in their home communities as well. Yet, they persist and many fight back, demanding services and programs to enhance their quality of life and ameliorate the disadvantage imposed on them by the larger society.

In this chapter, I make the arguments for self-determination and self-government of Indigenous peoples in Canada. Personally, I have no Indigenous ancestry and do not have a disability; I do not speak for or on behalf of Indigenous people, but through my research I attempt to speak with and promote the voice of Indigenous peoples with disabilities. Just as First Nations/Indigenous peoples have rights expressed in the Constitution and treaties, Indigenous peoples with disabilities have the right to self-determination, respectful lifestyles and human dignity. The first section of this chapter provides a brief overview of Indigenous peoples in Canada and is followed by basic statistics of Indigenous peoples with disabilities and the reasons for such high rates of disability. Hope's story is a case study of a woman of Cree descent with quadriplegia that examines her struggles and resistance to oppression. In the next section, Indigenous people share their experiences and perspectives about living with disabilities. In the final section, eight specific recommendations are provided that may help address the plight of Indigenous people with disabilities. It is important to be clear that the poor conditions of Indigenous peoples with disabilities are the results of a history of colonialism and racism. The conditions reflect the provincial and federal governments' failure to provide adequate health care, housing, employment and services for Indigenous peoples.

Aboriginal people accounted for 4.3 percent (1,400,685) of the total population of Canada enumerated in the 2011 National Household Survey, up from 3.8 (1,172,790) in 2006 (Canada 2013). The Indigenous people of Canada comprise numerous cultural and ethnic groups; all are diverse, with unique cultural systems and historical experiences. Seventy percent of the 997 First Nations reserves are small communities with less than 500 persons (Canada 2013). Fifty-three percent are urban, and in some cities, Indigenous peoples comprise 10 percent of the population and are highly visible in Winnipeg, Regina and Saskatoon. Ironically, the city of Toronto has close to 14,000 Indigenous people but one of the lowest percentages, 0.5 percent (Canada 2006). With such a low percentage, Indigenous people blend into the ethnic diversity of Toronto making them "invisible." The population is younger than the non-Indigenous population and is growing at a faster rate (Canada 2013). The number of Indigenous people increased by 20.1 percent between 2006 and 2011 whereas the general population increased by only 5.2 percent and mainly through immigration during the same time period (Canada 2011).

With the enactment of the federal Indian Act (1876) and the Constitution Act (1982), categories were developed to classify Indigenous people. The term "First Nations" is used to describe people who are Status or Registered Indians as defined by the federal Indian Act. First Nations people are under the fiduciary responsibility of the federal government. Status Indians are registered with the federal government and have special rights to income tax exclusion, health care, housing, and education relating to land claims and treaty rights. These apply when they live on-reserve; however, if they move off-reserve, many of the treaty entitlements are restricted. It should be noted that although First Nations people have special rights as enshrined in federal legislation, it is evident that they are often denied these rights.

The term "Indigenous peoples" is a broad term used to define all people who identify with Indigenous ancestry. The Indian Act (federal legislation) does not apply to Non-Status Indians (Indigenous peoples) and they receive benefits from the province in which they reside, as do all other Canadian citizens. Métis people are of mixed Indigenous and European heritage. Finally, Inuit are Indigenous peoples of the Arctic and sub-Arctic regions of the North and are under a special agreement to receive federal benefits under the Indian Act. Section 35 of the Constitution Act, 1982, recognizes three groups of Indigenous peoples of Canada: First Nations, Métis and Inuit.

Federal Bill C-31 was an Act passed in 1984 to reinstate Indigenous women, children and others who had lost their status as a result of off-reserve education, employment and marriage. The passing of this bill has led to a dramatic increase in the number of Indigenous people holding status in Canada.

Sadly, the federal government of Canada has taken a negative approach toward upholding the rights of Indigenous peoples. In September 2014, Canada was the only member of the United Nations to object to a landmark document in support of the protection of the rights of Indigenous peoples (Lum 2014). This U.N. document re-established human rights protection of Indigenous peoples and was based on an original document developed seven years earlier. In 2007, Canada, with three other nations, one of which was the United States, voted against the original human rights protection document; yet, in 2014, the other two nations supported the revised document. Canada stood alone with a consistent negative message about the rights of Indigenous peoples (Lum 2014). It is hoped that with a new federal government elected in the fall of 2015, there will be a significant warming of attitudes towards Indigenous peoples.

The contexts of Indigenous/First Nations peoples are complex: some are urban or rural, some on- and off-reserve, and the diversity of language and culture makes simple assumptions or generalizations misleading. However, the common experiences of Indigenous peoples are those of cultural oppression, racism, discrimination and marginalization across the country and throughout history. For over one hundred years, Indigenous children were stolen from their families and communities and placed in large residential schools. The removal from family and the abuse suffered in residential schools left permanent emotional scars that have only recently been acknowledged (Sinclair 2008, 2009: Truth and Reconciliation Commission of Canada 2015). The journey of healing has only started for many. The experiences of colonialism and the residential schools have left a lasting impact that is common to Indigenous peoples in Canada. It is critical that social workers and human service professionals recognize and acknowledge the harmful impact of colonialism and oppression.

As a result of this oppression and these structural barriers, Indigenous people have socio-economic characteristics that place them well behind non-Indigenous Canadians in just about every category. They have poorer health, lower education levels, overcrowded housing, shorter lifespans, higher unemployment, lower incomes and so on (Canada 2013a; Frideres and Gadacz 2012). Indigenous peoples have diabetes at a rate that is three to five times the national average (CDS 2012), and HIV infections are still increasing in some sectors such as Saskatchewan (Canada 2012). Their living conditions on reserves are sometimes described as "Third World" and many face significant barriers in addressing the disparities in their lives. However, statistics show improvements for some Indigenous people. There is an emerging urban middle class of educated and professional families (Durst 2010). High school and university completions are increasing, and some communities are seeing a rise in Indigenous lawyers, social workers and teachers (Canada 2013a, 2013b). In spite of the new urban lifestyle, most urban Indigenous peoples maintain strong connections to their Indigenous culture through Band and family contacts (Durst 2010a).

How disability is defined is a complex issue. Similar to a number of other contributors to this text, I argue that disability is a social construction and is inexplicitly connected to culture — society's customs, attitudes and beliefs (Stone 2005). Moreover, many definitions focus on the individual and take a biomedical orientation (Barnes 2012), which interprets "disability" as deficiency. Such an approach emphasizes finding a "cure" or "rehabilitation," since it assumes that the challenges encountered by people with disabilities are written into their bodies and minds. Therefore, a biomedical model ignores the ways that disability is socially created and ignores the violation of rights, societal exclusion and oppression that people with disabilities experience.

Consequently, medical definitions of disability are now broadly contested, and people with disabilities argue that it is not the disability that is the problem but how the society accepts and responds to disability. Among other perspectives, the social model of disability emphasizes that disability is the loss of a valued function and acknowledges that what is valued varies from culture to culture. Disability is a social and political construction. For instance, an Indigenous person with a disability who requests support for special needs education and is refused by both local Indigenous and provincial governments on jurisdictional grounds — each holding the other authority responsible — is effectively "disabled" by the dispute. The problem is not the "impairment" but the failure of governments to provide the support needed to be successful in school. Disability is thus a political and social issue and not an "individual" biomedical concern. In this chapter, I argue from a human rights perspective that emphasizes the respect and dignity of all individuals and promotes and facilitates the full and equal participation in society of all persons regardless of ability. It is critical that people who have physical or sensory impairments enjoy full and meaningful participation in their community just as any other citizen (DRPI 2010).

Differences between Indigenous culture and the dominant culture, and differences amongst Indigenous cultures, lead to variations in what is considered a disability, the cause and the appropriate intervention to support the person. For example, the Navajo culture emphasizes the cause of the disability and focuses less on the symptoms influencing the choice of interventions. Lovern and Locust (2013) note differences in the perception of disability due to one's culture; Indigenous peoples may not see themselves as having a disability, whereas the "trained professional" might. Gething (1995) attributes the lack of accurate data to variations in the personal definition of a disability between professionals and Indigenous peoples. Some think of only obvious and noticeable conditions such as an amputation or severe physical impairment as a disability. Subtle forms of disability such as fetal alcohol syndrome or mental health issues are not identified as such. "Disability is rarely seen as a separate issue, but is perceived as part of problems which are widespread and accepted as part of the life cycle" (Gething 1995: 81). In some cases, the disability is believed to be the outcome of offences in spiritual taboos, customs or traditions that bring disharmony in body, mind and spirit (Lovern and Locust, 2013).

Interestingly, some Indigenous languages do not have a word that translates as "disability" (Durst 2006; Lovern and Locust 2013; Steinstra 2012). Depending on the cultural beliefs and values, conditions that are classified as disabilities by dominant society may not be considered in the same context in a particular First Nations community. In some contexts, Indigenous culture does not accept biomedical causes for disabilities and instead understands them from a spiritual, Creator-given perspective (Lovern and Locust 2013; Thomas 1981). As such, the cultural definition of disability emerges out of social relationships, not out of rigid medical or physiological criterion. For example, the Hopi believe that a person born with a condition that inhibits mobility, but is still able to contribute to the functioning of the community, is not seen as being disabled (Dapcic 1995; Lovern and Locust 2013). There is also evidence that some disabilities are seen as special gifts from the Creator. Reflecting on a disfiguring disability, a Cree elder stated "to be born imperfect was a sign of specialness" (Wiebe and Johnson 1998: 423). An Indigenous person shared their perspective with the disability scholar, Tom Shakespeare (2014: 75):

> I do not explain disability as impairment, and I do not see impairment as determining. My approach is nonreductionist, because I accept that limitations are always experienced as an inter-play of impairment with particular contexts and environments.

Unfortunately, most non-Indigenous communities do not encourage participation of persons with a disability in daily life. Therefore, when examining issues pertaining to Indigenous peoples with disabilities, it is necessary to consider an Indigenous vantage point and not base perceptions on Euro-Western standards because they are simply not comparable.With the vast diversity of Indigenous peoples in Canada, it is inappropriate and even dangerous to apply sweeping generalizations about Indigenous beliefs and disability. However, the oppression and racism Indigenous peoples have experienced and resisted has influenced their perspectives toward disability in ways that we are only beginning to understand.

Indigenous Peoples with Disabilities

Approximately 4.8 million, or 13.7 percent, of Canadians reported having a disability and needing some assistance with everyday activities (Canada 2012a). Of course, the percentage of persons with disabilities increases with age. Only 4.7 percent of adults between fifteen to twenty-four years of age have a disability, whereas 56.3 percent of adults seventy-five years of age or older reported a disability. This chapter focuses on physical disabilities, but mental health and substance misuse disabilities are also prevalent in many Indigenous communities. For an overview of mental health issues in Indigenous communities see Borg, Sportak and Delaney (2010).

The participants of the Canadian Survey on Disability (Canada 2012a) had the option of identifying themselves as First Nations, Métis, Inuit or Indigenous (Table 1). Due to logistical issues in data collection, persons living on-reserve were not included, thus missing large populations of First Nations peoples living in isolated and poor living conditions. In addition, the data involving Inuit people was too small to be reliable and was not included in the survey report. Even with missing data, the survey found that the rate of disability among Indigenous peoples was close to twice that of non-Indigenous people. The Canadian Survey on Disability (Canada 2012a) collected data on ten types of disabilities listed in the following table. The column titled "Ratio" presents the over-representation of Indigenous people in each of the types of disabilities. For all types of disabilities, Indigenous persons report 1.8 times the frequency of non-Indigenous persons. As noted in Chapter 3 by Robertson, one must be wary of interpreting the data presented within particular surveys as hard "facts" due to the various methods employed, the construction of disability, and the in/exclusion of specific respondents.

As the reader will note, this survey does not include Indigenous peoples living on-reserve (Table 9.1). The last survey that included Indigenous people was conducted more than twenty years ago (Canada 1994). Unlike the Canadian Survey of 2012, this study focused on both on- and off-reserve Indigenous peoples, and I would argue that it is more representative of the demographics. It found that 31.4 percent of the Indigenous population reported specific aspects of disability, which is over twice the national average. There is no reason to believe that the numbers have decreased in the past two decades. Clearly, the rate of disability is high for this population and it increases significantly with age and gender (female). In 1994, approximately 66.5 percent of Indigenous peoples fifty-five years or older reported living with a disability (Canada 1994).

Of those surveyed in the Aboriginal Peoples Survey (Canada 1994), 72 percent classified their disability as mild, while 4 percent indicated a severe disability. Disabilities were most frequently caused by injuries, followed by aging and congenital factors (SK 1999). Lifestyle diseases associated with socio-economic conditions are quite prevalent (Frideres and Gadacz 2012). Although Indigenous peoples have genetic disabilities at about the same rate as the rest of Canadians, they have a higher rate of disability due to environment and trauma-related disabilities. Clearly, while not placing blame on individuals or Indigenous communities, the Royal Commission on Aboriginal Peoples reported that "the disparity between Indigenous and non-Indigenous rates of disability corresponds to disparities in rates of injury, accident, violence, self-destructive or suicidal behaviour and illness (such as diabetes) that can result in permanent impairment" (RCAP 1996: 148). Sadly, not much has changed in the twenty years since the Commission produced this 4000-page report.

Indigenous peoples are positioned at the lowest end of the socio-economic

Table 9.1 Percentages of Adults with Disabilities

Disability	Non-Indigenous Population	Total Indigenous Off-Reserve	Ratio
All Types	13.7	18.6	1.8 (adjusted for multiple responses)
Seeing	2.7	5.0	1.9
Hearing	3.2	4.9	1.6
Mobility	7.2	11.6	1.7
Flexibility	7.6	10.6	1.4
Dexterity	3.5	5.6	1.6
Learning	2.3	4.7	2.1
Pain	9.7	14.4	1.5
Developmental	0.6	1.1	1.8
Mental/Psychological	3.9	6.6	1.7
Memory	2.3	5.1	2.3

Source: Canada 2012a *Canadian Survey on Disability*

scale regarding education, employment, income and health through no fault of their own. Housing on many remote and rural reserves is inadequate, failing to meet basic housing standards for amenities and structure, and the unemployment rate is consistently higher than in less isolated communities (Frideres and Gadacz 2012). On average, Indigenous peoples have lower education and often live in poverty with poorer health than non-Indigenous Canadians. Again, this points to the history of oppression and marginalization of Indigenous people by the larger Canadian society.

Similar to Mike Touchie in Chapter 1, many Indigenous people with disabilities have moved to urban areas to access supports or to be closer to services. They find that accessible housing is scarce; education and training opportunities are inadequate, as are home care services, employment opportunities and transportation. In addition, they are isolated and have limited opportunities for social interaction. Generally, Indigenous people are a neglected and lost population in the overall health and social service systems.

Mobility has also been noted as a serious problem for all groups and is reported equally, except for the Inuit (Canada 1994). The Inuit primarily live in small Arctic communities where their perceptions of "getting around" are seen as less of a problem. They are also close to family so help is generally available. Since the definition of disability is a social construction, there is evidence to suggest that individuals may be under-reporting their disability and that the numbers may have actually been higher (Durst and Bluechardt 2001).

As indicated in the 2012 survey, hearing disabilities are also a concern and their prevalence is much higher among Indigenous persons. In the 2012 study, the percentage of non-Indigenous Canadians with hearing difficulties was 2.9, and the percentage of off-reserve Indigenous people with hearing difficulties was 4.9; twice the national average was reported among the Inuit in the Aboriginal Peoples Survey (Canada 1994). It is suspected that this is related to two environmental concerns. First, many children live in cramped quarters, and high rates of childhood ear infections have been consistently reported. These ear infections have resulted in permanent but preventable hearing loss. The lack of prompt action at the onset of the infant's infection can have permanent effects, demonstrating the need for education and prevention. For First Nations persons living on-reserve, limited access to timely medical services and inadequate housing further exacerbates the conditions for hearing loss. The data in Table 1 demonstrate the impact of poverty and poor living conditions of Indigenous persons. Like the occupations of mining and farming, hunting in hostile climates and environments also put Indigenous people at risk for injury.

The higher rate of visual disability (seeing) reported as twice the national average is also alarming (Canada 2012a, 1994). Many visual disabilities among Indigenous peoples are related to the high rates of Type 2 diabetes. The loss of vision has a high

personal cost and can lead to isolation and loneliness, in addition to the high financial costs associated with health care and caregiving. With careful insulin control
and appropriate diet in the early stages, many of these disabilities are preventable,
but it can be difficult where health services and health education are not readily
available or are inadequate, and nutritious food is unaffordable.

The categories of flexibility and dexterity raise definitional issues (Canada
2012a, 1994). Dexterity includes the person's ability to complete everyday personal and household activities. For example, it may include opening a can of soup,
completing personal hygiene such as brushing your teeth, making a bed and other
tasks that require some strength, flexibility and agility. With family supports and a
culture that encourages giving and receiving help (interdependency), individuals
are not expected to be totally independent and self-sufficient in all aspects of their
lives. As a result, one does not perceive him or herself to have a problem with flexibility or agility if they need help opening a jar of strawberry jam or putting on a
winter coat, as the assistance will be provided (Durst and Bluechardt 2001). This
example illustrates how the perception of disability is influenced by culture. In a
society that emphasizes individualism and self-sufficiency, the lack of these abilities
socially construct the "disability" that would not exist in a society that emphasized
mutual support and communal help.

Case Example — Hope's Story:
"Listen to what I am saying!"

In the section below, Hope's story, as directly conveyed by her, is shared to illustrate
a first person account of the experiences behind the statistics. As in Mike Touchie's
account (Chapter 1), the reader will appreciate the personal struggles, resilience and
strength of these two individuals, as well as the structural barriers and oppression
they have had to overcome. As part of a larger research project, the poignant story
of Hope emerged, and for a more detailed account with direct quotes, I refer the
reader to Durst, Morin, Wall and Bluechardt (2007). Hope is the pseudonym for a
First Nations woman with quadriplegia who lives alone in a western Canadian city
(Durst and Bluechardt 2001; Durst et al. 2007). Hope began her life on an isolated
reserve in northern Saskatchewan, and her life was without incident until she suffered a serious accident at the age of thirteen. She was with some other children
and one of them was playing with a rifle. The rifle fell to the floor and discharged.
The bullet cut through her neck and damaged her spinal cord. In severe pain, she
laid on the backseat of a car for the 400-kilometre journey on gravel roads to the
nearest hospital. During her hospital stay and rehabilitation, she noted that her
family and friends did not visit her, leaving her feeling abandoned. To this day,
she remembers this pain and loss of family, community and culture. For a short

time, she returned to her reserve community but did not receive the medical care and social supports she needed. She returned to the city where she remains today.

At a young age, child protection services brought her into care as a ward of the province and placed her in a number of foster homes. While in these homes and in the hospital she suffered abuse from other children and sexual abuse from adult so-called "caregivers." She later had the courage to attend university and reports experiencing further abuse by an instructor. She persevered and completed a Bachelor of Education degree but was unable to find meaningful employment. Hope has lived entirely on social assistance and tells her story of poverty. In her loneliness, she often thought of suicide and for a time she slept with a knife under her pillow. As she tried to create a life, she was consistently marginalized and ignored by people, and she felt invisible.

Later, Hope reports meeting a "nice man" and became pregnant. Sadly, the father was not committed to the relationship and soon abandoned her. He has not been seen since. She gave birth to a baby girl. Unfortunately, hospital staff tried to prevent her from bonding with her daughter and removed the baby; they even moved Hope's wheelchair so that she could not reach her child. Child protection services wanted to permanently remove the baby from her care, but Hope fought them, arguing that she could provide the essential emotional and physical care. Hope and most would agree that her daughter has grown into an intelligent and outstanding young woman. In spite of the pain and suffering, Hope has demon-strated resistance and resiliency. She is aware of, and fights for, her right to have an independent and fulfilling life.

Hope gives herself meaning through human contact, just as she picked her pseudonym *Hope*. She is regularly seen in her community selling raffle tickets in the mall, visiting other persons with disabilities and reaching out to others. In her motorized chair, she and her daughter "wheel" around the city taking groceries to, watching television with, or just visiting other marginalized city residents who have various forms of physical and mental disabilities. She advocates for others by doing things such as making calls to City Hall to request repairs to shifting and broken sidewalks. She has asked for help from her Band Council but feels they have abandoned her. She calls on First Nations governments to respond to the needs of this neglected and invisible population. Hope challenges the jurisdictional arguments between the federal, provincial, and Band governments that leave First Nations people "ping-ponging" from one agency to another.

Although Hope's story is filled with grief, abuse and poverty, it is also uplifting. It is a story of courage and resiliency in spite of significant structural barriers. For example, she was determined to strive for independent living. She fought the child welfare authorities to keep and raise her child. She resisted the racism and oppres-sion of public officials and private individuals to maintain dignity and self-respect, with the rights and responsibilities of any citizen. She resisted social isolation by reaching out to others and finding meaning as a mother, care provider and advocate for others (Durst et al. 2007). Hope's story is only one of many with similar experiences. She has lived the life of a marginalized and discriminated woman but maintains optimism and "hope." As she likes to say with a bright smile, "I have *wheeled the wheel* of Indigenous people with disabilities."

Issues Facing Indigenous Persons with Disabilities

The issues facing Indigenous peoples with disabilities are common to other people with disabilities; however, they are exacerbated by colonial oppression and the specific discrimination imposed on Indigenous peoples. The themes presented below emerged during research conducted by the author and colleagues in a Prairie city (Durst, Manuel South and Bluechardt 2006). The findings and discussions are based upon four focus groups involving eleven Indigenous participants who reported having a disability. The findings are widely supported by other similar studies. In this chapter, they have been organized under the following headings: Independent Living; Transportation; Employment and Income; Education and Training; Housing; and Personal Supports. The following quotations are a collection of the thoughts and perspectives of Indigenous peoples (Durst et al. 2006).

Independent Living

> *People with disabilities are working on the issues facing independent living in [this city] but they consistently encounter barriers to full and meaningful employment. Like with the attendant care issue, the government is totally against having individual funding for attendant care. (Female, Durst et al. 2006)*

The idea of *independence* is widely understood as the ability to be able to live a lifestyle that allows for individual choice and decision-making. Sadly, participants in this study felt discriminated against based on their Indigenous descent.

> *Being disabled is one thing, but being disabled and Indian is a whole other problem. Indian people do not have a very good reputation and it makes it hard on us to get ahead. The Bands don't want to help us once we leave the reserve, and the services in the city might not help you because they don't get funding for you. Also, if you are applying for a job, some employees are racist, so are some landlords. (Female, Durst et al. 2006)*

Living completely alone may not be realistic; however, being dependent on others for physical assistance does not mean that individual choice should be restricted. Social and physical barriers may become repressive, such that many people with disabilities are forced to deny their experiences and their reality of disability, and conform to the prejudices and images imposed by others (French 1993). These attitudinal barriers contribute to feelings of low self-worth and social isolation. Many individuals are trapped in a self-depreciating world of loneliness and hopelessness and other associated problems.

> *I didn't accept my disability for a long time, probably five years. I went through drinking a fair bit, drugs, and it was the only way I could cope with life. I wanted to be out to lunch all the time and not really care about myself. But then after a while I needed to take a really good look at my life and I don't want to be like this for the rest of my life, so then I started ... I stopped drinking, stopped doing drugs, stopped trying to be so dysfunctional. I found better ways to handle my disability. (Female, Durst et al. 2006)*

Many Indigenous people have never had the benefit of being full and active participants in mainstream society because of restrictive social and physical barriers. In turn, these attitudinal and systemic barriers have made it even more difficult to enjoy full community participation. With restricted and limited access to resources and services, Indigenous people with disabilities are forced to remain in a dependent role, and to have few of their basic needs met; this, in turn, makes it extremely difficult to attain independence.

Transportation
Access to transportation affects a person's ability to be independent in a number of ways. Without adequate and reliable means of travel, a person with a disability is restricted from participating in many aspects of community life, such as shopping, employment, education, training, medical appointments, and recreation (B.C. Aboriginal Network on Disability Society 1993).

> *If I have to wait for two days to book a ride [on para-transit], I don't get out that much, especially in the winter. Since getting around is either tough or costs too much, I tend to stay at home a lot. That affects a lot more than just not being able to get out of my apartment. I start feeling closed in and get down on myself. (Male, Durst et al. 2006)*

Canadian cities often have a wide array of transportation alternatives, but cost and accessibility are constant problems that are exasperated for Indigenous people. It is understood that people with disabilities have a right to reasonable transportation supports, but these supports are under increasing demand and are sometimes not welcoming to Indigenous people.

Employment and Income

Part of being independent is the ability to support one's self economically. The ability to be economically self-sustaining, in turn, depends upon success in the labour market. It has been estimated that the unemployment rate for Indigenous people is more than twice that of the average non-Indigenous workforce (Frideres and Gadacz 2012). The rate of unemployment is even greater for Indigenous people with disabilities, much for the same reasons, but also because of stereotypes and discriminatory hiring practices.

Research indicates that Indigenous people with disabilities who are fortunate enough to have employment tend to be concentrated in lower-skilled, lower-wage employment sectors (B.C. Aboriginal Network on Disability Society 1993). Participants who were previously employed before they acquired a disability commented on the physical barriers within work places that did not allow for a comfortable or accessible work environment. Such barriers consisted of low desks and counter tops that did not allow for wheelchair clearance, cramped work quarters, inaccessible washroom facilities, and nonadaptive technology.

> *Accessibility in the workplace and attendant services are necessary for me. If they are not available or accessible, then I am pretty restricted to where I can work. (Male, Durst et al. 2006)*

> *Some employers are uncomfortable with disabled people and even more uncomfortable with having an attendant present. With those kinds of attitudes, it makes getting a job pretty hard. (Male family member, Durst et al. 2006)*

The right to income security through employment or income assistance ensures adequate security and subsistence. People have the right to receive reasonable accommodation by employers in the workplace, but just as non-Indigenous people with disabilities find it difficult, the situation is even more frustrating for Indigenous peoples.

Education and Training

Education and training are critical in obtaining and securing economic self-sufficiency through employment. However, receiving financial support from some individual Band Councils has been difficult for many.

> *I'm continually fighting for education funding and training. I keep searching for a job but there are none with my experience and education level. But the Band does not want to give me any sponsorship because I live off-reserve. (Male, Durst et al. 2006)*

> *The Neil Squire Foundation [employment and training nonprofit agency]*

helped with my funding so I could get computer training because the Band would not support me. So after two years of fighting [with the Band] for some funding, I finally received help from the organization [Neil Squire Foundation]. (Male, Durst et al. 2006)

In recent years, there have been considerable improvements in making education and training more accessible to persons with disabilities. But these agencies are operated by non-Indigenous professionals, and Indigenous persons often feel excluded and unwelcomed. If they go at all, it just does not feel right for them — as one Indigenous individual reported: "It's for white people."

Housing
Housing for persons with a disability is not a problem for those who can afford it. It is not a question of the availability of adequate housing, but the problem of affordability caused by poverty. The cheaper rental units are often substandard and of poor quality; the better housing is just out of reach of most Indigenous peoples with disabilities.

What is needed is an allocation of more accessible and affordable housing to people with disabilities ... but usually their definition of wheelchair accessible is just a ramp to the door. They don't take into consideration that you need to use your chair to go into the washroom. Washrooms are so small in most apartments. Like getting under the sink. I can't do it where we live. I just wash up on my lap every day with a basin. (Female, Durst et al. 2006)

Often rental units that were advertised to be accessible for persons with disabilities were not, and sometimes landlords were noted as taking advantage of persons with disabilities.

The house I live in does not have a back door, steps or a porch ... it's just a drop and that is not safe. The landlord won't fix my entrance. The doorway is a struggle to get through, but the landlord says it's wheelchair accessible. He just keeps saying he has no money to do any renovations. Landlords use welfare people ... This house, I got it fixed up to be wheelchair accessible just to be able to get through the front door. He used the grant money to do renovations but did them sloppy to save the money for himself. (Female, Durst et al. 2006)

As illustrated by the above accounts, Indigenous people often face direct racism when seeking housing in major cities. With affordable housing in short supply, landlords can exploit the most vulnerable, and the right to decent accommodation is frequently denied to Indigenous peoples with disabilities.

Personal Supports

Personal supports, such as attendant care, equipment repair, service provision and counselling, are supposed to be available but these services are difficult to access. The responsibility often falls on family members, and many programs that provide financial support for attendant care will not allow family members to be reimbursed for this service.

> *There is not any compensation for the family and that's who you rely on or that's who you have to rely on. The family system can burnout really fast without help, and that has a big effect on the disabled person. (Male, Durst et al. 2006)*

> *About caregiving, it's really lacking ... I know [my husband] took a caregiving course three years ago. They started having their meetings and after a while everyone started saying they just didn't have the time because they had people at home they had to look after and there were no supports in place to help out during those times, when they had to be away from home. (Female, Durst et al. 2006)*

There is a cultural expectation in Indigenous communities that families care for their own, and, consistently, Indigenous people would prefer to have a family member provide personal supports. However, funding sources frequently deny financial assistance to family members and insist on the utilization of home care paraprofessionals who are often outside the culture. Subsequently, Indigenous people often make do without these critical supports.

Recommendations for Change

Self-government means the ability and inherent right of Indigenous peoples to govern themselves as they decide, creating and operating their social, administrative and economic institutions. The pursuit of independent living for Indigenous peoples with disabilities is similar. Self-government and local control over social, educational and health programs has been viewed as a positive step in making programs culturally appropriate and accessible, but at times it has been a turbulent journey (Durst 2010).

There is solid evidence of program improvement through self-government, but in a curious twist, the right to self-government supersedes the right to services and programs for persons with disabilities. For example, if the Band receives funding earmarked for disability programming, the Band has the right to re-allocate those funds to any program they choose. There are situations where federal funding for disabilities has been applied to capital expenditures such as new furniture, and there is nothing the people with disabilities can do about it. In many circumstances, disability issues are not viewed as a priority by the Chiefs and Band Councils, and with increasing Band administration in some communities, there is the possibility that people with disabilities may be further marginalized. This concern is succinctly expressed in the following quotes.

> Disabled people will altogether be forgotten about, because right now we are at the bottom of the pile, but with self-government we won't be in the pile at all. They aren't concerned with the disabled, they're more concerned with making money. Even though they are supposed to get additional funding for the disabled, we don't see any of that. (Female, Durst et al. 2006)

> It is necessary for the Bands, more specifically, Chief and Council, to become aware. Chief and Council are not very supportive because they are not aware or because disability issues are just not a priority to them. But that's where it starts because they could start creating services like counselling services and attendant services. They need to be willing to allocate money. Nowadays you hear about all those reserves getting land claim dollars back. You think they would have some dollars to help disabled Band members. (Female, Durst et al. 2006)

Overall, participants feared that as funding of services and programs are transferred to Band governments, their needs will be further ignored. It was suggested that they would be better off without First Nations status. However, in recent years, there have been some interesting and positive developments. Since the 1960s and until his death in 2001, Everett Soop was an active advocate for Indigenous persons with disabilities. Although he had muscular dystrophy, he promoted himself as abled and challenged society's structural inequities. In northern Saskatchewan, Gary Tinker, a Métis advocate with cerebral palsy, created a foundation advocating for Indigenous peoples. Literature searches soon find the decades of work by Doreen Demas, a blind activist who has spoken and written about disabled Indigenous peoples. The British Columbia Aboriginal Network on Disability Society (BCANDS) and organizations like the Native Women's Association of Canada have researched and been active in the Indigenous disability movement. At the time of this writing, the Disability Rights Promotion International (York University) is active in researching this topic and has just released its report, Expanding the Circle: Snapshot, that explores the issues facing Indigenous persons (DRPI 2014).

Much needs to be done, including challenging the inequities facing all Indigenous peoples in Canada. In the following section, eight specific recommendations are offered to address the complex issues facing Indigenous peoples with disabilities (see also DRPI 2014; Lovern and Locust 2013).

1. There is the need for education programs that increase awareness of disability issues for both Indigenous and non-Indigenous people. Indigenous peoples are often invisible and ignored by existing agencies. Agency leaders do not understand the subtle barriers facing Indigenous people from accessing their programs. Some professionals feel that they provide service equally to all but fail to understand the cultural barriers that Indigenous people experience. Increasing awareness can ameliorate some of the problems facing Indigenous people with disabilities.

2. There is a need for culturally sensitive health and social programs to meet the needs of Indigenous people with disabilities, and trained Indigenous people are required to deliver these programs. Many communities have a wide array of programs and services but they are not meeting the needs of this population. They need to make their agencies more culturally sensitive and appropriate for Indigenous people. This includes the hiring of Indigenous people with and without disabilities.

3. Indigenous people with disabilities need to be involved in the development and delivery of programs. As Hope says, "Listen to what I am saying!" Indigenous people need to be part of the planning and delivery of programs and services that affect their quality of life. This can be achieved by seeking their participation on planning councils, community agency boards and service committees.

4. There is a need for increased funding to cover the personal costs associated with having a disability. A sufficient and dependable income is a human right and a secure income would improve the standard and quality of living for Indigenous people with disabilities. There are many hidden and extra costs of living that need to be covered.

5. Many Indigenous people depend upon the support of family, and financial compensation should be made available to family supports. If family members were adequately compensated for their needed services, the quality of support and care could be greatly improved.

6. The funding based on political jurisdictional issues needs to be resolved so that First Nations, Indigenous, on-reserve and off-reserve persons can access the services they are entitled to receive. As it stands, each agency or department has its own mandate, and persons with disabilities are bounced from one agency to another. There needs to be agreements that allow services to be provided across agencies.

7. Increased funding for training programs and education is required to assist Indigenous people who wish to compete in the labour market to develop the necessary skills and knowledge.

8. There needs to be inclusion and enforcement of employment equity programs to ensure the hiring of Indigenous people with disabilities.

Clearly, it is through concrete and realistic steps that the barriers facing Indigenous persons with disabilities can be confronted, and their aspirations for participation in their communities can be attained. These recommendations challenge the larger systemic barriers that have created the conditions of disadvantage. Indigenous people with disabilities are seeking an improved quality of life, a life with meaning and joy, and equal rights with all citizens. They are entitled to receive benefits and services provided to non-Indigenous citizens. Indigenous people with disabilities are resilient and courageous and want their voices to be heard: some feel their disability is a "gift from the Creator" and they want to reduce the barriers to greater social inclusion and a full and rewarding life.

What can health and social service professionals do to help? Aside from engaging in broader structural change and creating a more just society, the answer is simple: advocacy. Indigenous persons with disabilities do not need social workers and professionals to practice their profession *on them* but need the knowledge and skills of professionals to access needed and entitled services and programs. They need a voice to advocate with an empowering anti-oppressive approach. They need help cutting through the red tape of jurisdictional barriers. It is an old cliché, but you are either part of the problem or part of the solution. As professionals, it is time to work together in advocating for Indigenous persons with disabilities. In the end, we create a more just society for all.

Chapter Summary

The rate of disabilities within the Indigenous population of Canada is twice that of the national average in all areas of disabilities, including physical, developmental and mental health issues. They encounter genetic disabilities at the same rate as non-Indigenous Canadians; however, it has been acknowledged that the higher rates of acquired disabilities are related to environmental causes related to experiences of racism, poverty and discrimination. Both on- and off-reserve Indigenous people with disabilities encounter barriers to services and are excluded from many services through jurisdictional disputes. Indigenous peoples with disabilities experience multiple oppressions: racism, ableism, sexism and geographic and jurisdictional disadvantage. Actions must be taken to improve services such as supporting independent living and personal supports, providing transportation, education and training, and accessible and affordable housing. It is critical that professionals hear the voice of Indigenous people with disabilities and respond from an anti-oppressive approach in order to confront ableism, racism and discrimination within policies and practice.

Discussion Questions

1. How has the history of colonialism and oppression had an impact on Indigenous people with disabilities today?
2. What could mainstream agencies do to invite, attract or reach more Indigenous persons with disabilities to their agencies?
3. How might social service agencies adapt their services to better meet the needs of Indigenous persons with disabilities? What policies or practices might they adopt?
4. How might Indigenous persons with disabilities understand independence and community differently than non-Indigenous persons?

References

B.C. Aboriginal Network on Disability Society. 1993. "Report on B.C. Aboriginal people with disabilities." Final Report to the Royal Commission on Aboriginal Peoples. B.C. Aboriginal Network on Disability Society.

Barnes, Colin. 2012. "Understanding the Social Model of Disability: Past, Present and Future." In Nick Watson, Alan Roulstone and Carol Thomas (eds.), *Routedge Handbook of Disability Studies*. Oxon, UK: Routledge, Taylor and Francis Group.

Borg, Darren, Jennifer Sportak and Roger Delaney. 2010. "A Context Sensitive Approach to Mental Illness: Towards a Wellness Model of Helping." In Keith Brownlee, Raymond Neckoway, Delaney Delaney, and Douglas Durst (eds.), *Social wWork and Aboriginal Peoples: Perspectives from Canada's Rural and Provincial Norths*. Thunder Bay, ON: Lakehead University Press.

Canada. 1994. *1991 Aboriginal Peoples: Disability and Housing*. Ottawa: Statistics Canada.

____. 2006. Statscan. *Persons with Disabilities*. <statcan.gc.ca/tables-tableaux/sum-som/l01/cst01/health71a-eng.htm>.

____. 2011. *National Household Survey, 2011*. Ottawa: Statistics Canada. <statcan.gc.ca/daily-quotidien/130508/dq130508a-eng.htm>

____. 2012. *First Nations Health: HIV and AIDS*. Ottawa: Health Canada. <hc-sc.gc.ca/fniah-spnia/diseases-maladies/aids-sida/index-eng.php>

____. 2012a. *Canadian Survey on Disability, 2012*. Ottawa: Statistics Canada.

____. 2013. *Aboriginal Demographics*. Ottawa, ON: Aboriginal Affairs and Northern Development Canada. <aadnc-aandc.gc.ca/DAM/DAM-INTER-HQ-AI/STAGING/texte-text/abo_demo2013_1370443844970_eng.pdf>.

____. 2013a. *Aboriginal Income Disparity in Canada: Strategic Research*. Ottawa, ON: Aboriginal Affairs and Northern Development Canada.

____. 2013b. *The Aboriginal Peoples Survey at a Glance: Strategic Research*. Ottawa, ON: Aboriginal Affairs and Northern Development Canada.

CDS. 2012. *Diabetes and Urban Aboriginal Populations in Canada*. Ottawa, ON: Canadian Diabetes Association.

Dapcic, B. 1995. *Socio-Cultural Understanding of d\Disability: Perspectives from Members of the Hopi Tribe*. Northern Arizona University.

Demas, Doreen. 1993. "Triple Jeopardy: Native Women with Disabilities." *Canadian Woman*

Studies 13, 4: 53–55.

DRPI (Disability Rights Promotion International). 2010. *UN Convention on the Rights of Persons with Disabilities and its Optional Protocol.* Toronto, ON: Disability Rights Promotion International, York University.

_____. 2014. *Expanding the Circle: Snapshot.* SSHRC Partnership Development Grant. Toronto, ON: Disability Rights Promotion International. York University.

Dunn, Peter A. 1999. *The Development of Government Independent Living Policies and Programs for Canadians with Disabilities.* Waterloo, ON: Faculty of Social Work, Wilfrid Laurier University.

Durst, Douglas. 2006. *Urban Aboriginal Families of Children with Disabilities: Social Inclusion or Exclusion?* Ottawa: National Association of Friendship Centres.

_____. 2010. "A Turbulent Journey: Self-government of Social Services." In Keith Brownlee, Raymond Neckoway, Delaney Delaney and Douglas Durst (eds.), *Social Work and Aboriginal Peoples: Perspectives from Canada's Rural and Provincial Norths.* Thunder Bay, ON: Lakehead University Press

_____. 2010a. "Urban Aboriginal Peoples in Canadian Cities." In Keith Brownlee, Raymond Neckoway, Delaney Delaney and Douglas Durst (eds.), *Social Work and Aboriginal peoples: Perspectives from Canada's Rural and Provincial Norths.* Thunder Bay, ON: Lakehead University Press.

Durst, Douglas, and Mary Bluechardt. 2001. *Urban Aboriginal Persons with Disabilities: Triple jJeopardy!* Regina, SK: Social Policy Research Unit, University of Regina. <uregina.ca/spru/spruweb/durst.html>.

Durst, Douglas, Shelly Manuel South and Mary Bluechardt. 2006. "Urban First Nations People with Disabilities Speak Out." *Journal of Aboriginal Health* 3, 1: 34–43.

Durst, Douglas, Georgina Morin, Sharon Wall and Mary Bluechardt. 2007. "A First Nations Woman with Disabilities: 'Listen to What I Am Saying.'" *Native Social Work Journal. Resistance and Resiliency: Addressing Historical Trauma of Aboriginal Peoples* 6: 57–77.

French, Sally. 1993. "Disability, Impairment or Something In Between." In John Swain, Colin Barnes, Sally French and Carol Thomas (eds.), *Disabling Barriers — Enabling Environments.* London: Sage.

Frideres, James S., and Rene R. Gadacz. 2012. *Aboriginal Peoples in Canada, Contemporary Conflicts* 9th edition. Toronto, ON: Pearson Canada, Inc.

Gething, Lindsay. 1995. "A Case Study of Australian Aboriginal People with Disabilities." *Australian Disabilities Review* 2, 1: 77–87.

Lovern, Lavonna L., and Carol Locust. 2013. *Native American Communities on Health and Disability: A Borderland Dialogue.* New York: Palgrave Macmillan Press.

Lum, Zi-Ann. 2014. "Canada is the Only U.N. Member to Reject Landmark Indigenous Rights Document." *Huffington Post,* October. <huffingtonpost.ca/2014/10/02/Canada-un-Indigenous-rights_n_5918868.html>.

NAND. 1994. *Little Mountain and If They Would Only Listen.* National Aboriginal Network on Disability, Ottawa.

RCAP (Royal Commission on Aboriginal Peoples). 1993. *Aboriginal Peoples in Urban Centres. Report of the National Round Table on Aboriginal Urban Issues.* Ottawa: Ministry of Supply Services.

_____. 1996. *Gathering Strength* Volume III. Ottawa: Ministry of Supply Services.

Shakespeare, Tom. 2014. *Disability Rights and Wrongs Revisited* 2nd edition. London, UK: Routledge Press.

Sinclair, Raven. 2008. "All My Relations — Native Transracial Adoption: A Critical Case Study of Cultural Identity." Doctoral dissertation, University of Calgary, 2007. Ann Arbor, MI: UMI Dissertation Services.

____. 2009. "Identity or Racism? Aboriginal Transracial Adoption." In R. Sinclair, M.A. Hart and G. Bruyere (eds.), *Wicihitowin: Aboriginal Social Work in Canada.* Halifax, NS: Fernwood Publishing.

SK – Saskatchewan's Women's Secretariat. 1999. *Profile of Aboriginal Women in Saskatchewan.* Regina, SK: Saskatchewan Women's Secretariat.

Stienstra, Deborah. 2012. *About Canada: Disability Rights.* Black Point, NS: Fernwood Publishing.

Stone, John H. (ed.). 2005. *Culture and Disability: Providing Culturally Competent Services.* Thousand Oaks, CA: Sage Publications.

Thomas, R. 1981. "Discussion." In F. Hoffman (ed.), *The American Indian Family: Strengths and Stresses.* Isleta, NM.

Truth and Reconciliation Commission. 2015. Justice Murray Sinclair, Winnipeg, MB: Truth and Reconciliation Commission of Canada.

Wiebe, Rudy, and Yvonne Johnson. 1998. *Stolen Life, The Journey of a Cree Woman.* Toronto: A.A. Knopf Canada.

Chapter 10

Mental Health Disability: The Forgotten Terrain

Grant Larson

An observation often made by students studying in the helping professions is that textbooks focusing on persons with disabilities rarely provide substantial content on mental health topics, and likewise, mental health literature makes minimal reference to other forms of disability. This observation highlights an interesting historical trend in the disability field — that mental health disability, although the most common form of disability, is often written about, responded to and understood as separate and distinct from other forms of disability. Mental health and disability legislation, policy, service organizations, professional practice orientations and even preparatory educational programs primarily exist as distinct fields of practice. This chapter will focus on mental health concerns as a form of disability, as the forgotten terrain in the disability field, and will argue that contemporary issues related to mental health disability parallel those facing other forms of disability and that the two fields of practice have much to learn from one another.

In 2014, the World Health Organization (WHO) reported that "the most common form of disability facing the globe is some form of mental illness" (WHO 2014). Although specific definitions of mental health and mental illness are contentious, there is little debate that mental health concerns touch all segments of Canadian society (Regehr and Glancy 2014: 1). In 2002, Health Canada reported that approximately 20 percent of Canadians would experience a form of mental disability sometime in their lives (Health Canada 2002). Canada spends over $14 billion annually on mental health services and supports (Institute of Health

Economics 2010), and the economic burden of mental health concerns in Canada was estimated in 2003 as $51 billion (Lim et al. 2008). Davis (2014: 46) reports that "about one in seven hospitalizations in Canada are related to the treatment of a mental illness," and unfortunately suicide remains as the second leading cause of death among 15–34 year olds (Navaneelan 2012). There is little doubt then that mental health disability is one of the most pervasive, serious and costly forms of disability facing the Canadian population.

The aim of this chapter is to introduce students to mental health concerns as a form of disability, and to show that language and discourse, theoretical frameworks, social attitudes and stigma, service responses, and controversial issues and ethical considerations are similar to the concerns faced by those with physical and cognitive disabilities. A progressive framework (critical theory) will be utilized to understand this form of disability, and an example will be provided to demonstrate principles and strategies of those wishing to engage in anti-oppressive and anti-ableist practice with those with mental health disabilities.

Language and Discourse

The editors of this book have had extensive discussions about the importance of language and terminology when referring to persons with disabilities. The terminology utilized in the mental health field is particularly contentious given the historical and professional dominance of the biomedical model. One might argue, however, that all language is deeply rooted in the context, social attitudes and time it was developed, and as such, what is deemed acceptable and appropriate at one time quickly becomes outdated, negative and disempowering to those most affected. In this chapter, the term "mental health disability" will be used rather than terms such as mental illness, mental disorder or specific diagnostic labels — schizophrenia, borderline personality, bipolar, and so on — when referring to people who have had different mental experiences. This terminology has been chosen because it is consistent with the values of anti-oppressive and progressive practice approaches. The experiences of those with mental health disabilities are subjective, variable and often influential in shaping identity (Riddell and Watson 2003), and the language used to describe such experiences must not label, stigmatize or disempower those being described.

The social constructions inherent in the terminology used to describe mental health disabilities are often derived from the dominant ideological and theoretical frameworks used to understand these social phenomena (Coppock and Dunn 2010). At first glance, many individuals, and even helping professionals, do not identify any negative connotations of terms such as mental illness or mental disorder. However, the word illness automatically places the discourse of mental health disability within a biomedical framework — a pathology-oriented approach that identifies and labels the whole person based on the presence of perceived deficits, diseases or problems (Davis 2014: 16). The language of illness and disorder then situates the discourse of mental health disability within a biomedical framework. Not only does this infer that the etiology of mental health disabilities lies in individual physiological pathology, a rather negative view of mental experiences, but it also reinforces a hierarchical health system whereby health providers hold more power than service users. Psychiatrists and other service providers have the power to assess, diagnose, treat and confine those with mental health disabilities. The language of mental disorder or mental illness, whether intentional or not, serves the function of reinforcing biological causes, medically oriented diagnostic and assessment tools, medicalized pharmacological treatments and power structures and roles whereby health professionals are the experts who make decisions, and service users are the receivers of those decisions. In like fashion, terms such as doctor, patient and diagnostic category — for example, schizophrenic — have the same effect of creating a power imbalance between professionals and service users.

Psychiatric survivor groups and the Mad People's Movement (LeFrançois, Menzies and Reaume 2013) illustrate how those who experience mental health disabilities are both reclaiming the language and discourse of their experiences and liberating themselves from a history of oppression, abuse, inequality and human rights violations that was, and sometimes still is, present in traditional and dominant mental health care systems. These survivors of psychiatric services

> incorporate all that is critical of psychiatry from a radical socially progressive foundation in which the medical model is dispensed with as biologically reductionist whilst alternative forms of helping people experiencing mental anguish are based on humanitarian, holistic perspectives where people are not reduced to symptoms but understood within the social and economic context of the society in which they live. (Menzies, LeFrançois and Reaume 2013: 2)

The author of this chapter, then, will resist the temptation to specifically define mental health disabilities because to do so would give in to the modernist tendency of categorizing and labelling those who experience diverse mental experiences. Instead, it may be fair to recognize that those with mental health disabilities represent a wide range of mental health experiences and are variably excluded, stigmatized and discriminated against by larger society.

To conclude this discussion about language and discourse, it is important to recognize that the language used by practitioners in working with those with diverse mental experiences is incredibly important as attitudes and stigma quickly become attached to terminology. It is important that workers continually challenge the language they use to ensure that it is respectful, sensitive, egalitarian and empowering for individuals and families who use mental health services.

A Progressive/Critical Approach

One of the aims of this book is to challenge the dominant ways of thinking about and responding to those with disabilities. Theoretical and conceptual frameworks for understanding mental health disabilities have both similarities and differences with the models commonly used with physical and developmental disabilities. Disability studies texts often refer to frameworks such as a social model, a personal tragedy model, and a rehabilitation model (see Hanes, Chapter 4). Mental health literature commonly refers to a biomedical model, a stress-vulnerability model, a biopsychosocial model, cognitive behavioral theory, and perspectives such as feminist theory, anti-oppressive practice, and ecological systems theory. Many mental health theories, like a biomedical model, take an individualized approach to understanding and treating mental health concerns. A biomedical model suggests that mental health and mental health disability reside within the individual as objective physical processes, and it ignores the subjective, cultural and societal context within which they take place (Davis 2014: 16). In recent times, however, a simple biomedical model has been replaced with a biopsychosocial model, or even a stress-vulnerability model (Davis 2014), which considers the importance of social factors in the development of mental health disabilities. However, in actual practice, one could argue that even with these approaches, biological determinants and a medical understanding of mental health disability are primary and social factors secondary. As well, one cannot ignore the influence and power of pharmaceutical companies in reinforcing a biomedical approach by their promotion of psychotropic medications as the most important treatment for mental health disabilities.

Critical perspectives such as feminist theory, anti-oppressive practice and structural theory focus on the larger issues of class, gender, race, sexual orientation and socio-political context that determine and alter the quality of life for those labelled as "mentally ill." With these progressive frameworks, mental disability is understood as not belonging to the individual, but as the result of the social and economic structures in society which create exclusion, discrimination and disadvantage for those with a different set of experiences.

Hanes, in Chapter 4, presents a full discussion of what he coins as the "Post-social Model of Disability." This model incorporates a social model of disability (Oliver 1996) with structural social work theory (Mullaly 2007; Moreau 1979; Lundy 2004) to focus not only on the socio-political inequalities and environmental factors but also on the lived experience of those with disabilities. The approach acknowledges both the immediate needs of those with disabilities and the larger structural issues which are responsible for the barriers and disadvantage created for those with disabilities. When applied to mental health disabilities, this perspective means understanding and responding with compassion in humanitarian and holistic ways to the real experience of those with "mental anguish" (LeFrançois, Menzies and Reaume 2013) and at the same time challenging the social structures in mental health systems and larger society that stigmatize and discriminate against service users. Such an approach does not deny that multiple factors — such as biological, social, socio-economic, stigma and social location — interact to create mental disability, but they do not reduce complex mental experiences to singular and individualistic explanations. In a similar way, Larson describes an anti-oppressive practice approach for working with those who have mental health disabilities. This progressive approach identifies the following principles as key elements for responding to both the lived experience of those with mental health disabilities and the social structures which create inequality and disadvantage:

- Inviting service users to be full participants in all aspects of mental health service.
- Using language and discourse that is respectful, egalitarian and empowering.
- Actively deconstructing the medical model with service users and their families and encouraging alternative healing perspectives and strategies.
- Establishing just working relationships.
- Promoting education.
- Embracing cultural diversity and strengths perspectives in practice.
- Promoting principles of social justice. (Larson 2008)

Progressive/critical approaches are consistent with a human rights approach to mental health (see Murphy, Chapter 5), which places equality, citizenship and full participation in society as essential rights for persons with disabilities. This is a particularly important approach for working with people with mental health disabilities, because historically, like people with other forms of disability, they have been locked up against their will, abused and treated harshly, had treatments administered without their consent, and been denied their basic human rights and dignity. In the larger society, those with mental health disabilities have been labelled, stigmatized and discriminated against in areas such as housing, employment and social relationships. Today, mainstream psychiatric systems for responding to and treating those with mental health disabilities are kinder, more humane and more respectful of human rights, but many mental health systems and professionals continue to understand the experiences of mental health service users through narrow singular explanations which stigmatize and disempower. What is needed to reform the mental health system is the full participation and the voices of those who have the lived experience with mental health disabilities (Schneider 2010).

Stigma and Social Exclusion

It is well known that individuals with mental health disabilities often indicate that the stigma attached to their diagnosis is worse than the disability itself. Capponi (2003: 110) described being diagnosed with a mental illness as a "traumatic death sentence." Barbara Shooltz Kendzierski (2002: 61) calls her life with a mental health disability "a death interrupted," and Scott Simmie (Simmie and Nunes 2001) referred to mental illness as "the last taboo" and wrote a book by this title. Stigma refers to the negative beliefs and attitudes about mental health disabilities that lead to prejudice, stereotyping and discrimination (Charbonneau et al. in Davis 2014: 61). Much of the survivor literature documents the stigma, exclusion and discrimination that those with mental health disabilities have experienced. The Canadian Mental Health Association (CMHA) actively promotes anti-stigma education and indicates that the most common public misperceptions about those with mental health disabilities are that they lack intelligence, cannot hold meaningful employment, are violent and unpredictable, lack will power and volition to change, and that they will be always "sick" (CMHA n.d.). These are similar myths and misperceptions experienced by many persons with other forms of disabilities. Davis (2014) suggests that this is one of the reasons why individuals with mental health disabilities avoid seeking treatment for mental health concerns. One of the most subtle forms of stigma involves social exclusion, the practice of creating social distance between the person with a mental health disability and those within their social and familial circle. This often takes the form of both overt and covert withdrawal of social contact, communication and participation. Individuals may no longer be invited to participate in social gatherings and may feel like outsiders. Current friends and coworkers and even romantic partners may be seen as not wanting to associate with them (Davis 2014). Social exclusion becomes a powerful factor in reinforcing the misperceptions and myths about those who experience diverse mental experiences. This kind of stigma may become internalized and a source of "self-stigma" that further exasperates mental health disabilities. Simmie writes, "Stigma was, for me, the most agonizing aspect of my disorder. It cost friendships, career opportunities, and — most importantly — my self-esteem. It wasn't long before I began internalizing the attitudes of others, viewing myself as a lesser person" (Simmie and Nunes 2001: 63).

The media has been a powerful source in the perpetuation of stigma and discrimination for those with mental disabilities. For example, the Sandy Hook School tragedy in the United States or the Vince Li Greyhound Bus killing in Canada headline the mental health aspects of these horrific events. In so doing, the general public associates acts of violence with mental health disabilities. In like fashion, popular movies and television shows often portray individuals with schizophrenia, depression or post-traumatic stress as violent and unpredictable people who cannot be trusted. The sensationalized Hollywood version of what it is like to experience a mental health disability is often far from reality and tends to reinforce commonly held myths. While many mental health organizations work diligently to provide realistic and accurate information about mental health disability to destigmatize the experience, popular media may be seen as promoting stigmatizing beliefs for the purposes of entertaining or selling news stories.

In recent years there have been significant efforts of governments, policy makers and nongovernmental organizations such as the Canadian Mental Health Association to change public attitudes toward mental health disabilities. What is surprising is that recent research does not indicate that stigma has been reduced through these efforts (Regehr and Glancy 2014: 37). Research evidence shows that individuals are becoming more comfortable in seeking help when that have a mental health concern, and that people generally have more knowledge of mental health concerns, but there is little evidence to suggest that public attitudes to mental health disabilities are becoming more positive. A well-publicized survey in the United States comparing public attitudes toward mental disability in the 1950s with those of 1996 found that stigmatizing beliefs had actually increased (Phelan et al. 2000). In addition to the observation that popular media representations of mental disability actually perpetuate stigma, Davis (2014: 71) suggests that "the problem of increasing stigma lies with the explanatory model. Neurobiological conceptions of mental illness have not helped diminish stigma, and some now suggest that this conception has actually made the problem worse." He goes on to present evidence that people who accept a biomedical model of mental health disabilities "may feel sorry for the individual but still not want to associate with him or her" (Davis 2014: 71). The voices of those with mental health disabilities, through such projects as the *Hearing (Our) Voices* participatory research project, are needed to challenge dominant public perceptions of those who have a different set of mental health experiences (Schneider 2010).

Practice Trends and Recent Innovations

Like other disabilities, the history of treatment of those with mental health concerns has been characterized by incarceration, forced hospitalization, forced treatment, isolation, stigmatization and discrimination. Until the 1970s, many of those with mental health disabilities were housed in large psychiatric hospitals (up to five thousand residents) such as Riverview Hospital in Coquitlam, British Columbia. Deinstitutionalization saw the closure or downsizing of these institutions in the same way as institutions for those with developmental disabilities. The move toward community integration and community treatment was welcomed by those who recognized how poorly these institutions treated individuals. Unfortunately, governments and policy makers in Canada and the Western world did not provide the resources to support alternative approaches in the community (Lester and Glasby 2010; Davis 2014). As well, the discovery of antipsychotic medication that was observed to decrease hallucinations, delusions and paranoia, further entrenched a medical model as a response to this type of disability, but did provide the opportunity for some individuals to live in the community. Canadian provincial mental health legislation was rewritten during the 1960s and 1970s, but it tended to define the roles and authority of psychiatrists and psychiatric facilities in the treatment of those with mental health disabilities and the terms for involuntary psychiatric admission rather than focus on the protection of service users' rights. However, the *Canadian Charter of Rights and Freedoms* (1982) did provide a human rights framework to protect the rights of those with mental health disabilities. Provincial mental health acts are required to conform to the Charter (Davis 2014).

The 1960s and 1970s saw a rise in the anti-psychiatry movement with the works of Thomas Szasz and R.D. Laing, and more attention was given to the humane treatment of those with mental health concerns. Pharmacological treatments rose dramatically as well as attention to the social context of mental health disabilities. Practitioners realized that medication alone was not the answer, and that through supportive housing, social relationships, recreation and meaningful activity, individuals with mental disabilities had a better prognosis (Davis 2014). However, the 1990s saw a return to biomedical understandings of mental health and medical practitioners as the dominant decision-makers concerning those with mental health disabilities. Unfortunately, the voices of those most affected may still be the last to be heard when decisions about individual treatment are made (Schneider 2010). Common treatment strategies utilized today for those suffering from mental health disabilities include psychotropic medication, electroconvulsive treatment, occupational therapy and life skills training, and various forms of individual and group psychotherapy, such as cognitive behavioral treatment.

Recent innovations in the mental health field include recovery approaches, assertive community treatment, integrated services for those with substance use issues and mental health concerns, and culturally safe practice. These approaches are more consistent with a progressive/critical approach to mental health treatment and will be briefly explored below.

Recovery Model

An attempt to shift treatment approaches away from a negative pessimistic view of mental health disability to one that emphasizes strengths and abilities is the "recovery movement" (Davis 2014; Lester and Glasby 2010). Although those espousing recovery approaches may still accept biomedical explanations for mental health disabilities, they see recovery "as a process of personal growth and development" that "involves overcoming the effects of being a mental health patient, with all its implications, to regain control and establish a personally fulfilling meaningful life (Schrank and Slade in Davis 2014: 88). Recovery is not viewed as an outcome such as a remission of psychiatric symptoms, but rather as a process whereby the individual manages not only their mental experiences but also the social consequences — stigma and exclusion — of being labelled (Lester and Glasby 2010). As such, a recovery orientation emphasizes hope, client strengths, resilience, self-management, taking control, and an optimistic view by professionals who believe that service users can live productive meaningful lives (Davis 2014; Regehr and Glancy 2014). Although recovery approaches gained prominence in community mental health practice in the 1990s and 2000s and grew largely from grassroots movements of survivor groups, they are unfortunately not yet fully embraced by mainstream traditional psychiatric services (Davis 2014). Recovery approaches are largely consistent with progressive/critical understandings of mental health disability and provide an opportunity for service users to gain decision-making power and to live functional meaningful lives.

Assertive Community Treatment

An interesting and somewhat controversial new trend for those with "serious, persistent mental illness" (B.C. Ministry of Health 2002) is a service delivery method known as assertive community treatment (ACT). This labour-intensive approach aims to keep those with mental health disabilities in the community rather than in institutions by providing low client-to-staff ratios, 24-hour-per-day outreach services in the community, life skills training, a multidisciplinary team approach, and comprehensive and continuous services (Lafave, deSouza and Gerber 1996; Davis 2014). Considered less expensive that traditional institutional care but more expensive that typical community care, ACT is viewed both positively and negatively by service users and families. With this model, those with severe mental health disabilities are able to live in the community closer to their families, learn useful life skills and maintain a lifestyle that has many of the features of other citizens. However, regular monitoring of service users by mental health practitioners in their homes is viewed as intrusive and coercive with a threat of hospital admission if they refuse medications or other treatments (Davis 2014). From a progressive/critical lens, ACT is a positive practice in that it integrates those with mental health disabilities into community life, and provides more autonomy and independence than hospital-based care for service users. However, it is inconsistent with progressive approaches in that it utilizes an individualistic biomedical approach and minimizes social and structural determinants of mental health. As well, the lack of client autonomy in decision-making and the threats of hospitalization make it inconsistent with recovery approaches (Salyers and Tsemberis 2007). This approach, like traditional hospital-based care, raises both ethical and human rights concerns when implemented within the context of current mental health law and policy regarding involuntary certification and treatment without consent.

Integrated Mental Health and Substance Use Services

A third trend in current mental health practice involves responses to those with substance use concerns and mental health disability. Many Canadian provinces, like British Columbia, have begun a process of integrating all services for those with mental health and/or substance use concerns (B.C. Ministry of Health 2012). In the past, those with substance use concerns received treatment in specialized addiction organizations by addiction workers rather than mental health practitioners, who utilized treatment approaches unlike those used in mental health treatment. Research as shown, however, that 50 percent of people seeking treatment for an addiction also suffer from a mental health concern, and that up to 20 percent of people with a mental health disability have a substance use issue (Canadian Centre on Substance Abuse 2009).

Literature on this topic suggests a complex relationship between substance use and mental health whereby substance use may be viewed as a form of self-medication for a mental health concern, or both may arise from complex biological, psychological, social and structural factors (Davis 2014). Regardless, stigma, social attitudes and discrimination remain much the same for those with a mental health disability, substance use concerns or both. As well, those with mental health disability and substance use issues "have not typically been well-served by the health care system, or in particular, by mental health practitioners" (Davis 2014: 258). Treatment philosophies, education and training of practitioners, bureaucratic systems and policies, as well as public perceptions of the causes of problems prevent significant practical integration of services. This situation has been largely recognized by the practice community, yet barriers to the integration of services and responses remains high. A progressive/critical analysis suggests that an integration of services may de-emphasize singular individualized explanations for substance use and mental health disabilities, and look to larger social factors as instrumental in creating the conditions of disadvantage for those with these experiences. However, it will take time and transformation of mental health care systems to actually integrate addiction and mental health services.

Culturally Safe Mental Health Services

A final theme worth noting has to do with the predominance of Western cultural understandings of mental health disabilities in Canada, and the lack of cross-cultural and culturally safe mental health services. The Mental Health Commission of Canada (MHCC 2009) has recognized the barriers that exist in Canada for those coming from other cultural traditions — other than dominant Euro-Western cultures — who seek help for mental health concerns. The MHCC (2009) framework notes that mental health policy and treatments should include cultural safety and cultural competence. This issue is particularly important for Indigenous (First Nations, Inuit and Métis) populations in Canada. They have not only been marginalized and oppressed generally in Canadian society, but also highly pathologized in regard to mental health concerns. Rather than looking to systemic racism and discrimination as determinants of mental health disabilities, mental health systems in Canada have continued to view mental health concerns of Indigenous people as the products of individual, family and community pathology and disorganization. This issue is also significant for Canada's multicultural and immigrant population. Statistics Canada in 2010 (cited in Davis 2014) reported that by 2031, 30 percent of the Canadian population will be members of a visible minority and at least 25 percent of Canadians will not have been born in Canada. A monocultural understanding of mental health disability then excludes a significant proportion of the Canadian population needing service.

As stated previously, the dominant perspective in mental health policy and practice in Canada stems from a Western biomedical conception of mental health. Tools like the Diagnostic and Statistical Manual (DSM) are used to diagnose and label mental health concerns, pharmacological treatments are predominantly used, and treatment plans are put into place by highly educated and powerful practitioners. These practices do not recognize the many different cultural explanations and conceptualizations of mental health disability, varying help-seeking strategies, alternative treatments and responses, spiritual components of mental health, and coping mechanisms particular to specific cultures. As a result, research has substantiated that people from nondominant cultures are underrepresented in mental health treatment and are often reluctant to seek help (Davis 2014).

In addressing nursing care with Indigenous peoples of New Zealand, Smye and Browne (2002) propose the concept of cultural safety. In contrast to cultural competence whereby practitioners learn the skills, attitudes and knowledge necessary to work effectively across cultures, cultural safety proposes a process of reflection where the practitioner examines the lens through which mental health concerns, policies, organizations and practices are viewed (Smye and Browne 2002). In so doing, the practitioner transforms their practice to ensure that oppressive, disempowering practices and policies are eliminated or reduced. This view postulates that one never fully reaches competence but that one must constantly reflect on their practice to ensure that oppressive elements are not automatically and subtly reinforced. Although the MHCC has clearly recognized the need for transformation of the Canadian mental health care system in regard to cultural safety, actual practice lags far behind.

The four trends noted above regarding mental health practice and policy in Canada do suggest a shift away from traditional conservative approaches to this form of disability. However, systems are slow to change, and much of the most meaningful work being done in the mental health field is directly influenced by the specific attitudes and values of those who work first-hand with mental distress. The following example is provided to explore how practitioners, families and mental health service users themselves might work together in anti-oppressive and anti-ableist ways.

Case Example — Darren

Darren is a 38-year-old male who works as a machinist for a small locally owned company that manufactures custom-made equipment for the oil and gas industry. He has been with this company for eight years and makes a reasonable wage. He was diagnosed with schizophrenia at age nineteen, and his parents indicate that he has always been different than their other four children. He is the third eldest and no other member of his family has experienced a serious mental health concern, although his father indicates that he had had a "nervous breakdown" when he was about thirty. Darren has been hospitalized in a psychiatric facility four times; the longest duration was six months when he had his first reported psychotic episode. Prior to these four hospitalizations, Darren reported experiencing hallucinations, delusions and some paranoia. Darren sees a psychiatrist monthly and is on an antipsychotic medication that he takes daily. Although infrequent, Darren reports that he still "hears voices" and becomes delusional (grandeur) on occasion. Darren periodically overindulges in alcohol, marijuana and crack cocaine. He is aware of the interaction of these street drugs with his medication, but indicates that he sometimes just wants to get high. Darren also states that he has "made peace" with his voices, and that they generally leave him alone.

Darren has been living with his girlfriend, Marla, in a small apartment for the past four years. Marla also experiences a mental health disability and has been diagnosed with schizophrenia, bipolar disorder, borderline personality disorder and schizoaffective disorder. She is also on antipsychotic medication but is considered "noncompliant" by her psychiatrist as she frequently neglects to take the medication. Both Darren and Marla have their ups and downs but manage to live independently with the support of both sets of parents. Marla would like to find steady employment but unlike Darren, she is unskilled and her mental health disability is often seen by others as a barrier in seeking and maintaining employment.

Darren's mother and father indicate that Darren has a "bad time" about once every four months, he becomes delusional and invites many strangers into his home. These bad times often become chaotic with a lot of conflict, screaming and yelling, neighbors calling the police, and the family coming to sort out the conflicts. Although Darren's father has recently retired, his mother, Lisa, works as the business manager for the same company that employs Darren. This arrangement allows Lisa the opportunity to support Darren at work and provide rides to and from work as Darren is often unable to drive. Over the years Lisa has been able to speak frankly with the other workers (engineers and machinists) about Darren's mental health disability and his need for understanding and accommodation. For example, as Darren's medication often makes him extremely drowsy in the morning, Lisa has advocated for Darren to begin work two hours later than the other workers and to stay two hours longer at the end of the day. Darren gets along well with the other workers, but indicates that they are not really his friends, just coworkers who understand him. Darren's technical supervisor (not his mother) reports that Darren is an excellent machinist — the best they have — as he does the work with incredible precision and accuracy; the company has never had a complaint about Darren's products.

A community mental health social worker is periodically involved with the family, usually when Darren has a "bad time." The family reports that this involvement is generally unhelpful and often viewed by Darren and the family as monitoring, interfering, unsupportive and threatening. The social worker often tells Darren that if he continues to hear voices and have delusions, then he will have to go back to a psychiatric hospital. Darren's brothers and sister are supportive of Darren and Marla and often visit their home and invite him to their places. The family does not view Darren as "mentally ill" as he maintains an excellent job, lives independently, has had a stable relationship with his partner for several years, and is generally pleasant and friendly to be around. Rather, the family takes the view that Darren and Marla are simply afforded different sets of mental experiences than their own, and that sometimes this does cause conflict, frustration and upset. They are quick to report that Darren has incredible strengths and that they prefer to focus on those rather than his limitations. That being said, the family also indicates that when Darren is having a "bad time," they would like to just "throw the towel in" as it is difficult. When asked if they would consider a residential or institutional setting for Darren, they clearly indicate it is out of the question and totally unnecessary. Darren's parents express frustration and annoyance with the mental health system that they say attempts to treat him like a "schizophrenic" rather than a well-functioning person. All in all, Darren and his family report a happy and meaningful life with its ups and downs; they state this is just how life is and they prefer to make the best of it.

An analysis of this example indicates many of the frustrations and barriers that individuals with mental health disabilities face on a daily basis, yet it also reflects the strength, resilience and creativity of Darren and his family in overcoming the stigma and barriers before them. Many of the myths and misperceptions about those with mental health disabilities mentioned earlier in this chapter are refuted. Darren is not violent and unpredictable, he maintains steady meaningful employment, he has a stable relationship with a girlfriend who also presents with mental health concerns, which might be considered a poor combination by many mental health workers, he is bright, articulate and skilled, and he maintains a close relationship with his family. In most ways, Darren's life is like that of any other 38-year-old. Darren's workplace accommodates his needs, understands his difference and applauds his strengths. Darren's family are incredibly supportive of his independence and need for his own life, yet they seem to know when to support and assist. Several years ago, it is likely that Darren and Marla would both have been institutionalized in a psychiatric facility or group home, and be "psychiatrized" as incapable and unable to manage on their own. Although Darren has been diagnosed with schizophrenia, this has not become his identity, and the family refuses to allow others to label him in this way. He is just Darren and Marla is Marla. One might ask what lessons can be learned from this couple and family about how to work in empowering, supportive and respective ways so that those with mental health disabilities can live meaningful independent lives.

Chapter Summary

A mental health disability is one of the many forms of disability in Canada whereby those experiencing one have been stigmatized, discriminated against, disempowered and misunderstood. Although there has been significant movement away from punitive, harsh and institutional responses in the last fifty years, what remains is essentially a medically dominated mental health system that situates the receiver of service and their families in a powerless position. Individualistic pathology-oriented conceptions of mental health continue to dominate, and in spite of anti-stigma campaigns and mental health education, public attitudes toward mental health disability remain negative.

A progressive/critical approach to mental health recognizes and addresses not only the immediate lived experience of those with different mental experiences, but also the larger social, structural and contextual factors related to the experience. Transformation of the mental health system is needed that involves the full participation and input of service users and families, and new cultural understandings of mental health experiences. Anti-oppressive practice principles need to be incorporated into the mental health system in ways that provides egalitarian and humanitarian responses to those with different mental experiences.

In recent years, practice strategies such as recovery approaches, assertive community treatment, integrated substance use and mental health services, and culturally safe perspectives indicate a move toward strength-based community alternatives which are client-centred and culturally sensitive. However, just as substantial societal change is slow, so too is change in mental health policy and practice. At the core of a progressive approach to mental health practice are the specific values, attitudes and actions of individual mental health workers. As an eternal optimist, it is the position of this author that in spite of traditional conservative mental health care systems, individual mental health workers can make a difference by working in anti-oppressive anti-abliest ways to assist those with mental health disabilities to live meaningful and fulfilling lives.

Discussion Questions

1. Discuss the benefits and limitations of using each of the following terms: mental disorder, mental illness, mental disability, disabling conditions of mental health, mental distress, patient, client, service user.
2. How are stigma and social exclusion similar and different for those with mental health disabilities and those with other forms of disability?
3. Critique a progressive/critical perspective toward mental health from a mental health worker's perspective.
4. From the case example, explain specifically how mental health services might assist Darren, Marla and their families, rather than create barriers for them.
5. What does it mean to "hear the voices" of those with mental health disabilities?
6. What does an anti-oppressive practice approach mean in terms of working with persons with mental health disabilities?

References

B.C. Ministry of Health. 2002. *Assertive Community Treatment.*

_____. 2012. "Integrated Models of Primary Care and Mental Health & Substance Use: Care in the Community." <health.gov.bc.ca>.

Canadian Centre on Substance Abuse. 2009. *Substance Abuse in Canada: Concurrent Disorders.* Ottawa: Canadian Centre on Substance Abuse.

Canadian Charter of Rights and Freedoms. 1982. Part I of the *Constitution Act,* Being Schedule B to the *Canada Act 1982* (U.K.) 1982, c. 11 [Charter].

CMHA (Canadian Mental Health Association). n.d. "Myths and Misconceptions of Mental

Illness." <cmha.ca>

Capponi, Pat. 2003. *Beyond the Crazy House — Changing the Future of Madness.* Toronto: Penquin Canada.

Charbonneau, M., et al. 2010. "The Psychiatrist's Role in Addressing Stigma and Discrimination." *Canadian Journal of Psychiatry* 55 Insert.

Coppock, Vicki, and Bob Dunn. 2010. *Understanding Social Work Practice in Mental Health.* London: SAGE Publications.

Davis, Simon. 2014. *Community Mental Health in Canada* revised and expanded edition. Vancouver: UBC Press.

Health Canada. 2002. "A Report on Mental Illness in Canada." Ottawa.

Institute of Health Economics. 2010. "The Cost of Mental Health and Substance Abuse Services in Canada." <ihe.ca/documents/Cost%20of%20Mental%20Health%20 services%20in%20canada%20Report%20June%202010.html>.

Lafave, H., H. deSouza and G. Gerber. 1996. "Assertive Community Treatment of Severe Mental Illness: A Canadian Experience." *Psychiatric Services* 47: 757--759.

Larson, Grant. 2008. "Anti-Oppressive Practice in Mental Health." *Journal of Progressive Human Services* 19, 1.

LeFrancois, Brenda, Robert Menzies and Geoffrey Reaume. 2013. *Mad Matters — A Critical Reader in Canadian Mad Studies.* Toronto: Canadian Scholars' Press.

Lester, Helen, and Jon Glasby. 2010. *Mental Health Policy and Practice* 2nd edition. New York: Palgrave MacMillan.

Lim, K-L., P. Jacobs, A. Obinmaa, D. Schopflocher and C. Dewa. 2008. "A New Population-Based Measure of the Burden of Mental Illness in Canada." *Chronic Diseases in Canada* 28, 3.

Lundy, Colleen. 2004. *Social Work and Social Justice: A Structural Approach to Practice.* Toronto: Broadview Press.

MHCC (Mental Health Commission of Canada). 2009. Toward Recovery and Well-Being: A Framework for a Mental Health Strategy for Canada. <mentalhealthcommission.ca>.

Moreau, Maurice. 1979. "A Structural Approach to Practice." *Canadian Journal of Social Work Education* 5, 1.

Mullaly, Bob. 2007. *The New Structural Social Work.* Toronto: University of Toronto Press.

Navaneelan, T. 2012. *Suicide Rates: An Overview.* Ottawa: Statistics Canada.

Oliver, Michael. 1996. *The Social Model in Context. Understanding Disability: From Theory to Practice.* New York: St. Martin's Press.

Phelan, J., et al. 2000. "Public Conceptions of Mental Illness in 1950 and 1996: What Is Mental Illness and Is It to Be Feared?" *Journal of Health and Social Behavior* 41.

Regehr, Cheryl, and Graham Glancy. 2014. *Mental Health Social Work Practice in Canada.* Don Mills, ON: Oxford University Press.

Riddell, S., and N. Watson. 2003. *Disability, Culture and Identity.* London: Pearson Prentice Hall.

Salyers, M., and S. Tsemberis. 2007. "ACT and Recovery: Integrating Evidence-Based Practice and Recovery Orientation on Assertive Community Treatment Teams." *Community Mental Health Journal* 43, 6.

Schneider, Barbara. 2010. *Hearing (Our) Voices — Participatory Research in Mental Health.* Toronto: University of Toronto Press.

Schrank, B., and M. Slade. 2007. "Recovery in Psychiatry." *Psychiatric Bulletin* 31.

Shooltz Kendzierski, Barbara. 2002. "Death Interrupted." In Elayne Clift (ed.), *Women's Encounters with the Mental Health Establishment — Escaping the Yellow Wallpaper.* London: Hawortth Press.

Simmie, Scott, and Julia Nunes. 2001. *The Last Taboo — A Survival Guide to Mental Health Care in Canada.* Toronto: McClelland & Stewart Ltd.

Smye, Vicki, and Annette Brown. 2002. "'Cultural Safety' and the Analysis of Health Policy Affecting Aboriginal People." *Nurse Researcher* 9, 3.

World Health Organization. 2014. <who.int>.

Chapter 11

Empowering Strategies for Change: Advocacy by and for People with Disabilities

Irene Carter

This chapter on advocacy is intended to assist persons with disabilities, those who support persons with disabilities, and professionals, such as social workers, to employ advocacy in the process of accessing services supported by disability rights. In this process, the goals of this chapter include:

- To define advocacy and its use in the area of disability at micro and macro levels.
- To review the social model of disability.
- To discuss the use of advocacy by, and for, persons with disabilities.
- To employ advocacy as an empowering process for persons with disabilities.
- To provide a step-by-step process for applying advocacy.
- To suggest implications for professionals who work with persons with disabilities.

Definitions of advocacy are followed by a discussion of models of disability, and a brief history of Canadian advocacy for and by persons with disabilities. Canadian social influences on disability and how different types of advocacy are practiced by various Canadian groups are discussed. The significance of developing empowerment is followed by approaches and strategies for advocacy using an example of the challenges a person diagnosed with an intellectual disability faces during childhood and as they transition into adulthood. Lastly, implications for social workers in working with persons with disabilities are considered.

Definitions of Advocacy

Advocacy is defined "as to speak on behalf of, to speak in favour of, or to recommend publicly" (Neufeldt 2003: 13). Hoefer (2012: 2) defines advocacy practice as taking "action in a systematic and purposeful way to defend, represent, or otherwise advance the cause of one or more clients at the individual, group, organizational, or community level in order to promote social justice." In social work practice, advocacy takes place at both the micro or macro level. Barker (2003) explains advocacy activities at the micro level as helping to solve challenges faced by individuals, families, and small groups, while advocacy activities at the macro level aim to bring about improvements and change in general society through political action, community organization, public education and social service agencies. Jansson (2011) presents efforts to change policies in legislative, agency, and community settings by establishing new policies, improving existing policies, and defeating the policy initiatives of others as policy advocacy. He distinguishes policy advocacy as aiming to help relatively powerless groups improve their resources and opportunities. He cautions advocates not to restrict their advocacy to the problems of individuals, arguing an advocate must strive to address societal factors, such as social injustice, that lessen inequality. To do otherwise, he suggests, would allow other groups with values and perspectives in opposition to the needs of clients to dominate public policy.

Advocacy is a process that historically changed social attitudes and developed and maintained progressive advancements in disability rights. Despite advances in disability rights, disabled Canadians still experience significant obstacles to achieving their human rights, continuing to experience disability as poverty, isolation and abuse (Stienstra 2012). This chapter will review how advocacy instrumentally helps to resolve various issues faced by persons with disabilities.

Background to Canadian Disability Advocacy

Thomas (2007) explains how the concept of a disabled person as a social deviant has persisted through history to the present. Thomas suggests that persons with disabilities were viewed as having conditions that needed to be remedied. Medicalization of disability increased with the rehabilitative intervention of doctors and other professionals. In order to overcome discrimination, the only choice for many persons with disabilities who could not be "fixed" was to become more socially acceptable by striving to appear normal (Wolfensberger 1983).

Advocacy in Canada began in the mid-eighteenth century when optimism that lasted to the mid-1920s arose about improving possibilities for persons with disabilities (Neufeldt 2003). For example, the Quebec government funded and monitored institutions by the end of the eighteenth century, while the Atlantic provinces built residential institutions modelled on British laws and practices (Neufeldt). At the turn of the twentieth century, the Canadian government increasingly developed their role in the care of persons with disabilities, although interest waned somewhat with the emphasis on economic survival from the Great Depression until the end of World War II. Significantly, in 1945, veterans unhappy with the care they received during the war formed an organization entitled the Canadian Paraplegic Association, "the first to develop broad public support for their rights" (Neufeldt 2003: 19).

The period between the 1950s to the 1970s was characterized by the push for deinstitutionalization and community services. Following World War II, parents of children with disabilities grouped together to raise awareness about the needs of their children with disabilities, promoting their children's access to education, group homes, and employment preparation and training. Stienstra (2012) recalls how the advocacy of mothers of people with intellectual disabilities resulted in the Canadian Association for Community Living (CACL), an early and important Canadian disability organization that continues its work today. The CACL laid the groundwork for the emphasis on disability rights by introducing a plan of comprehensive, community-based services.

In the 1970s, disability rights emerged as a reaction to a long history of exclusion, institutionalization and paternalism (Stienstra 2012). Large disability social movements arose with members who viewed their situation as unjust, which later warranted a change in public policy (Prince 2009). Emphasis was placed on the development of the consumer movement for independent living and school inclusion (Prince 2009).

As outlined in Chapter 5 by Murphy, in the 1980s, Canada included the rights of people with disabilities in the *Canadian Charter of Rights and Freedoms* (1982). Disability rights advocates fought at the national level for disability to be included in the Charter. In 1980, Canada's federal government planned to call on the British Parliament to patriate Canada's constitution, a British statute that could only be amended by the U.K. Parliament and to entrench in it a new *Charter of Rights*. Lepofsky (2004) explains how Section 15 of the proposed *Charter of Rights* included a new constitutional guarantee of equality rights for Canadians, but did not originally include protection against discrimination because of disability. At the time, disability advocates, groups and organizations strongly advocated that Section 15 of the Charter be amended to include constitutional protection against discrimination for persons with disabilities. The federal government was persuaded to amend the Charter, Section 15, to include equality rights for persons with disabilities. Lepofsky explains that although this change in the Charter wording aided disability advocates in removing attitudinal barriers for persons with disabilities, its limitations due to lengthy, bureaucratic and costly legal procedures resulted in continued frustration for persons with disabilities in removing barriers.

During the period that the *Canadian Charter of Rights and Freedoms* (1982) was being developed and introduced to the Canadian public, Henry Enns established the first Independent Living Centre in Kitchener, Ontario (Phillips 2003). In expanding the Canadian Association of Independent Living Centres (CAILC) across Canada, key objectives included empowerment of persons with disabilities in learning how to advocate on their own behalf. Although the main goals of CAULC were individual advocacy and self-advocacy, the CAULC took on the role of advocate for its members as well in providing programs that included information and referral, peer support, individual advocacy and service development.

The Council of Canadians with Disabilities (CCD) also became a major national advocacy organization of people with intellectual disabilities. Currently, under the leadership of the CACL and the CCD, one hundred organizations have come together to create a National Action Plan, stressing deinstitutionalization and disability supports, and the alleviation of poverty (Stienstra 2012). Presently, the disability movement continues to question state and professional practices through negotiation and consensus (Neufeldt 2003) as disabled people continue to be marginalized (Stienstra 2012). Effort is also being made to introduce knowledge about disability in post-secondary social work and interdisciplinary programs (Carter, Hanes, and MacDonald 2012). The Canadian disability movement of today is active and collaborative in addressing obstacles, inclusion, equality rights, citizenship and accessibility, which is evident in the advocacy of service agencies, group claims and university-based research (Prince 2009).

Social Model of Disability

Advocacy is employed in advancing the rights of persons with disabilities in the context of the social model of disability, a progressive approach to exploring what can be done about the negative impact of environmental barriers and social attitudes on people with disabilities (Oliver 1990). The social model of disability counters the vision of disabled persons as sick, deficient and dependent, perceptions often associated with the medical model. Although a medical perspective has also been beneficial in helping persons with disabilities, it has maintained a focus on minimizing the disability by locating it solely within the individual. Since most adaptation to permanent disabilities happens outside of medical intervention, it is no longer adequate or desirable to focus on the medical rehabilitation processes alone to help people with disabilities adapt to life in society.

The social model emphasizes social, cultural, political and environmental factors that limit the disabled person more than their impairment does, and views the environment as creating and perpetuating the disabling condition (Rothman 2003). Describing persons with disabilities as an oppressed and marginalized group (Gilson and DePoy 2002), the social model led to progressive social policy that could reduce and address oppression (Goodley 2000). It resulted in legislation that outlaws discrimination based on a person's disability and promoted accessibility for persons with disabilities (Prince 2004; Roeher Institute 2003). As Roy Hanes writes in Chapter 4, although the social model is about socio-political and economic change and the removal of structural and attitudinal barriers, it is less about individual people who have difficulty achieving access. Hanes argues that the social model does not take into account the lived experiences of individuals and families.

Thomas (2007) suggests the social model of disability promoted the division of impairment — the characteristics of the body — from disability, restrictions imposed on the individual by society. Crow (1996) writes that the rejection of impairment is the social model's flaw as it causes disadvantage for some people, such as children with disabilities. Crow argues that if the constraints of disability ended, impairment would remain, and individuals would still require resources and social support. In cases where removal of impairment is not possible, such as persons with intellectual disabilities, Crow suggests there are insufficient formal and informal resources to accommodate the impairment. The social model needs to incorporate patterns of impairment as experienced by different groups to ensure development of appropriate services, employing advocacy where support is under-resourced. Thus, although the social model represents a collective commitment to social justice and accessibility, and it provides a pathway to advocate for the rights of persons with disabilities, it must continue to evolve to take into account particular impairments and lived experiences of persons with disabilities.

Discrimination and Disability

Discrimination implies the negative treatment of others based on identifiable characteristics. In the case of disability, it might imply one recognizes a difference in another and treats the other differently and unfairly based on this difference. We may choose to use difference to deny or exploit others (Mullaly 2010) or celebrate differences by appreciating diversity. Mullaly explains that when "diversity is based on difference there is always a possibility of difference leading to discrimination in a negative and unfair way rather than to a celebration" (2010: 35). When severe limitations are placed on a person or group with disabilities by another group who has more power, the result is devaluation, exploitation and deprivation, or oppression. Mullaly clarifies that oppression exists

> when a person is blocked from opportunities to self-development, is excluded from full participation in society, does not have certain rights that the dominant group takes for granted, or is assigned a second-class citizenship, not because of individual talent, merit, or failure, but because of his or her membership in a particular group or category of people. (2010: 40)

Thus, oppression serves to ensure and preserve the subordination of particular groups, such as persons with disabilities.

Broad social influences contribute to the ongoing discrimination of people with disabilities. In Canada, discrimination against persons with disabilities is sustained by individual and institutional attitudes, evident in the areas of social assistance, health care, education, childcare, taxation, building codes, Aboriginal rights, immigration, development assistance, information technologies and housing (Stienstra 2012).

Prince (2009) views Canadian discriminatory practices as largely attributed to neoliberal ideas of independence and individualism. Prince views the Canadian disability movement as liberal because it reflects appreciation for autonomy and individualized development, tolerance of values, market relations, the rule of law and representative government, evident in the perception of legislated rights-based advocacy. Because the Canadian disability movement supports groups and group rights, evident in the perception of disabled persons as consumers of services, Prince also describes it as social. Prince explains that the Canadian disability movement is a "style of activism distinguished by values and beliefs which are a form of social liberalism" (2009: 1) that emphasizes self-development, the community, and rights of numerous political social groups. He considers how neoliberalism interacts with social liberalism in looking at how the disability movement promotes a socio-political model that results in "a politics of socio-economic redistribution" (2009: 122). Although Prince views most disability activism as functioning within conventional political and governmental structures, he also sees it as resisting neoliberalism, using group tactics and engaging with political parties to advance social and economic disability policy. Thus, the Canadian disability movement is seen as offering a social liberalism that calls for a renewed role for government in addressing discrimination and a more accessible and just society by employing advocacy.

Presently, the Canadian government influences the advocacy work of nonprofit disability organizations by limiting their political activities. The Canada Revenue Agency (2014) limits charitable status to organizations with a political purpose, creating an environment of struggling nonprofit organizations encouraged to become less political and distance themselves from ideas of advocacy. Endorsing activist language on an individual or organizational level is difficult in this climate (Kelly 2013). Despite these obstacles, Kim (2010) found disabled women's advocacy organizations have brought about significant gains in the recognition of disabled women with advances in gender-sensitive approaches to disability policy, suggesting such networking will continue to grow. Kelly contends that more radical forms of activism for persons with disabilities have been forced to operate outside government-sponsored organizations to work in lesser-known groups. Thus, Kelly suggests that disability activism includes varied political tactics, demonstrating the resourcefulness among disability groups in Canada, such as the work of DAMN (Disability Action Movement Now), a cross-disability, Toronto-based, radical, anti-capitalist organization with a strong stance grounded in poverty mobilization.

Advocacy Needs for Persons with Disabilities

Stienstra (2012) describes how achieving education for disabled persons involves removing stigma and increasing accessibility with appropriate interventions at preschool, school, and post-secondary institutions. She acknowledges, although limited, there are other areas where accessibility needs to improve, such as trans-portation, telecommunications, health care and disability supports, income and employment.

As for transportation, Stienstra (2012), indicates that 25 to 30 percent of people with disabilities do not experience accessibility with the existing transportation system. Although urban areas have door-to-door access, accessible transportation in rural and remote areas is very limited. With respect to telecommunications and the ability to connect with others, in Canada, inaccessible equipment continues to be an economic barrier. Health care limitations include coverage for medication, disability aids and uninsured visits to health professionals. Improved employment opportunities for persons with disabilities are crucial. As in the United Kingdom, United States and Australia, 51 percent of people with disabilities in Canada are employed compared to 75 percent of people without disabilities (Stienstra). As outlined by Mike Touchie in Chapter 1 and Durst in Chapter 9, Indigenous people with disabilities experience even greater challenges with respect to transportation, health care and employment.

O'Day and Goldstein (2005) found that advocacy research leaders considered the impact of poverty on persons with disabilities a major disability agenda chal-lenge. With one million Canadians excluded from work due to disability and one half of the welfare caseload consisting of people with disabilities, Stienstra insists significant barriers, such as workplace accommodation and the loss of benefits when they become unemployed, such as health care, present major obstacles that need to be removed for persons with disabilities. To address the above issues, Stienstra challenges Canadians to incorporate the rights of disabled persons in policies that reflect existing accessibility legislation, such as the 2005 Accessibility for Ontarians with Disabilities Act and other human rights legislation.

Advocacy in Nonprofit Organizations

Canada's voluntary disability groups with a particular purpose, such as self-help groups, service providers and advocacy organizations are part of five thousand disability-specific organizations (Canadian Abilities Foundation 2007, as cited in Prince 2009). Additionally, other groups that support persons with disabilities include groups of families and friends, private for-profit organizations and professional organizations that provide support and fundraising assistance, and public policy think tanks (Prince 2009). Many organizations in the community are concerned with the provision of services for persons with disabilities and the acquisition of funds, staff, volunteers and other resources. Some organizations combine service delivery with advocacy, while the orientation of others is mainly political with an aim to influence public policy.

Nonprofit organizations consist of "social agencies, professional associations, and social change organizations" (Barker 2003: 297). Nonprofit organizations are usually private, voluntary social agencies that fulfill a social purpose other than monetary reward. They are funded from a variety of sources including clients and government grants. Kelly (2013) views nonprofit organizations as filling gaps left by the influence of neoliberal policies upon the provision of government services for persons with disabilities. She describes Canadian disability advocacy as primarily concerned with changes in legislation and policy by working side-by-side with the government and their representatives in various levels of government, seeking incremental rather than radical change.

Kimberlin (2010) stresses that advocacy is an important activity for a nonprofit organization, whether it is lobbying or providing indirect education. Schmid, Bar and Nirel (2008) suggest local and national decision makers were politically influenced when there were large numbers of volunteers associated with nonprofit organizations. They also noted that the more dependent the organizations were on local authorities for funding, the lower the level of advocacy and political activity that took place. In Canada, Yundt (2012) writes that Canadian charities can generally put 10 percent of their resources toward non-partisan political activities that further their purposes, commenting that the lack of clarity between sharing views and advocating for a change of law creates an "advocacy chill" among charitable agencies. The Canada Revenue Agency (2014) states that a charitable agency's activities "must be [nonpartisan] and connected and subordinate to the charities' purpose." Thus, charitable agencies are restricted in communicating a call to action, supporting existing law or policy, or placing pressure on an elected representative or government official to change a law or policy to 10 percent of their organization's activities. Exceptions include charitable organizations with an income of $200,000 or less that stipulates 20 percent for organizations below $50,000, 15 percent for organizations between $50,000 and $100,000, and 12 percent for organizations between $100,000 and $200,000. The above rule necessitates that charitable organizations devote most of their income to their charitable purposes, restricting opportunities for political activity to promote change, to public awareness campaigns and speaking with elected officials from 10 to 20 percent of the time, depending on the charitable agency's income.

Silverman and Patterson (2011) added to the understanding of how nonprofit organizations interface with the constraints placed on them by larger institutions in society in relation to the balance between programmatic and advocacy work. They examined the perceptions of executive directors with respect to funding an organization's programs, heavily reliant on public funding, for minority and disadvantaged groups. They found advocacy activities were sustainable when a strong individual donor base was in place, suggesting the stability of grassroots resources counters institutional pressures to reduce advocacy.

Advocacy by Family Members
The development of advocacy for persons with disabilities has been encouraged by families, particularly mothers, "who identified the impact of discriminatory practices on the exclusion of their child" (Panitch 2003: 273). Parents identify deficiencies in environments and provide support to other parents unaware of their children's rights. They engage in research and create strategies to help bring about greater reform. Parents are a potent influence in shaping legislation for children with disabilities (Trainor 2010). When parents are provided with knowledge about services and their rights, they become better equipped to advocate for the services their child and family needs. Banach, Iudice, Conway and Couse (2010) found that the average mean scores on the Family Empowerment Scale increased in a six-session, co-facilitated, support group regarding advocacy and self-efficacy of parents coping with a child's diagnosis.

Parents often react strongly when they receive a diagnosis that their child has a significant disability and need follow-up services and support to help them adapt and meet their needs and their children's needs (Banach et al. 2010). Acts of parental advocacy include requesting enhanced help from professionals, which is often experienced as stressful for parents (Prezant and Marshak 2006). The attitude of school stakeholders is particularly challenging for parents. In presenting their child's learning needs, parental advocates are often at odds with the school system

(Esquivel, Ryan and Bonner 2008; Munn-Joseph and Gavin-Evans 2008). School personnel often intimidate parents with the use of professional jargon, creating a power differential (Trainor 2010).

Although parental advocacy often decreases stress levels (Neely-Barnes and Dia 2008), the ability for parents to advocate is determined by factors such as parents' occupational flexibility, economic resources, knowledge of social networks and access to transportation (Leiter and Krauss 2004). Parents identified barriers in parental advocacy that include a lack of knowledge and resources or drive to try new tactics (Brotherson, Cook, Erwin and Weigel 2008). For many parents, going through the day-to-day struggles had more relevance than planning new strategies. Moreover, Zhang (2005) found cultural factors to be a mediating factor. Zhang suggested that families from European American backgrounds were more involved in encouraging personal independence activities than families of Asian or African American backgrounds. Huang, DeLambo, Kot, Ito, Long and Dunn (2004) found Asian American parents of children with developmental disabilities scored lower in assertiveness and self-advocacy skills than their non-Asian American counterparts. Parental advocacy skills were positively correlated to the social support they received and negatively correlated with the reported disability-based discrimination experienced.

Advocacy by family members does raise some concern for professionals with respect to when and how others may speak on behalf of persons with disabilities. For example, in a study that looked at the online publishing activities of adults with learning disabilities, Seale (2007) revealed that participants were being supported in their online publishing activities by family who included the home page as part of a bigger family website and took major responsibility for writing the home page narrative. Youth with autism have reported that behavioural interventions, such as applied behaviour analysis for up to forty hours a week, encouraged by their parents to enhance personal, social, and academic skills was overly invasive. They asked for the right to be accepted for who they are (Canadian Broadcasting Corporation 2010). These examples point to the need to distinguish between the needs of persons with disabilities and the needs of their family members.

Brotherson et al. (2008) found that families can provide outlets in the home for their family members with disabilities to practice making choices and decisions to foster a sense of control over their environment. They suggest that the fostering of self-determination, such as opportunities to make choices when selecting food items or toys, helps to encourage self-determining acts. Families often promote and facilitate interaction in social contexts, providing informal education about disability and creating a valued social identity for their children through involvement in community recreation and social activities (Baker and Donnelly 2001).

Empowerment and Self-advocacy

Empowerment "is associated with self-efficacy, awareness, control, participation, advocacy, and change" (Cohen and Hyde 2014: 29). Empowerment is "the process of helping individuals, families, groups, and communities increase their personal, interpersonal, socio-economic, and political strength and develop influence toward improving their circumstances" (Barker 2003: 142). Individual empowerment provides the opportunity to achieve a greater sense of self-esteem and self-control. Collectively, people become more resilient as they gain "greater personal, interpersonal, and environmental control over their lives" (Gitterman and Shulman 2005: xiv).

Closely linked to the personal and collective aspects of empowerment is the strengths perspective, an orientation that "emphasizes the client's resources, capabilities, support systems, and motivations to meet challenges and overcome adversity" (Barker 2003: 420). The strengths-based approach emphasizes the importance of hope in developing empowerment (Saleebey 2006). For example, with hope, persons with disabilities view themselves as having the strength to face challenges and to develop their own problem-solving skills to deal with misfortune and stress. Collectively, they can develop a greater voice to address oppression and to influence external organizations by emphasizing the need to remove injustice and inequality.

The term "empowerment" represents the belief that one can change one's environment. If individual and collective goals are not achieved, the disappointment can create ambivalence about participating in advocacy. Persons with disabilities need to be supported effectively in order for them to pursue and sustain advocacy and empowerment. For example, in a study of persons with intellectual disabilities and advocacy where the aim was empowerment, advocacy was influenced by the availability of support (Llewellyn and Northway 2008). One major perspective to promoting self-advocacy skills among persons with disabilities is the social model of disability. It provides authentic support as it empowers us to see that progressive social policy could lessen and address oppression (Goodley 2011).

The Internet provides additional support and empowerment for persons with disabilities with access to engage in self-advocacy work. In reviewing evolving virtual communities initiated by persons with autism, Jordan (2010: 222) described the Internet as a medium for self-advocacy for individuals with autism who were "seizing the opportunity to represent themselves." The participants presented their opinions, such as their thoughts on how autism is portrayed in the media, on their blogs and websites. Jordan found that online discussion forums functioned as supportive communities and lessened autistic symptoms. Both self-advocacy efforts by persons with autism and Jordan's findings suggest that self-representation and advocacy by persons with autism on the Internet can be beneficial. Web-based activities by persons with disabilities can support advocacy, used independently or collectively, in small or large groups.

Case Example — Andrew

Each situation involving a person with a disability is somewhat different, and the most appropriate advocacy strategies given the context will likely differ in intensity and variety. The following common fictional case example of a boy with autism named Andrew provides opportunities from diagnosis to adulthood for a disabled person, a family member, or an advocate, individually or collaboratively, to intervene appropriately and effectively. This case stresses the need to support families and individuals to advocate for themselves wherever possible and appropriate by applying advocacy strategies.

Andrew was first diagnosed at the age of three with moderate autism. The young, Canadian parents were high school students that knew little about autism and longed for someone to help them navigate through the system of policies, social agencies, and services. A parental separation two years following the diagnosis left the mother with most of the responsibility in raising Andrew, and the father's involvement was limited to financial support. Daycare supports proved difficult to achieve with respect to acquiring a support worker with the skills to apply behavioural interventions. Although early intervention was eventually arranged in day care, there was a delay and lack of appropriate support when Andrew went to public school.

In middle school, a short drive from his home, where he was well known and appreciated for his uniqueness, support was appropriate and meaningful. Andrew was placed in a class with other children with developmental disabilities and taught life skills in a supportive environment with adequate facilities, space and a high student/teacher ratio. In high school, Andrew's support at school deteriorated. The transition involved an early bus ride to a large, noisy classroom of about twenty adults with intellectual disabilities with a support worker assigned to every four students. Over the next year, on several occasions, Andrew tried to run out of the classroom and as a result, the school staff described him as an "elopement risk." Soon, Andrew refused to get on the bus to go to school. Andrew received minimal intervention from the school during his high school years, contributing to his growing problems due to lack of appropriate support. At the same time, Andrew's mother became depressed, and, consequently, Andrew's life became increasingly isolated. The home was in disarray, and dark without routine or structure. Andrew's behaviour worsened, with him often reacting to neglect by developing regressive toileting habits, and expressing his frustration by screaming or attempting to leave the home. At this time, Andrew's mother refused most help. Increased formal support, such as appropriate behavioural interventions at school and respite for his mother, as well as financial assistance for the family unit and the involvement of a supportive social worker, would have helped to prevent the exacerbation of Andrew's behaviour.

Eventually, with the involvement of a social worker, Andrew was taken to live in a large rehabilitative centre with other individuals with autism, 241 kilometres from his mother's home. Andrew exercised patience while his new caregivers and professionals learned how to interact with him. On the average, Andrew returned home to visit his mother once a month for a weekend. His grandmother visits him three times a year and takes him on mini holidays, including a two-week holiday in the summer at her cottage. Andrew tries to leave with his mother or grandmother when they return him to the group home. Although being employed is a requirement at the institution where he lives, after six months Andrew is still pending employment despite his family's suggestion that Andrew would enjoy tasks such as gardening. Andrew's length of stay at this rehabilitative centre was regarded as indefinite by the social worker as there was a lack of sufficient resources to adequately support his care in a facility closer to his mother's home. When Andrew's mother and grandmother inquired about and advocated for a transfer closer to his mother's home one year later, the staff indicated that Andrew really only required supervision and had no behavioural problems. The social worker at the rehabilitation centre suggested that, although there may be a waiting period, paperwork should commence to ensure a transfer for Andrew to a lesser level of care as soon as possible, such as a group home closer to his mother's residence.

The above case example presents many issues about how Andrew's needs were neglected or supported, as well as opportunities to improve Andrew's circumstances through the use of advocacy as he transitioned through different stages in his life. In planning advocacy, Hoefer (2012) views the advocate as taking the following five steps:

1. Identify what is needed.
2. Determine the targets of advocacy, or who can provide what is needed.
3. Assess when to act.
4. Understand what action is required to get what is needed.

5. Gather the appropriate information and incentives to influence decision makers.

In applying Hoefer's advocacy steps to Andrew's early years of school, the advocate may identify behavioural support and guidance as needed. Next, the advocate may determine that the school principal is one of the targets who can secure the behavioural intervention and support. Third, the advocate may decide the best time to act is when Andrew's Individual Educational Plan (IEP) is being developed. Fourth, the advocate may find it necessary to have all those concerned about Andrew to attend a meeting about his need for behavioural intervention and support. Fifth, the advocate would gain support from others and research to support Andrew's need for behavioural intervention, including the proposal for a pilot project involving Andrew. It is also critical to consider how the context may not meet Andrew's needs and that particular "behaviours" may serve a purpose for Andrew as his means of communication in some circumstances. People need to reframe their notions of preferred or acceptable communication to incorporate diverse ways of communicating. The focus must include the context as well as the individual; otherwise the needs and strengths of individuals are neglected and they are perceived as the "problem."

One can employ advocacy, as needed, on a short- or long-term basis in varying degrees when well prepared with knowledge and effective communication and negotiation skills. Individual and group advocacy is most helpful when advocates are prepared to sustain the goal of seeking social justice. Andrew's mother, as a young mother, was easily intimidated by professionals and suspicious of their intervention for fear she may be found inadequate to care for Andrew. She required the support of other family members and parent support groups to access the information and support she required. For example, initiating consultation with institutional and community social workers in the process of arranging a transfer for Andrew to a group home closer to his family's residence is initially seen as a difficult task to his mother. With support from others, his mother can work to revise existing or new policy, supported by research and work with government personnel, in promoting the most successful community living arrangements for Andrew. Advocating for changes in policy includes efforts to change policies in legislative, agency and community settings by suggesting new policies, improving existing ones, or altering existing policies. In advocating for changes to policy, the advocate helps another from a relatively powerless group to become an advocate in improving their resources and opportunities, consistent with a social justice approach.

Engagement in direct self-advocacy or advocacy work with or on behalf of people with disabilities as a family member, particular advocacy group or organization can initially seem like a daunting task. In the beginning, advocacy is best approached from the perspective of stages with a beginning stage of getting involved and understanding the issue. During this stage, Hoefer (2012) suggests the advocate needs to consider what individuals want and who can assist them in securing these resources or having these needs met. During the middle stage of planning and advocating, the advocate considers when they should act and how they should act, producing long- and short-term goals. Collaboration with other professionals, such as social workers, may be appropriate and useful; however, support and training for people with disabilities and their families to advocate on their own behalf, whenever and wherever possible, is essential. Lastly, the advocate assesses what action to take with the aim to improving the success of future advocacy projects. The above steps will make advocacy manageable as well as rewarding in the development of empowerment at the individual or organizational level.

Implications for Professional Social Work Practice

Historically, social workers often contributed to the negative psychosocial and emotional issues faced by persons with disabilities. As Mullaly (2010: 37) explains, social work "has attempted to deal with difference by accepting the dominant group as the norm and any differences to be the result of deviance, with the treatment plan being to restore the deviant individual or group to (dominant group) 'normalcy.'" Moreover, Mullaly expresses concern that social work has recently overemphasized difference, having the effect of concealing similar characteristics among oppressed groups, and resulting in competition among groups for limited resources in social work curriculum development. Mullaly criticizes the use of an identity model that characterizes groups of people according to limited characteristics that overlooks the diversity within groups and encourages social work to use a theory of difference that examines the diversity within subordinate groups, noting the intersectional effects of oppression as discussed in Chapter 8 by MacDonald.

Social workers use an anti-oppressive approach in attempts to alleviate the negative effects of the liberal/neoconservative capitalistic system placed on individuals and groups in society (Mullaly 2007). Using a structural approach, social workers strive to change the effect of negative social structures thought to be oppressive at personal, cultural and institutional levels (Mullaly 2007). Such an approach is supported by the Canadian Association of Social Work Code of Ethics that states a social worker should "act to reduce barriers and expand choice for all persons, with special regard for those who are marginalized, disadvantaged, vulnerable, and/or have exceptional needs" (Mullaly 2007: 5) and "specifically challenge views and actions that stereotype particular persons or groups" (Mullaly 2007: 5).

Mullaly (2010: 221) cautions that "how-to-do-it recipes do not help the social worker engage with complexity and individuality." Social workers need to allow for significant differences within a group, such as persons with disabilities, to assess the extent to which a client may be challenged by oppression. In anti-oppressive social work, a critical framework allows the social worker to consider individual narratives and expose the injustices that exist within them. Ungar (2011: 34) describes narrative therapy as "an approach that integrates postmodern epistemology and social constructionism." A postmodern epistemology suggests to the social worker that we are constantly evolving a sense of self through experiences that are seen as positive or negative. Further, Ungar suggests social constructivism plays a role in postmodern counselling by emphasizing the differences in people and "the decolonization of a Eurocentric bias" (Ungar 2011: 34) as the truth. Narrative therapy allows the social worker to see the person as affected by the problem instead of being the problem, exposing social structures affecting clients negatively as the client's narrative is examined.

Once aware of social injustice, it is often difficult for social workers to transfer anti-oppressive knowledge to practice in helping to bring about social change. Altholz and Golensky (2004) found social workers exhibited a lack of knowledge about counselling, support and advocacy for clients with disabilities, suggesting that social workers engage more in ethical practice by taking on a greater advocacy role. Jurkowski, Jovanovic and Rowitz (2002) looked at the leadership of persons with physical disabilities in their ability to gain increased access to health care, attendant care and social services. Their findings suggested that those who advocated felt their advocacy improved access to health care, attendant care and social services, highlighting the value of consumer/citizen participation. They stressed how this action can be collaborated with social work professionals to bring about change. For example, in the case of Andrew, his mother became more confident about change that could bring improvement in the quality of life for her son and herself through involvement and collaboration with other family members, parental advocates and social workers.

Social workers can use a combination of therapeutic approaches in applying anti-oppressive practice to bring about change. For example, Sue and Sue (2012) used a model, the Racial/Cultural Identity Development (R/CID) to address oppression at the personal and cultural levels. The R/CID model assesses where individuals are in their cultural identity and is applicable to address issues of oppression, such as gender or disability, with individuals who may not be able to articulate the degree of oppression they are experiencing.

The R/CID model assists clients in moving through the five stages of conformity, dissonance, resistance and immersion, introspection, and integrative awareness. In the conformity stage, individuals prefer dominant cultural values, often developing negative views of their own cultural group. At the dissonance stage, individuals begin to experience conflict between the dominant cultural values they prefer and their own cultural values and beliefs. In the resistance and immersion stage, clients begin to appreciate their own culture and to reject dominant cultural values, often feeling guilt, shame and anger, and motivation to address oppression. At the stage of introspection, individuals are described as feeling uncomfortable with previously held rigid views and focus on understanding themselves and their cultural group. In the final stage of integrative awareness, Sue and Sue describe individuals as having positive feelings about both their own culture and the dominant culture, and expressing commitment to end all forms of oppression and discrimination.

In this process, the social worker remains cognizant that most people have a cultural identity and assesses where the client currently falls in the model as a starting point for intervention. Using an integrated approach in anti-oppressive practice provides opportunities to assess the degree of oppression caused by oppressive social structures and to help the client understand and address oppression (Mullaly 2010; Sue and Sue 2012; Ungar 2011).

The delivery of health and social services often presents challenges for the social worker in assuming the role of advocate. Payne and Pithouse (2006) suggest the needs of persons with disabilities are often not met well because access is a competitive process with other groups in need of health care, such as persons with acute health care needs. Moreover, social workers committed to advocacy often face dilemmas in making choices between the objectives of their agency and the welfare of persons with disabilities. Thus, Meinert and de Loyola (2002) have suggested social workers learn more about advocacy organizations and where they are compatible with social work. Further training in policy advocacy at the curriculum and practicum levels in social work training would enhance strategies for change at the institutional level. Challenging stereotypes and decreasing disabling barriers often requires the affiliation with supportive organizations in developing or altering existing policy regarding persons with disabilities. An advocate seldom works alone. They work with individuals with disabilities, families, advocacy groups or with those who have experience in policy advocacy.

In creating supports to enhance functioning or quality of life, it is essential the advocate develop effective support systems in partnership with the individual in receipt of the intended services (Jansson 2003). Jansson explains how becoming a policy advocate is a developmental process using analytic, political, interactional and ethical reasoning skills. Change in policy that is unjust is understood as a developmental process from deciding what is right and wrong, navigating existing policy, setting an agenda, analyzing problems, developing proposals, enacting policy tasks, implementing policy, and assessing policy. Jansson describes policy advocacy as vital to the future of social work as social injustice, the pinnacle of social work, has increased the need to reform existing social policy. An effective social work policy advocate that works in cooperation with persons with disabilities and supportive agencies persistently seeks opportunities for advocacy supported by a vision and a set of advocacy skills.

Listed below are practice implications for social workers to help persons with disabilities to reduce barriers to accessibility:

- Social workers need to increase their knowledge of disability issues and develop collaborative relationships with persons with disabilities.
- Social workers need to enhance their cultural competence regarding persons with disabilities and work together with persons with disabilities in applying advocacy.
- Social workers need to develop dynamic and creative, integrative, anti-oppressive approaches to reinforce assertiveness, positively, in persons with disabilities and their families in seeking change.
- Social workers need greater accessibility to disability studies and further training on how to interact with persons with disabilities, taking care to avoid the detrimental effects of jargon.
- Social workers need training as policy advocates and opportunities to work with advocacy organizations in volunteer roles or as students in field-based practicums.

Chapter Summary

In conclusion, advocacy provides a vehicle to support persons with disabilities in Canadian society in their efforts to increase social inclusion and to address their lack of accessibility to resources. Advocacy by persons with disabilities has resulted in creative, innovative legislation and programs to address pressing problems and to provide an example for individuals, families, organizations and social workers to create further change. Advocacy is supported by the social model of disability and challenged by continuing discriminatory social practices. Advocacy, in attaining equality and social inclusion, whether by nonprofit organizations, family, persons with disabilities, or social workers, helps to mitigate the effects of stigma and discrimination. Using a case example, step-by-step approaches to advocacy were outlined to illustrate the lack of accessibility for children with developmental disabilities. Improvement of the use and practice of advocacy by social workers, using integrated approaches involving structural social work practice, in collaboration with persons with disabilities were also outlined in the implications for professional social work practice section.

Discussion Questions

1. If you realize that a child with an intellectual disability is not receiving the disability supports the child needs in the educational system or the community, how would you go about advocating for the child's needs as a parent — for example, as in Andrew's case example — or as a representative of a nonprofit agency, or as a social worker?

2. As a social worker, what strategies would you teach a group of youth with intellectual disabilities to assist them in learning how to self-advocate?

3. In assisting parents with advocacy for their children with disabilities, what important considerations does your assessment have to take into account?

4. What major obstacles or strengths do you foresee for your future practice regarding your role as an advocate?

5. What major obstacles do you foresee to greater accessibility for persons with disabilities?

References

Accessibility for Ontarians with Disabilities Act. 2005. S.O. 2005, c. 11.

Altholz, Suzanne, and Martha Golensky. 2004. "Counseling, Support, and Advocacy for Clients Who Stutter." *Health & Social Work* 29, 3: 197–205.

Baker, K., and M Donelly. 2001. "The Social Experiences of Children with Disability and the Influence of Environment: A Framework for Intervention." *Disability & Society* 16, 1: 71–85.

Banach, M., J. Iudice, L. Conway and L Couse. 2010. "Family Support and Empowerment: Post Autism Diagnosis Support Group for Parents." *Social Work with Groups* 33, 1: 69–83.

Barker, Robert. 2003. *The Social Work Dictionary* fifth edition. Washington, DC: NASW Press.

Brotherson, Mary, Christine Cook, Elizabeth Erwin and Cindy Weigel. 2008. "Understanding Self-Determination and Families of Young Children with Disabilities in Home Environments." *Journal of Early Intervention* 31, 1: 22–43.

Canada Revenue Agency. 2014. "Political Activities." <cra-arc.gc.ca/chrts-gvng/chrts/plcy/cps/cps-022-eng.html#N1038D>.

Canadian Association of Social Workers. 2005. *Code of Ethics.* Ottawa: CASW.

Canadian Association of Social Work. 2013. "Code of Ethics 2005." <casw-acts.ca/en/what-social-work/casw-code-ethics>.

Canadian Broadcasting Corporation. 2010. "*Positively Autistic.*" <cbc.ca/thenational/indepthanalysis/story/2009/10/06/national-positivelyautistic.html>.

Canadian Charter of Rights and Freedoms. 1982. The Constitution Act, 1982, being Schedule B to the Canada Act 1982 (U.K.), 1982, c. 11.

Carter, Irene, Roy Hanes and Judy MacDonald. 2012. "The Inaccessible Road Not Taken: The Trials,Tribulations and Successes of Disability Inclusion within Social Work Post-Secondary Education." *Canadian Journal of Disability Studies* 1, 1: 109–142.

Cohen, Marcia, and Cheryl Hyde. 2014. *Empowering Workers & Clients for Organizational Change*. Chicago, IL: Lyceum Books, Inc.

Crow, Liz. 1996. "Including All of Our Lives: Renewing the Social Model of Disability." In Colin Barnes and Geoff Mercer (eds.), *Exploring the Divide: Illness and Disability*. Leeds, England: The Disability Press, University of Leeds.

Esquivel, Shelly, Carey Ryan and Mike Bonner. 2008. "Involved Parents' Perceptions of Their Experiences in School-Based Team Meetings." *Journal of Educational & Psychological Consultation* 18, 3: 234–258.

Gilson, Stephen, and Elizabeth DePoy. 2002. "Theoretical Approaches to Disability Content in Social Work Education." *Journal of Social Work Education* 38, 2: 153–165.

Gitterman, Alex, and Lawrence Shulman. 2005. "Preface." In Alex Gitterman and Lawrence Shulman (eds.), *Mutual Aid Groups, Vulnerable and Resilient Populations, and the Life Cycle*. New York: Columbia University Press.

Goodley, Dan. 2000. "Self-Advocacy in the Lives of People with Learning Difficulties." In Len Barton (ed.), *Disability, Human Rights and Society Series*. Philadelphia, PA: Open University Press.

____. 2011. *Disability Studies: An Interdisciplinary Introduction*. California, CA: Sage Publications.

Hoefer, Richard. 2012. *Advocacy Practice for Social Justice* 2nd. edition. Chicago, IL: Lyceum Books.

Huang, Weihe, David Delambo, Ricky Kot, Ineko Ito, Henry Long and Karen Dunn. 2004. "Self-Advocacy Skills in Asian American Parents of Children with Developmental Disabilities: A Pilot Study." *Journal of Ethnic & Cultural Diversity in Social Work* 13, 1: 1–18.

Jansson, Bruce. 2003. *Becoming an Effective Policy Advocate: From Policy Practice to Social Justice* fourth edition Pacific Grove, CA: Thomson Learning.

Jordan, Chloe. 2010. "Evolution of Autism Support and Understanding Via the World Wide Web." *Intellectual and Developmental Disabilities* 48, 3: 220–227. doi: 10.1352/1934-9556-48.3.220.

Jurkowski, Elaine, B. Jovanovic and L. Rowitz. 2002. "Leadership/Citizen Participation: Perceived Impact of Advocacy Activities by People with Physical Disabilities on Access to Health Care, Attendant Care and Social Services." *Journal of Health & Social Policy* 14, 4: 49–61.

Kelly, Christine. 2013. "Towards Renewed Descriptions of Canadian Disability Movements: Disability Activism Outside of the Non-Profit Sector." *Canadian Journal of Disability Studies* 2, 1: 1–27.

Kim, Kyung. 2010. "The Accomplishments of Disabled Women's Advocacy Organizations and Their Future in Korea." *Disability & Society* 25, 2: 219–230.

Kimberlin, Sara. 2010. "Advocacy by Nonprofits: Roles and Practices of Core Advocacy Organizations and Direct Service Agencies." *Journal of Policy Practice* 9, 3–4: 164–182.

Leiter, Valerie, and Marty Krauss. 2004. "Claims, Barriers, and Satisfaction: Parents' Requests for Additional Special Education Services." *Journal of Disability Policy Studies* 15, 3: 135–146. Lepofsky, David. 2004. "The Long, Arduous Road to a Barrier-Free Ontario for People with Disabilities: The History of The Ontarians with Disabilities Act — The First Chapter." *National Journal of Constitutional Law* 15, 2: 125–333.

Lepofsky, David. 2004. "The Long, Arduous Road to a Barrier-Free Ontario for People With Disabilities – The First Chapter." *National Journal of Constitutional Law* 15.

Llewellyn, Penny, and Ruth Northway. 2008. "The Views and Experiences of People with Intellectual Disabilities Concerning Advocacy: A Focus Study." *Journal of Intellectual Disabilities* 12, 3: 213–228.

Meinert, R., and S. de Loyola. 2002. "The National Protection and Advocacy System: What Social Workers Need to Know." *Journal of Social Work in Disability and Rehabilitation* 1, 1: 15–26.

Mullaly, Bob. 2007. *The New Structural Social Work*. Toronto: University of Toronto Press.

____. 2010. "Chapter 2 Oppression: An Overview." *Challenging Oppression and Confronting Privilege* 2nd edition. Toronto, ON: Oxford University Press.

Munn-Joseph, Marlene, and Karen Gavin-Evans. 2008. "Urban Parents of Children with Special Needs: Advocating for Their Children Through Social Networks." *Urban Education* 43, 3: 378–393.

Neely-Barnes, Susan, and David Dia. 2008."Families of Children with Disabilities: A Review of Literature and Recommendations for Interventions." *Journal of Early and Intensive Behaviour Intervention* 5, 3: 93–107.

Neufeldt, Alfred. 2003. "Growth and Evolution of Disability Advocacy in Canada." In Deborah Stienstra and AileenWight-Felske (eds.), *Making Equality: History of Advocacy and Persons With Disabilities in Canada*. Concord, ON: Captus Press.

O'Day, Bonnie, and Marcie Goldstein. 2005. "Advocacy Issues and Strategies for the 21st Century: Key Informant Interviews." *Journal of Disability Policy Studies* 15, 4: 240–250.

Oliver, Mike. 1990. *The Politics of Disablement*. New York: St. Martin's Press.

Panitch, Melanie. 2003. "Mothers of Intention: Women, Disability and Activism." In Deborah Stienstra and Aileen Wight-Felske (eds.), *Making Equality: History of Advocacy and Persons with Disabilities in Canada*. Concord, ON: Captus Press.

Payne, H., and Andrew Pithouse. 2006. "More Aspiration than Achievement? Children's Complaints and Advocacy in Health Services in Wales." *Health and Social Care in the Community* 14, 6: 563–571.

Phillips, Cassandra. 2003. "Steering Your Own Ship." In Deborah Stienstra and Aileen Wight-Felske (eds.), *Making Equality: History of Advocacy and Persons with Disabilities in Canada*. Concord, ON: Captus Press.

Prezanta, F., and L. Marshak. 2006. "Helpful Actions Seen Through the Eyes of Parents of Children with Disabilities." *Disability & Society* 21, 1: 31–45.

Prince, Michael. 2004. "Canadian Disability Policy: Still a Hit-and-Miss Affair." *Canadian Journal of Sociology* 29, 1: 59–82.

____. 2009. "The Canadian Disability Community: Five Arenas of Social Action and Capacity." In *Absent Citizens: Disability Politics and Policy in Canada*. Toronto: University of Toronto Press.

Roeher Institute. 2003. *Towards a Common Approach to Thinking About and Measuring Social Inclusion*. Toronto, ON: Roeher Institute.

Rothman, Juliet. 2003. *Social Work Practice Across Disability*. Boston: Allyn & Bacon.

Saleebey, Dennis. 2006. *The Strengths Perspective in Social Work Practice* 4th edition. Toronto, ON: Pearson Education.

Schmid, Hillel, Michal Bar and Ronit Nirel. 2008. "Advocacy Activities in Nonprofit

Human Service Organizations: Implications for Policy." *Nonprofit and Voluntary Sector Quarterly* 37, 4: 581–602.

Seale, Jane. 2007. "Strategies for Supporting the Online Publishing Activities of Adults with Learning Difficulties." *Disability & Society* 22, 2: 173–186.

Silverman, Robert, and Kelly Patterson. 2011. "The Effects of Perceived Funding Trends on Non-Profit Advocacy: A National Survey of Non-Profit Advocacy Organizations in The United States." *International Journal of Public Sector Management* 24, 5: 435–451.

Stienstra, Deborah. 2012. *About Canada: Disability Rights.* Halifax, NS: Fernwood Publishing.

Sue, Deward Wing, and David Sue. 2012. *Counseling the Culturally Diverse: Theory and Practice* 6th edition. Toronto, ON: John Wiley and Sons.

Thomas, Carol. 2007. *Sociologies of Disabilities and Illness: Contested Ideas in Disability Studies and Medical Sociology.* New York: Palgrave MacMillan.

Trainor, Audrey. 2010. "Diverse Approaches to Parent Advocacy during Special Education Home-School Interactions: Identification and Use of Cultural and Social Capital." *Remedial and Special Education* 31, 1: 34–47.

Ungar, Michael. 2011. *Counseling in Challenging Contexts: Working with Individuals and Families Across Clinical and Community Settings.* Belmont, CA: Brooks/Cole.

Wolfensberger, Wolf. 1983. "Social Role Valorization: A Proposed New Term for the Principle of Normalization." *Mental Retardation* 21, 6: 234–239.

Yundt, Heather. 2012. "The Politics of Advocacy: Are Charities Apathetic or Afraid?" Charity Village. <charityvillage.com/Content. aspx?topic=The_politics_of_advocacy_Are_charities_apathetic_or_afraid>

Zhang, Dalun. 2005. "Parent Practices in Facilitating Self-Determination Skills: The Influences of Culture, Socioeconomic Status, and Children's Special Education Status." *Research and Practice for Persons with Severe Disabilities* 30, 3: 154–162.

Chapter 12

Reflections and Final Thoughts

Grant Larson and Jeanette Robertson

A progressive approach to supporting persons with disabilities involves shifting the viewpoint from one primarily focused on the individual to one focused on the barriers and structures of society. Workers and volunteers in the disability field need to be acutely aware of the real practical limitations imposed on people with disabilities and respond in ways which empower and counter the negative forces of society. For too long, Canadian society, and professional helpers in particular, have placed their focus on what persons with disabilities cannot do, rather than on their strengths, resilience and ability.

We began this book in Chapter 1 by introducing readers to four individuals — Melanie Thomas, Mike Touchie, Jaclyn Porter and Lorea Regan — as each in their own voice articulated their story as a person in Canadian society with a disability. Melanie Thomas relayed the struggles of a person with an "invisible" disability and how she went through the stages of grief and loss in dealing with her hearing loss. She also spoke of the joy of having good friends who were determined that her hearing loss would not have any impact on their friendships and showed that they would include her in all their activities. She described how in fact her disability became her "ability" and changed her life positively. Mike Touchie enlightened us with his experience as an Indigenous man with a spinal cord injury. He explained how the most difficult things to deal with were the ignorance and the assumptions of other people, including health care professionals, about his disability. Others frequently assumed that he could not do things for himself and that he could not even talk for himself. Mike also described how important the support of other people with disabilities was to his rehabilitation and to his ability to live with chronic pain. He unapologetically confronted the negative barriers created by society with courage and resilience and is now a strong advocate for others with disabilities. Jaclyn Porter reminded us not only of the struggles of having a mental health disability, but the conundrum of having to choose between medication that made her "fat and numb" or the sinking symptoms of depression. She also related how difficult it was to overcome the expectations of others to "snap out of it" as well as the expectations she placed on herself as she struggled with the label of bipolar. Interestingly, Jaclyn described how she found solace and confidence as she discovered that many others struggled with mental health disabilities but still lived productive meaningful lives. Jaclyn is now a successful practicing social worker who offers courage, understanding and help to others in need.

And finally, Lorea Regan conveyed her struggles and triumphs as a person born missing one arm just below her elbow. She has never let this get in the way of trying many activities and endeavours, such as raising three children, becoming a long-term care aide, and learning to drive a standard vehicle, despite the attitudinal and structural barriers imposed on her by others. Although she was provided with a prosthetic arm twice, she found that it actually got in her way and she preferred not to wear it. As she emphasized, she was born with a disability and adapted without knowing any different. She also spoke of her ability to conceal the absence of her arm so well that people had a difficult time adjusting their perceptions of her when they noticed her arm was missing. Although Lorea admitted to experiencing frustration in her life, the object of this frustration was not the fact that she was born with one arm; rather, it was the ableist attitudes and practices that denied her disability — such as governmental disability screening processes that questioned her absence of an arm — and a society that assumed that she "suffered" from a disability.

In like fashion in Chapter 7, Kevin Lusignan explained the process and dynamics of family life when a family member had a disability. He communicated not only his own life experience as a father of a child with a disability, but also his knowledge and experience from years of community advocacy and leadership regarding services to families with disabilities.

The voices of all these individuals portray people who have lived with and broken the stereotypes of people with disabilities, and confronted many of the barriers that others placed before them. They are successful citizens who make meaningful contributions to the lives of others. One must be careful, however, not to "romanticize" these individuals or generalize that all persons with disabilities can overcome any of the barriers and injustices placed before them. Many people with disabilities continue to struggle with the attitudes, structures and barriers in society and this imposes more of a burden on individuals than their specific disability.

We began the book with the voices of people who live with the realities of a disabling society every day to emphasize that their knowledge, their experiences and their suggestions are in fact the ones that count. Anti-oppressive and anti-ableist practice is premised on principles of egalitarianism where those being served are not "othered," nor are they put into lesser positions of power and influence. Rather, they are viewed as "the experts" and are invited to be full participants (Larson 2008) in all aspects (policy, administration, practice) of service provision.

Predominant Themes

In addition to the "first-person accounts," the first half of the book (chapters 2 to 6) provides the larger context for thinking about disability and social change in Canada — historical perspectives, current demographics, theoretical frameworks, human rights and a legal framework, and the Canadian social policy context. Two major themes become evident as the authors provide specific information about each of these important topics. The first is that due to social and political action, Canadian society has made significant progress toward integrating people with disabilities into the mainstream of Canadian life, and moving toward a more collectivist and egalitarian society. Evidence of this lies in the history of deinstitutionalization, the integration of people with disabilities in schools, workplaces and community activities, and through the legal protection of people with disabilities though social policy, the *Charter of Rights and Freedoms*, and provincial human rights legislation.

However, the second theme of these chapters indicates that as much as we should celebrate the work of advocates, social movements and disability coalitions, we should also recognize the growing trend toward neoliberalism in the Western world that reinforces social and economic inequality. This alarming conservative trend continues to divide societies into unequal groups and categories, and asks them to compete in the marketplace for needed resources, income and status. It encourages nation-states like Canada to return to individualistic pathology-oriented medical models for understanding and responding to people with disabilities.

In Chapter 2, Dunn and Langdon outline some of the important changes in disability history, from the collectivist orientation of Indigenous peoples to the individualistic focus of European colonization and widespread institutional care and then deinstitutionalization. The current move towards fully integrating people with disabilities into the community marks a progressive return to a more collectivist orientation. As noted, these changes in attitudes and policies are the result of activist pressure, coalition building and social movements. In Chapter 3, Robertson addresses the controversy of how disability is conceptualized, how people become classified as people with disabilities, and how these aspects are constructed. It is stressed that it is critical to acknowledge how disability demographics represent snapshots in time. And these snapshots only provide a limited and skewed representation of "facts" based on how disability is defined, the respondents included in the surveys, and the interpretations applied to these responses. Furthermore, it is emphasized that there is no generally accepted definition of disability in Canada or within the international community.

In Chapter 4, Hanes outlines a conceptual and theoretical model — the post-social model of disability — that combines the best of a social model of disability with an understanding of the "lived experience" of those with disabilities. Hanes recommends, as noted earlier, that we shift our view from the dualistic thinking of accepting either an individualist deficit-based medical model, or a broader social model, which focuses on the environment and social attitudes as the creators of the concept of disability. Instead, he suggests we accept both the individual and collective lived experience of people with disabilities and recognize the structural elements in the creation of disadvantaging conditions. We are compelled then to respond to both the immediate needs of those with disabilities as well as the larger structural factors that create barriers and disadvantage for those with disabilities. The post-social model of disability provides a new paradigm for responding to disability, and a theoretical foundation for the remaining chapters, which focus on the experiences of people with disabilities in Canadian society.

In Chapter 5, Murphy notes that transformational approaches to disability were developed in the 1990s in international and national regulatory bodies, yet the reality is that the practical work with people with disabilities still focuses on rehabilitation models which attempt to help people with disabilities adapt or fit into mainstream society. Furthermore, as noted by Murphy, new areas of contention, in particular the "death with dignity movement" to legalize assisted suicide, may open up discussions that have been largely avoided about autonomy and self-determination for people with disabilities. What is needed is a transformation of ableist values and attitudes in society to move beyond simple words and into actual practice.

As indicated by Prince in Chapter 6, a déjà vu discourse on disability policy issues has consequences for social change in Canadian affairs. This discourse conceals the incremental change and slow pace of reforms in disability policy and practice. More troubling, the discourse conceals the erosion and decline of existing programs and benefits to persons with disabilities. The neoliberal language of "shared social responsibility" for addressing disability issues further reinforces a limited role for governments and places the responsibility for meeting the needs of people with disabilities on individuals with disabilities themselves, their families, or on other institutions such as local not-for-profit community agencies.

In Chapter 8, MacDonald explores intersectionality and disability with a consideration of how gender, sexual orientation and race intersect with disability, resulting in multiple oppressions for individuals. Each of these intersections is explored with respect to oppressive aspects of violence, poverty and embodiment that impact individuals' lives in devastating ways. Durst (Chapter 9) provides an examination of the status and experience of Canada's Indigenous peoples, who are reported to experience disability at twice the national average. The voices of Indigenous peoples are shared to highlight the unique jurisdictional issues, service issues, and concerns experienced. With these voices in mind, Durst makes a series of recommendations to improve services to Aboriginal people with disabilities, and he encourages social work and other human service professionals to recognize these voices and respond with practical advocacy as allies of Indigenous people with disabilities.

Larson, in Chapter 10, provides insights into an area not often considered in disability texts: the experiences of those with mental health disabilities. He stresses the importance of language and discourse and the similarities of treatment to those with physical, cognitive and mental health disabilities. In addition to a brief review of innovative progressive mental health practices, Larson returns us to the need to work with people with disabilities in anti-oppressive and empowering ways. And finally, in Chapter 11, Carter emphasizes the importance of advocacy for persons with disabilities and the relationship of advocacy to the social model. She suggests micro and macro level approaches to access necessary services and supports that can be adopted by persons with disabilities and those who support them. Moreover, advocacy to attain equality and social inclusion challenges continuing discriminatory social policies and practices, while addressing the lack of accessibility to resources.

Challenges and Opportunities Ahead

The challenge to changing the viewpoint in how we understand and respond to persons with disabilities in our society remains embedded in ableist values, social structures and policies. Unfortunately, this is as true for social workers, nurses, physicians and others who provide support to persons with disabilities as it is for the general public. The difference, however, is that those working in the field have the opportunity through their work experience, professional development and interactions with people with disabilities to alter their approach to work in ways that resist and counteract the damage done by larger society and the troubling practices of many human service and medical service providers. It takes courageous professionals, with or without disabilities, who understand themselves and others in relation to progressive frameworks, and who are willing to take unpopular and necessary positions to privilege the voices of people with disabilities. In the end, what means the most is that those with disabilities are respected, valued and treated as full citizens in our society. Although gains have been made in recent years in recognizing the human rights and citizenship of people with disabilities, long-standing ableist traditions and values are slow to change.

We briefly return to the assumptions outlined in the Introduction to restate and re-emphasize what we believe are the key principles and beliefs for working from a progressive approach to supporting people with disabilities. These assumptions begin with the belief that disability is not inherently negative. Although acquiring a disability involves major life changes, including loss as well as gain, it is not the end of a meaningful and productive existence as illustrated by the voices in Chapter 1. Likewise, people with disabilities experience segregation, isolation and discrimination as a result of other people's prejudice and institutional ableism, not because of the disability itself. Additionally, cultural norms, social beliefs and media images about intelligence, physical ability, beauty, communication and behaviour often negatively influence the way people with disabilities are treated. Neoliberal expectations about self-sufficiency and economic productivity devalue persons who are not able to work, and denies other contributions they may make to family and community life. Although independence and dependence are relative concepts, subject to personal definition, something every person experiences, neither is inherently positive or negative. In fact, without affirmative messages about who they are, persons with disabilities are susceptible to internalizing society's negative ableist messages about disability. Moreover, although law now protects persons with disabilities' rights to inclusion in the mainstream of our society, they are still not treated as full and equal citizens (Chouinard 2009; Rioux and Valentine 2006).

It is our hope that this book has awakened the reader to altering their perceptions to recognize "misfortunes" as injustices, and to begin the process of developing and adhering to an anti-oppressive and anti-ableist framework for practice. We also hope the authors have motivated those who work in the field to think beyond their current practice and policy frameworks to be open to new ways of understanding disability, and especially to hearing the *voices* of those they work with, persons with disabilities.

References

Chouinard, Vera. 2009. "Legal Peripheries: Struggles over DisAbled Canadians' Places in Law, Society, and Space." In Tanya Titchkosky and Rod Michalko (eds.), *Rethinking Normalcy: A Disability Studies Reader*. Toronto: Canadian Scholars Press.

Larson, Grant. 2008. "Anti-Oppressive Practice in Mental Health." *Journal of Progressive Human Services* 19, 1.

Rioux, Marcia H., and Fraser Valentine. 2006. "Does Theory Matter? Exploring the Nexus between Disability, Human Rights and Public Policy." In Dianne Pothier and Richard Devlin (eds.), *Critical Disability Theory: Essays in Philosophy, Politics, Policy, and Law*. Vancouver: University of British Columbia Press.

Index